Publishing in Joyce's *Ulysses*

European Joyce Studies

VOLUME 26

The titles published in this series are listed at *brill.com/ejs*

Publishing in Joyce's *Ulysses*

Newspapers, Advertising and Printing

Edited by

William S. Brockman
Tekla Mecsnóber
Sabrina Alonso

BRILL
RODOPI

LEIDEN | BOSTON

Library of Congress Cataloging-in-Publication Data

Names: Brockman, William S., editor. | Mecsnóber, Tekla, editor. | Alonso, Sabrina, editor.
Title: Publishing in Joyce's Ulysses : newspapers, advertising and printing / edited by William S. Brockman, Tekla Mecsnóber, Sabrina Alonso.
Description: Leiden ; Boston : Brill, [2018] | Series: European Joyce studies ; VOLUME 26 | Includes bibliographical references and index.
Identifiers: LCCN 2017048758 (print) | LCCN 2017048898 (ebook) | ISBN 9789004359062 (E-book) | ISBN 9789004359048 (pbk. : alk. paper)
Subjects: LCSH: Joyce, James, 1882-1941. Ulysses. | Publishers and publishing in literature. | Newspapers in literature. | Advertising in literature. | Printing in literature.
Classification: LCC PR6019.O9 (ebook) | LCC PR6019.O9 U6864 2018 (print) | DDC 823/.912--dc23
LC record available at https://lccn.loc.gov/2017048758

Typeface for the Latin, Greek, and Cyrillic scripts: "Brill". See and download: brill.com/brill-typeface.

ISSN 0923-9855
ISBN 978-90-04-35904-8 (paperback)
ISBN 978-90-04-35906-2 (e-book)

This book is printed on acid-free paper and produced in a sustainable manner.

Contents

List of Illustrations VII
List of Abbreviations X
Notes on Contributors XI

Introduction 1

1 George Newnes's Most Entertaining Publication 11
Judith Harrington

2 Bloom, the Dandy, the Nymph and the Old Hag: *Tit-Bits* and *Photo Bits*, Reflections of the Victorian Press in James Joyce's *Ulysses* 25
Elisabetta d'Erme

3 Types of News Events 47
Fritz Senn

4 Newspapers, Print, Language: Steganography in Joyce 57
Jolanta Wawrzycka

5 Classified Advertising in Joyce 77
David Spurr

6 "But Who Was Gerty?" Intertextuality and the Advertising Language of "Nausicaa" 89
Matthew Hayward

7 Advertising in *Ulysses* 107
Sabrina Alonso

8 "Aeolus" – A Sightseeing Tour 130
Harald Beck

9 "Aeolus", Interrupted: Heady Headlines and Joycean Negotiations of Closure 143
Tamara Radak

10 **The Self-Reflexive Text of "Aeolus"** 156
Sangam MacDuff

11 **"Clio's Clippings": From Newspaper to Press Cutting** 175
William S. Brockman

12 **The Ineluctable Modernity of the Visible: The Typographic Odyssey of *Ulysses* in Interwar Print Culture** 192
Tekla Mecsnóber

Index 225

List of Illustrations

4.1 Sample of a "crossed" letter 75
4.2 Title page of the 1621 printing of Trithemius's *Steganographia* 75
7.1 Nineteenth century travelling showcart for Cherry Blossom 111
7.2 Nineteenth century advertising wagon 111
7.3 The re-designed college sports advertisement as imagined by Bloom 114
7.4 Joyce's notes on optical illusions 115
7.5 Bridgewater's original for Joyce's copy, page 29 116
7.6 Bridgewater's original for Joyce's copy, page 30 116
7.7 Joyce's notes about posters 116
7.8 Joyce's notes on attention 117
7.9 Advertisement for Eyebrowlin in *Lloyd's Weekly News* (1916) 119
7.10 Advertisement for nose shaper (1916) 119
7.11 The Barclay & Cook shoe advertisement featuring in the reconstructed Dublin *Evening Telegraph* of 16 June 1904, produced in 2004 to celebrate the centenary of Bloomsday 126
8.1 Map showing Bloom's route in "Aeolus" from the cab stand through the *Freeman*'s offices and on to Dillon's in Bachelor's Walk. (1) The Prince's Stores, (2) The *Freeman* offices and printing works, (3) The Oval, (4) Williams's Row, (5) Dillon's auction rooms, (6) Mooney's, (7) The Irish Catholic, (8) Graham Lemon, confectioner 131
8.2 Map indicating destroyed structures (shaded areas) and remains of the *Freeman* building 132
8.3 Irish Rebellion, May 1916, ruined Prince's Stores and *Freeman's Journal* 132
8.4 Nelson's Pillar on Sackville Street 133
8.5 Main entrance to the *Freeman*'s public office, facing Sackville Street 134
8.6 This enlargement from a picture of the Hotel Metropole shows the Prince's Stores and the entrance to the *Freeman* office familiar from the drawing above 134
8.7 A 1910 plan showing the location of the *Freeman's* public office where Bloom and Murray discuss Keyes's ad 135
8.8 Bloom's possible route (blue arrow) through the buildings from North Prince's Street to Middle Abbey Street (not more than a suggestion). *Insurance Plan of the City of Dublin* (London: Charles E. Goad, 1893), vol. 1, sheet 7 136
8.9 Printing Press "Victory" web newspaper machine, with folding apparatus 137

8.10 A view of the composing room at the *Freeman's Journal*, taken between the mid-1890s and 1904 138
8.11 A view showing the complete destruction of the linotypes 138
8.12 Bloom's destination is on the quays at J. Dillon, auctioneer, 25 Bachelor's Walk, the seventh house from the right 140
8.13 83 Middle Abbey Street from Sackville Street 140
8.14 Excerpt from *Thom's Dublin Directory* (1910): 1461, third column 141
8.15 Statue of John Gray in the middle of Sackville Street. Mooney's is on Lower Abbey Street to the right 142
10.1 Opening of "Aeolus" printed in the *Little Review* of October 1918 159
10.2 Opening of "Aeolus" printed in the 1922 edition 159
11.1 Romeike Press Clipping Bureau readers' room, from *American Magazine* 93 (February 1922): 15 176
11.2 Romeike Press Clipping Bureau slip 178
11.3 Beginning of article; Oscar Schwarz, "Di un poeta irlandese a Trieste," *L'era nuova* (14 August 1919), 2 180
11.4 End of article; Schwarz, "Di un poeta irlandese," 2 180
11.5–6 From *Extracts from Press Notices of "Ulysses" by James Joyce*. See footnote 21 183
11.7 Advertisement for *Modern Society*. *Newspaper Press Directory* (1905): 499 186
12.1 Prospectus issued by the Odyssey Press in 1932 193
12.2 Type used for the "POST NO BILLS" passage in the first edition of *Ulysses* printed in 1922 by Shakespeare and Company (page 146) 198
12.3 Type used for the "POST NO BILLS" passage in the 1932 Odyssey Press edition (page 156) 198
12.4 Front cover for the *Little Review* of March 1918 200
12.5 Front cover for the *Little Review* of July 1919 201
12.6 Front cover for the *Egoist* of January–February 1919 202
12.7 Front cover for the *Egoist* of July 1919 203
12.8 Extract from page 44 of the "Hades" episode printed in the *Egoist* issue of July 1919, set in Caslon and using archaic ligatures 204
12.9 Front cover of the first edition of *Ulysses* published by Shakespeare and Company in 1922 206
12.10 Subscription prospectus for the 1922 edition of *Ulysses* issued by Shakespeare and Company 207
12.11 Front cover of the first (July 1926) issue of Samuel Roth's *Two Worlds Monthly*, advertising "The FIRST CHAPTER of ULYSSES By JAMES JOYCE" 209
12.12 Cover for *Dubliners* published by Albatross Press in 1932 210

12.13 Sans serif block capitals used for the headings of "Aeolus" in the Odyssey Press edition of 1932 211
12.14 Dust jacket design by Ernst Reichl for the Random House edition of *Ulysses* published in 1934 212
12.15 Title spread of the Random House edition of *Ulysses* published in 1934 213
12.16 Random House advertisement for *Ulysses* placed in the *New York Times Book Review* issue of 28 January 1934 214
12.17 Random House promotional folder for the 1934 *Ulysses* 216
12.18 Random House advertisement for *Ulysses* placed in the *New York Times Book Review* issue of 18 March 1934 217
12.19 Title page of the Limited Editions Club *Ulysses* issued in 1935 218
12.20 Headlines of the "Aeolus" episode printed in the Limited Editions Club *Ulysses* 219
12.21 Title page of the Bodley Head edition of 1936 220
12.22 Bodley Head advertisement for *Ulysses* placed in the *Observer* issue of 11 October 1936 221
12.23 Dust jacket (front and spine) for the reissue of *Ulysses* in the Modern Library series of 1940 222

List of Abbreviations

References in the text to works by or about James Joyce employ the following abbreviations:

D	*Dubliners: Authoritative Text, Contexts, Criticism*. Edited by Margot Norris. Text edited by Hans Walter Gabler with Walter Hettche. New York: W.W. Norton and Company, [1914] 2006. References give story and line number, e.g. (*D* 11.23).
FW	*Finnegans Wake*. New York: Viking Press; London: Faber and Faber, 1939. References give page and line number, e.g (*FW* 254.7).
JJII	Ellmann, Richard. *James Joyce*. New and revised edition. New York: Oxford University Press, 1982.
JJA	*The James Joyce Archive*. Edited by Michael Groden et al. New York and London: Garland Publishing, 1977–1979. References give volume and page number following the volume numbering specified by the *James Joyce Quarterly*, e.g. (*JJA* 62:50).
Letters	*Letters of James Joyce*. Volume I. Edited by Stuart Gilbert. New York: Viking Press, 1957; reissued with corrections 1966. Volumes II and III. Edited by Richard Ellmann. New York: Viking Press, 1966. References give volume and page number, e.g. (*Letters III* 140).
P	*A Portrait of the Artist as a Young Man: Authoritative Text, Backgrounds and Contexts, Criticism*. Edited by John Paul Riquelme. Text edited by Hans Walter Gabler with Walter Hettche. New York: W.W. Norton and Company, [1916] 2007. References give chapter and line number, e.g. (*P* V.1746).
SH	*Stephen Hero*. New edition. Edited by John J. Slocum and Herbert Cahoon. New York: New Directions, 1963. References give page number, e.g. (*SH* 55).
SL	*Selected Letters of James Joyce*. Edited by Richard Ellmann. New York: Viking Press, 1975.
U	*Ulysses*. Edited by Hans Walter Gabler et al. New York: Garland Publishing, 1984, 1986. References give episode and line number, e.g. (*U* 18.144).
U-G	*Ulysses*. Edited by Hans Walter Gabler et al. New York: Garland Publishing, 1984. References to the Foreword, Critical Apparatus, Textual Notes, Historical Collation or Afterword cited parenthetically by page number, e.g. (*U-G* 1872).

Notes on Contributors

Sabrina Alonso
holds a degree in English from the University of Zurich, has taught in higher education, worked in the field of product design and been employed at the Zurich James Joyce Foundation. She has published in the journal *Medien und Zeit* (2012) and in the collection *Parallaxing Joyce* (2017). She maintains the progress report for the Zurich *Finnegans Wake* reading group, accompanied by *Wake*-derived collages (http://thursdayswake.blogspot.ch), and is currently compiling the "alphybetty," a collection of Joyce's alphabet-letters as found in his correspondence and manuscripts, to be consulted when reading Joyce's handwriting (http://joycehand.blogspot.ch).

Harald Beck
worked on the team of *Ulysses: A Critical and Synoptic Edition* under Hans Walter Gabler in Munich and has translated *Dubliners*, parts of *Ulysses* and *Finnegans Wake* into German. He has also contributed to Clive Hart and Ian Gunn's *James Joyce's Dublin: A Topographical Guide to the Dublin of "Ulysses"* (2004), published notes on *Ulysses*, and edited a selection from *Dubliners* and an annotated version of the "Penelope" episode. He co-edits *James Joyce Online Notes*, an open-access electronic journal, with John Simpson, former Chief Editor of the OED and has revised the 1976 German translation of *Ulysses* by Hans Wollschläger for Suhrkamp Verlag with Ruth Frehner and Ursula Zeller of the Zurich James Joyce Foundation.

William S. Brockman
is Paterno Family Librarian for Literature at Pennsylvania State University. He has been Bibliographer for the *James Joyce Quarterly* since 1991 and edits the "James Joyce Checklist" (http://norman.hrc.utexas.edu/jamesjoycechecklist), a comprehensive online bibliography of publications by and about Joyce. He has lectured at the Joyce School in Trieste and is a Trustee on the Board of the International James Joyce Foundation. He has published essays and articles on Joyce in *James Joyce Quarterly*, *Joyce Studies Annual*, *Journal of Modern Literature*, *Papers of the Bibliographical Society of America*, *Genetic Joyce Studies* and the collection *James Joyce in Context* (2009). He is co-editor of a forthcoming edition of Joyce's correspondence.

Elisabetta d'Erme
lives in Trieste. She is a journalist and an independent scholar. Her research is focused on James Joyce and Victorian culture. She is the author of *Trieste*

Vittoriana: Ritratti (2017) and *Tit-Bits: James Joyce, un'epoca e i suoi media* (2008). Her essays and articles have been published in *Joyce Studies in Italy, Mediazioni, Circolare* and *Angelica*. She has been among the speakers at international conferences in Rome, Genoa, Zurich, Bagni di Lucca and Perugia.

Judith Harrington
is an independent scholar who has spoken at many Joyce conferences and symposia since the early 1990s, where she has especially enjoyed the close *Ulysses* and *Finnegans Wake* reading groups. Her essays have appeared in the *James Joyce Literary Supplement* and the *James Joyce Quarterly*. Her *James Joyce: Suburban Tenor* was one of the centenary monographs published by the National Library of Ireland. She also spent two decades at the weekly Berkeley Tuesday Night *Wake* Group and was lucky enough to attend five stimulating August Workshops in Zurich.

Matthew Hayward
is Lecturer in Literature at the University of the South Pacific, Fiji. Recent essays on Joyce, modernism and Irish consumer culture have appeared in *James Joyce Quarterly, Texas Studies in Literature and Language, Modernism/modernity, English Studies, Dublin James Joyce Journal* and in the edited collection *James Joyce in the Nineteenth Century* (2013). He is currently working on the monograph *Joyce in Business*, and co-editing (with Maebh Long) the collection *Oceanic Modernism*.

Sangam MacDuff
is an Assistant in Modern English Literature at the University of Geneva, where he wrote his doctoral thesis on James Joyce's epiphanies. He read English at Trinity Hall, Cambridge University, before completing a Masters in English Literature and Creative Writing at the University of Edinburgh. He has published on Joyce and literary modernism in the *James Joyce Broadsheet* and *Swiss Papers in English Language and Literature*, with essays forthcoming in the *James Joyce Quarterly, Genetic Joyce Studies* and *Genesic Fields: James Joyce and Genetic Criticism*.

Tekla Mecsnóber
teaches at the University of Groningen in the Netherlands and has co-edited, with R.B. Kershner, volume 22 of the *European Joyce Studies* series, entitled *Joycean Unions: Post-Millennial Essays from East to West* (2013). Her current research projects involve investigating *Ulysses* and *Finnegans Wake* in the context

of the changing linguistic and typographic landscapes of Europe between 1900 and 1938, and more general aspects of typography as memory practice and ideological tool.

Tamara Radak
is Lecturer and PhD candidate at the University of Vienna. She is currently preparing a monograph on closural and anti-closural narratives in the novels of James Joyce, Flann O'Brien, Virginia Woolf and Ernest Hemingway, titled *No(n)Sense of an Ending? Modernist Aporias of Closure*. She was the host organiser of *Irish Modernisms: Gaps, Conjectures, Possibilities* (University of Vienna, 2016) and has published in *James Joyce Quarterly*, *James Joyce Literary Supplement* and the Flann O'Brien-themed *Parish Review*. Her most recent essay, published in *Flann O'Brien: Problems with Authority* (2017), applies hypertext and possible worlds theory to Flann O'Brien's *The Third Policeman*.

Fritz Senn
has been in charge of the Zurich James Joyce Foundation since its inception in 1985. He has written mainly on Joyce. Publications include: *Joyce's Dislocutions: Essays on Reading as Translation*, ed. John Paul Riquelme (1984); *Inductive Scrutinies: Focus on Joyce*, ed. Christine O'Neill (1995); *Joycean Murmoirs: Fritz Senn on James Joyce*, ed. Christine O'Neill (2007); *Ulyssean Close-ups* (2007); *Noch mehr über Joyce: Streiflichter* (2012).

David Spurr
is Emeritus Professor of English at the Université de Genève. A board member of both the Zurich and International James Joyce Foundations, he has published widely on Joyce and on modern literature in general. Among his recent books are *Architecture and Modern Literature* (2012) and *Joyce and the Scene of Modernity* (2002). He has held visiting appointments at the universities of Basel, Zurich, Innsbruck and Iceland and curated the international exhibition *Frankenstein, créé des ténèbres*, at the Bodmer Foundation in Geneva from May to October 2016.

Jolanta Wawrzycka
is Professor of English at Radford University, Virginia. She lectured at the Joyce Schools in Dublin and Trieste and currently serves as Trustee on the Board of the International James Joyce Foundation. She co-edited *Gender in Joyce* (1997), guest-edited the *James Joyce Quarterly* translation issue (Summer 2010) and

two issues of *Scientia Traductionis* (2010; 2012). She wrote on Kundera, Barthes and Joyce, contributing chapters to, among others, *ReJoycing: New Readings of "Dubliners"* (1998), *Twenty-First Joyce* (2004), *The Reception of James Joyce in Europe* (2004) and *Joyce in Context* (2009). She translated works of Roman Ingarden, Joyce's *Chamber Music* and poems by Czesław Miłosz and W.B. Yeats.

Introduction

> Nothing like *Ulysses* has ever met the face of type.
>
> *Scots Pictorial*, quoted in *Extracts from Press Notices of "Ulysses" by JAMES JOYCE*, 1922

∴

Published at a time of rapid change in the printing and publishing industries, *Ulysses* exploited and exemplified facets of those industries in ways that become increasingly evident nearly a century after the book's publication. Its employment of typographic design, awareness of advertising techniques, adaptation of journalistic style and explicit inclusion of newspapers as elements of setting and plot make it a virtual museum of 1904 media. James Joyce himself was extraordinarily – for a writer – involved with printers, newspapermen and designers throughout his life, giving him a familiarity with the early twentieth century communication industries that not only pervaded the content of his fiction but also determined how it appeared in print.

Joyce himself came to learn a great deal about the industry. As an amateur publisher, he oversaw the printing and distribution of two early broadsides: *The Holy Office* and *Gas from a Burner*. As a reporter in Dublin, he drew material for the story "After the Race" from an interview with a race car driver. In Dublin and later in Trieste he reviewed books and published essays on literature and Irish politics. Throughout his life, Joyce was an avid reader of newspapers and a collector of press clippings. Always a self-promoter, he put to good use his interest in the press to compile excerpts from reviews for compilation in leaflets to publicize his books. He took great care with the typographic design of his books, arguing for the use of quotation marks rather than dashes to introduce characters' speech and involving himself heavily in the printing of the first edition of *Ulysses*. He was a fan of advertising and the popular press, on the one hand collecting magazines and illustrations and on the other studying diligently a textbook of advertising.

None of this is news to readers of Joyce. But serious interest in Joyce and the press has only begun to emerge in the last couple of decades, paralleling the evolution of the discipline of book history, the burgeoning of cultural studies and the growing sophistication of genetic criticism – all of which embed Joyce and his work in a material culture of letters, manuscripts, proofs,

 | DOI 10.1163/9789004359062_002

publicity, reviewing and a growing body of documentation of the ways in which Joyce's writing reached his readers. An indication of the change in focus is in the first volume of Joyce's *Letters*, where editor Stuart Gilbert routinely omitted passages dealing with the details of printing and publishing – number of copies printed, royalties, negotiations with publishers – as being irrelevant to concerns of the artist.[1] Readers in recent years have come to feel that this kind of information, formerly seen as dull and inconsequential, can provide a vivid perspective of Joyce's understanding of publishing and an equally vivid perspective on the published works.

In none of Joyce's works is this as evident as in *Ulysses*. Terence Killeen expresses this concisely: "*Ulysses* teems with references to the popular press of the day and is thoroughly immersed in the world of print".[2] Newspapers and the publishing industry pervade the book, propelling the plot, acting as leitmotifs, providing settings and characters, even serving as toilet paper and kneeling cushion. *Ulysses* brims with innovative features of typographic design such as the headlines in "Aeolus", "Ithaca's" terminal dot and "Penelope's" lack of punctuation and sporadic capital letters. Despite the developing problems with his vision, Joyce was keenly attentive to such details in his feverish revisions to the *Ulysses* proofs. A note to printer Darantiere's assistant bears a complaint about how frequently the letter "f" was printed imperfectly (*JJA* 25:103). In places, even the characters envision themselves typographically. Master Dignam takes some pleasure in knowing that his classmates will see his name in his father's obituary ("Then they'll all see it in the paper and read my name printed and pa's name" [*U* 10.1159–60]), Buck Mulligan hands out calling cards ("he handed round to the company a set of pasteboard cards which he had had printed that day at Mr Quinnell's bearing a legend printed in fair italics: *Mr Malachi Mulligan. Fertiliser and Incubator. Lambay Island*". [*U* 14.658–60]), Bloom recalls composing lines beginning "*An ambition to squint / At my verses in print…*" (*U* 17.396–401) and Molly remembers practicing her future name to see how it would look printed on a visiting card ("I never thought that would be my name Bloom when I used to write it in print to see how it looked on a visiting card" [*U* 18.840–42]).

1 For example, in his transcription of a letter from Joyce to Harriet Weaver (*Letters I* 187), Gilbert omitted "I have not checked the paging from p. 680 on as my head was reeling after the effort. The corrections in black pencil are mistakes in the setting. Mr Rodker wants the proof at once so will you please let him have it" (28 September 1922, Add MS 57346, Harriet Shaw Weaver Papers, British Library).

2 Terence Killeen, "From the '*Freeman's General*' to the 'dully expressed': James Joyce and Journalism", *Irish Journalism before Independence: More a Disease than a Profession*, ed. Kevin Rafter (Manchester: Manchester University Press, 2011), 209.

In relation to the newspaper there was a decisive transition in Joyce's life which partly informs the compilation of this collection. For years he had a journalistic career, writing newspaper articles, reviews and political pieces for British and Italian papers from 1900 to 1912. After a series of his articles had appeared in the Trieste newspaper *Il Piccolo della Sera* on Irish political topics in 1907, Joyce remarked to his brother Stanislaus: "I may not be the Jesus Christ I once fondly imagined myself, but I think I must have a talent for journalism" (*JJII* 255). A decade later, in a letter of 5 August 1918 sent from Zurich addressing "Madame" (recipient unknown; Stuart Gilbert suspects Mlle Guillermet of the *Journal de Genève*), he replied to an invitation to contribute an article by explaining that he never writes articles, not even literary ones, to say nothing of others ("je n'écris jamais d'articles – pas même d'articles littéraires pour ne parler pas d'autres"; *Letters I* 118). This did not mean, however, that he had turned his back on newspapers or even lost interest in them: numerous references throughout his letters and the substantial collection of press clippings held at the University at Buffalo testify to the attention he paid them. His outrage at the newspapers' attention to his marriage in July 1931[3] was conversely matched by his irritation at not receiving mention in the papers for sending a wreath for George Moore's funeral in January 1933 (*Letters I* 335).

This collection situates itself biographically after Joyce's transition away from being a journalist and historically during a time of rapid evolution in newspaper and typographic design.[4] More newspapers – both titles and issues – than ever before were being produced. Production had become cheaper thanks to the gradual abolition of taxes on newspapers between the 1830s and the 1860s. Technological advancements such as the introduction of the telegraph and the wide development of the railroad system had enhanced the speed and efficiency of news-gathering and newspaper distribution. An increasingly literate reading public brought about by the 1870 Education Act, a rise in disposable income and greater leisure time due to a shortening of the average working week enlarged the demand for newspapers. Newspapers targeted an increasingly varied reading public, seeking particular audiences and introducing changes in layout, illustration and typography. Articles in mass-distribution newspapers like the *Daily Mail* became more concise and compact.

---

3 James Joyce to Giorgio Joyce, 9 July 1931, Hans E. Jahnke Bequest, Zurich James Joyce Foundation.

4 Information in this paragraph on changes in the printing and publishing industries is taken from Kevin Williams, *Read All About It! A History of the British Newspaper* (London: Routledge, 2010), 125–48.

Most of this collection's essays focus on or make reference to the "Aeolus" episode of *Ulysses*, set in the offices of the 1904 *Freeman's Journal* and the *Evening Telegraph*. These newspapers' formats, though about to be superseded by the design of the popular press with headlines, illustrations and the placement of news rather than advertising on the front page, were typical of the time. Joyce's addition of headlines, or crossheads, to the "Aeolus" episode in the summer of 1921 after it had been published without these features in the *Little Review* of 1918 was an innovation typical of the mass-circulation London dailies. Headlines tended to be used relatively sparingly and deliberately in British newspapers, but crossheads, breaking up long articles, were becoming more common. "By breaking up long columns of text, the centered and boldface crosshead served as a visual aid to readers and a device for foregrounding eye-catching items in the body of an article. ...Although now commonplace, crossheads were relatively novel in 1904, a recognizable symptom of the recent sea-changes in British journalism".[5]

The essays collected in this volume derive from the 2013 annual summer Workshop of the Zurich James Joyce Foundation whose theme for that year was "Newspapers". Given the informal nature of the Workshop, at which the reading of papers is strongly discouraged, authors of the essays had the opportunity to interact with each other. At the editors' invitation to Joyce scholars – some from the Workshop, some not – each of the authors in this volume contributed an essay for a collection examining some aspect of *Ulysses* in relation to the press: newspaper publishing, advertising, typography, newspapers as props in the book.

Judith Harrington opens the collection with a snapshot of the media landscape and the newspaper publishing industry at the turn of the century and demonstrates how some of it is reflected in *Ulysses* and *Finnegans Wake*. Her focus on the three major newspaper publishers of the time – George Newnes, publisher of *Tit-Bits*, Arthur Pearson, publisher of *Pearson's Magazine*, and Alfred Harmsworth, publisher of *Answers to Correspondents* and later the *Daily Mail* – shows both how much Joyce was aware of them and how his books reflect the pervasive mass medium of the printed papers of the time. By beginning with the shrewd inventiveness of such entrepreneurs as Newnes, Pearson and Harmsworth and the publishing ideas they developed to foster the sale of their weeklies and journals, the essay reflects the times of transformation and innovation that shaped a large part of British publishing of the time. Joyce was

5 Stephen Donovan, "'SHORT BUT TO THE POINT': Newspaper Typography in 'Aeolus'", *James Joyce Quarterly* 40, no. 3 (Spring 2003): 527. Information regarding crossheads is adapted from Donovan.

fascinated with these three major publishers and their weeklies and absorbed them into his works. As Harrington points out, at least sixty-five newspapers and other periodicals are mentioned in *Ulysses*, *Tit-Bits* being the most salient.

Elisabetta d'Erme focuses in on some things mentioned by Harrington, specifically on the two late Victorian penny weeklies *Tit-Bits*, with its puzzles, contests and readers' contributions, and *Photo Bits*, with its slightly risqué illustrations. The essay discusses the vital role these two publications play in the writing of *Ulysses*, particularly in Joyce's adaptation of their style, by which he assembled and integrated various types of texts from the mass media, as well as in the treatment he gives the figure of the prize-winning writer and contributor to *Tit-Bits* Philip Beaufoy. He was interested in *Photo Bits*, a periodical heavily illustrated with advertisements and often titillating photographs, for providing traits that resurface in the more erotically charged episodes like "Calypso", "Nausicaa", "Circe", "Ithaca" and "Penelope". The appendix to the essay provides a comprehensive list of Philip Beaufoy's works.

The engagement that d'Erme finds in the readership of *Tit-Bits* as well as the pervasiveness of papers in people's daily lives is what Fritz Senn recognizes in a news item of 16 June 1904 which reported a major event at the time and receives treatment in *Ulysses*. The General Slocum disaster (a shipboard fire in New York's East River that had happened the previous day and killed over a thousand people) is a recurrent element in the book, although it never appears centre stage. It is present in what Senn calls "parallactic diversion", reflected and deflected through various characters. The news report is in the minds of several of them, as becomes evident from what they talk and think about, and they would have had their information from the newspapers. An instance of a news item which receives more explicit, although by no means unpuzzling treatment in *Ulysses* is provided by Miles Crawford in "Aeolus": an account of the report about the code used to encrypt the escape route on which "Skin-the-Goat" supposedly drove the car for the Invincibles following Dublin's Phoenix Park murders in 1882. It involved placing an advertisement superimposed on a map of Dublin, so that a prominent letter in the advertisement pointed to a specific place in the city, a letter in an ad to a location in Dublin. Senn terms this device "superimposition" and shows that, in itself, it points to the overall technique of the book and that it can be seen as a thumbnail sketch by which to read *Ulysses*.

Superimposition is code through overlay – in the case discussed by Senn, an ad laid over a map of Dublin. Jolanta Wawrzycka delves further into the fascination with code evident in Joyce's writings. With a particular interest for visual clues that the graphics of print can provide, like typographic features and arrangement of characters, the essay focuses on veiled information and secret communication. Joyce's writing often involves playing with code, which can serve as a system of communication but also of encryption and of deception. The essay considers such instances as Bloom's getting caught in the act of writing to Martha and his subsequent strategies of cover-up, dissimulation and deceit. The discussion places these within the context of secret writing and strategies of encoding, but also of codes as representing one more way to configure language, a recurrent preoccupation of *Ulysses*. In particular, it suggests reading Joyce's writings from a steganographic point of view. Steganography, the practice of hiding information from unintended eyes and doing so in plain sight (thereby concealing the very fact that a message is being sent at all), offers a valuable tool to appreciate numerous veiling strategies and textual stratagems. Wawrzycka discusses passages that draw attention to themselves as texts in *Ulysses* (such as the acrostic cipher, the boustrophedon, acronyms, anagrams, Ogham writing) and of secret communication codes (such as jargon and slang, concealed messages, textual and visual semagrams) and demonstrates how Joyce employs a variety of veiling methods, thus introducing a series of steganographic tests which probe and engage the reader.

The opportunity for flirtation offered by codified writing in *Ulysses* and seized by Bloom is illustrated by David Spurr's essay, at the same time opening the section in this volume concerned with advertising. In his consideration of Bloom's classified ad searching for a "smart lady typist" in "Lestrygonians" (which resurfaces in a rewritten form in the "Shem the Penman" chapter of *Finnegans Wake* at *FW* 181:27–33), of the imaginary ad written by Molly offering £5 for an imagined runaway Bloom in "Ithaca", and of a passage in HCE's boastful speech which bears resemblance to the language of the rooms-to-let ad of newspapers, Spurr discusses the way in which the advertisement is used as a kind of code. It offers an invitation to a secret erotic exchange and an opportunity for indulging in clandestine behaviour, a language which Martha Clifford seems quick enough to understand. He further discusses how the newspaper is used as cover, when Bloom, in "Sirens", uses it to conceal the letter he is writing in reply to Martha while pretending to answer an ad for a town traveller, thus trying to evade the inquiring gaze of a fellow diner. The classified ad, although originally functioning as communication about goods and services, also provides a particular language which can be re-used and re-appropriated, for example for erotic purposes. Spurr's essay shows how the treatment the classified ad receives in Joyce, operating as a means of negotiation between the private and the public sphere, diverts it from its original function as an investment to providing a mode of concealment and alibi for illicit private communication. In *Finnegans Wake*, the potential of the classified ad to function as a vehicle for parody is taken even further.

Like Spurr, Matthew Hayward focuses on the language of advertising but with attention on "Nausicaa", particularly the language and style of the first half of the episode. The essay challenges an assumption often held in scholarly criticism that, with Gerty, Joyce is depicting a realistic figure who has either been shaped by or shapes herself according to the dictates of consumerism. Hayward shows that, in "Nausicaa", the style is foregrounded in such a way that the episode emerges as being parodic of other styles. It therefore demands that it be read against these other texts. Indeed, by returning to the language of women's advertisements in the early decades of the twentieth century the essay shows that the episode is more thoroughly intertextual than has been recognised. It moves away from naturalistic conceptions of Gerty as a depiction of a real-life, early twentieth-century female consumer – modelled upon a historical type: the deluded, fashion-attentive young woman of the early twentieth century – and it resists the conventional interpretation of the "Nausicaa" episode as a critique of the young, consuming female. It argues that Joyce's text is aimed not at a presumed female consumer, nor exactly at the culture within which she consumes, but at a certain kind of style – that of the language of advertising – which is itself constructed and projected onto a particular subject, and it explains what the implications of this are for a less naive reading of the episode.

A different angle on the subject is taken in Sabrina Alonso's essay, which studies Joyce's use of advertising in *Ulysses* as it is filtered through Bloom's perspective. It focuses on prominent instances of the practice as they feature in the novel, but also reads them against the background of the notes Joyce took on the issue. He listed them under the heading "Advertising" in his "Notes on Business and Commerce" (*JJA* 3:474–617) and had copied them from Howard Bridgewater's book *Advertising, Or the Art of Making Known*. These remarks used to be explained as part of Joyce's preparation for his employment at a private bank in Rome between 1906 and 1907, but the identification of their source (i.e. a series of advertising guides published in London at the beginning of the century) allows a different contextualization.[6] Bridgewater offers a popularised version of the science of advertising based on the theories of the day. A number of experiments with them can be found in *Ulysses*. The essay elucidates the way in which Joyce's use of advertising lends itself to highlight typical features of the whole book.

Among the same pages of Joyce's notebooks, and also taken from Bridgewater, are entries referring to the printing world, for example, short paragraphs

6 Matthew Hayward, "The Bloom of Advertising: Joyce's 'Notes on Business and Commerce' and *Ulysses*", *Dublin James Joyce Journal* 5 (2012): 50.

headed “Letter Heading”, “Illustration”, “Space”, “Catchlines”, “Line Block”, “Half Tone”, “Stereos and Electros”, “Three-Colour Process”, “Lithography”. Whatever Joyce had in mind – to use them for his construction of Bloom, to characterise some of the other press-men, to use the information for himself – he had some personal knowledge of the printing world. His own experience as publisher, promoter of self and others, his early experience as a journalist, his several visits to the offices of the *Freeman's Journal* and the *Evening Telegraph* in 1909, gave him further material to draw from and to rework into “Aeolus”. Harald Beck's essay reconstructs details of the newspaper offices. Although “Aeolus” is set in the newspaper production venue, we learn relatively little about how the newspaper is produced, the layout of the office and the way in which a journalist works. Beck traces Bloom's walk through the offices of the *Freeman's Journal* and documents the route with reproductions of contemporary maps, photographs, extracts from *Thom's Directory* of 1910 as well as other contemporary sources like history books and novels. His materials and illustrations are valuable documents to portray the premises of the *Freeman's* building, particularly so as much of what was there in Joyce's time is now lost since the destruction of the offices in the Easter Rising of 1916.

Following Beck's reconstructions of the venue of the physical creation of the paper and its assimilation into the text of “Aeolus”, Tamara Radak's essay takes us further into the episode. It discusses how the artistic devices employed in “Aeolus” are used to enact a typical feature of Joyce's writing, that of evading the definitiveness of a fixed form. Both form and content of the chapter work toward keeping it in a state of tension between linear progression and circularity. With particular attention to elements that stand out formally from the rest of the text and, thus, draw attention to themselves as linguistic devices – such as onomatopoeia, interruptions, the newspaper form of the episode – the essay studies two seemingly opposed tendencies which they sustain. On the one hand, they give structure to the narrative and drive it forward while, at the same time, they provide instances of the text intruding upon itself and disturbing its own linear progress. The text thus draws attention to itself as artefact, acquires a self-reflexive quality and introduces a circular element, thereby making the reader aware of the constructed nature and provisional quality of any set form. “Aeolus” constantly re-negotiates the form, essentially rejecting closure and propagating openness.

That “circulation” is not only a recurrent motif but a governing principle in *Ulysses* is developed further by Sangam MacDuff in his discussion of the nature and role of language in “Aeolus”. He explains how two major aspects of the episode's form, that of its language and that of the makeup of the newspaper, contribute to the self-reflexive awareness of the text as a whole. Linguistic elements such as onomatopoeia or the boustrophedon, and the form of the newspaper – with its use of headlines, references to typesetting, to the printing of text, its distribution and recycling – are devices which both draw attention to themselves and reflect on writing conventions. They thus contribute to enhancing the self-conscious quality of the text, a technique that brings language to the forefront and gives it a prominent position. Language is a major concern from the start in *Ulysses*, of course, but it takes "Aeolus" to make this evident. The essay argues that self-reflexivity turns out to be the real focus of the episode, underscored by Joyce's return, not without ironic undertones, to the biblical origins of speech and writing.

Language or print calling for attention is, on a more figurative level, reminiscent of its simpler embodiment in the "puff" or "par" that Bloom mentions to the newspaper editor, "a par to call attention in the *Telegraph*" (*U* 7.973–74). Such calls became of growing interest to Joyce himself. As his works were published and he was beginning to receive treatment in the press, he became increasingly attuned to press coverage, both collecting articles clipped from the newspapers and supplied by the press cutting services, and sending them as enclosures in his letters. As William Brockman's essay elucidates, one of Joyce's main means of communication with supporters was via clippings, especially with Ezra Pound and Harriet Weaver. His essay examines how Joyce uses clippings in his works, from an early instance in "A Painful Case" to the three clippings that are enumerated in the "Ithaca" episode and some remnants of press notices which appear in *Finnegans Wake*. Extracting them from their original sources, Joyce puts them to a variety of uses and offers them to be viewed from multiple perspectives.

Although Joyce knew how to use the print media to foster attention to his book and tried to exert some influence on the design of the printed text, he was not always directly involved in decisions regarding the material shape *Ulysses* was going to receive. Yet, his interest in visual aspects of the written word did have an impact on the novel's text in print. The final essay in this volume takes the reader out of the text to physical and external considerations of the book as a printed object. Tekla Mecsnóber's essay examines the significance of typefaces in designing and promoting *Ulysses*. It traces some of the important changes that accompanied the novel's development from its first serialisation in the little magazines of the 1910s to its appearance as a book in various editions during Joyce's lifetime. The essay highlights a number of visual clues that the typographic form of the novel and the printed publicity materials would have provided as to the nature and value of the novel. This study of the significance of type draws on contemporary and later assessments of the "character" of relevant typefaces and anchors the early editions of Joyce's work among the design trends of the interwar years, during the increasingly mature and ultimately decisive emergence of a modern visual language in Europe and North America. It suggests that, whereas the typography of most of the earlier editions as well as their publicity materials tended to rely on historicising typefaces to convey connotations of classic dignity, artistic quality and craftsmanship, editions in the 1930s began to borrow from modernist typographic trends to promote the book as a modern work.

While *Finnegans Wake* drew upon some of the many typographic and journalistic threads woven thickly in *Ulysses*, its treatment of these elements is muted by the sea of other cultural reference points. *Ulysses* remains an encyclopaedic compilation negotiating uniquely between its focus on Dublin during a day in 1904 and the contemporary media, between portrayals of quotidian characters and their lives amid the equally quotidian presence of the evolving publishing environment.

CHAPTER 1

George Newnes's Most Entertaining Publication

Judith Harrington

Abstract

James Joyce was greatly interested in the weekly journals of his time. Three prominent publishers of the day, whose promotional schemes were shrewd and inventive, were George Newnes, publisher of *Tit-Bits*, Arthur Pearson, publisher of *Pearson's Magazine*, and Alfred Harmsworth, publisher of *Answers to Correspondents*. Joyce was fascinated with their publications and knew how to draw from them. All three publishers appear together in one sentence in *Finnegans Wake* and at least sixty-five journals feature in *Ulysses*, *Tit-Bits* being among the most salient. Much of Bloom's attention revolves around it, its appeal, its makeup, its featured writers, its prize-winning stories, its uses (including that of serving as toilet paper). The significance that these three major publishers and their weeklies had for Joyce can be appreciated by outlining how he worked them into his own creative writing.

Keywords

Ulysses – George Newnes – *Tit-Bits* – prize stories – ads – accident insurance – other competitors – "Villa Toryism"

George Newnes (1851–1910) was an innovative nineteenth century English publisher of periodicals, magazines, pamphlets and books. His first publication was *Tit-Bits* in 1881, which quickly became an enormous success. Readers of *Ulysses* usually remember Bloom using a torn piece of *Tit-Bits* instead of toilet paper (*U* 4.537). This early example of recycling might engage those working on Joyce and eco-criticism; however, the publication itself was what caught Joyce's attention as well as mine.

George Newnes was born in 1851 in Matlock, Derbyshire, where his father was an active Congregational minister.[1] This town in the East Midlands was

1 Kate Jackson, *George Newnes and the New Journalism in Britain, 1880–1910: Culture and Profit* (Aldershot: Ashgate Publishing Limited, 2001), 21; Hulda Friedrichs, *The Life of Sir George*

 | DOI 10.1163/9789004359062_003

close to the Derwent River's cotton mills and warm springs. The spas nearby attracted well-known tourists including Queen Victoria, various members of the Wedgewood and Darwin families as well as Byron and Ruskin.[2] Between 1857 and 1866 George Newnes attended Silcoates, a Congregational school near Wakefield in West Yorkshire, where William T. Stead was also a pupil for two of the same years.[3] Newnes also attended a school in Warwickshire as well as the City of London School.

During these years each Congregational church was entirely autonomous and free of any higher authority or governance – which I am tempted to see as a positive influence on Newnes in shaping his impressive career – which was *not* obvious in his first job at the age of sixteen, working as a commercial traveller with a clerk's salary and limited prospects. However, his energy and talent in sales soon found him working as a wholesaler in Liverpool and then in Manchester, where he settled, married and prospered. His next venture (remember that this was in 1881) was to open a vegetarian restaurant in a Manchester basement. Within six months Newnes was able to cash out with enough money to begin his real career as a publisher.

Tit-Bits from All the Most Interesting Books, Periodicals and Contributors in the World was launched on 22 October 1881 – charmingly promoted by one hundred boys wearing head-bands labelled "The *Tit-Bits* Brigade", while men in Newcastle-on-Tyne touted the paper with sandwich-board ads. It is curious that Newnes was shocked to learn that people were tittering over the *Tit-Bits* name – nicely contradicting all those travelling salesmen jokes. The *OED* tells us that a seventeenth century "tyd bit" was a "toothsome morsel", but by 1743 the word "tid-bit" came to mean a brief interesting item of news or information.[4] I was surprised to learn that initially there were no ads in the sixteen page penny weekly; however, fairly quickly Newnes added advertisements to several sections of the paper. This income from ads along with sales averaging five hundred thousand issues a week soon made Newnes a wealthy man.

In 1885 he moved his family and paper to London – to launch other publications while also serving three times in Parliament as a Liberal MP. He had

---

Newnes, Bart (London: Hodder and Stoughton, 1911. San Bernardino, California: Ulan Press, 2013 reprint). Both books provide biographical details although Jackson's also discusses what is going on in journalism during this period. Although Friedrichs worked for Newnes and had access to his notes, her book unfortunately smothers the facts amidst her sentimental, poorly written prose. Unless otherwise noted, all biographical details are from Jackson's book.

2 "Matlock Bath", accessed 6 December 2016, https://en.wikipedia.org/wiki/Matlock_Bath.

3 Stead later claimed that Silcoates taught him "Christianity, cricket and democracy"; Jackson, *George Newnes*, 21.

4 "Tit-bit / tid-bit", *OED Online*, accessed 6 December 2016, http://oed.com.

expensive homes in London along with a slowly developed and extravagant country estate on the North Devon coast – unfortunately named "Hollerday House". The location and views were enhanced with elaborate landscaping, tennis courts, croquet lawns and bowling greens. He also financed a small local railway for easy access. In "Ithaca" as Bloom thinks about improvements in the Dublin area – he imagines that "narrow gauge local railways" (*U* 17.1722–23) – along the coast – might help to attract more tourists. Among the many details for *his* fantasy estate in the country Bloom wanted to have "a tennis and fives court" (*U* 17.1552).[5] Could he have been following some of the press coverage about Newnes? The 1880s and 1890s saw a number of new, cheap, entertaining papers which Matthew Arnold pungently described this way: "The New Journalism … is full of ability, novelty, variety, sensation, sympathy, generous instincts: its one great fault is that it is featherbrained".[6] Newnes certainly helped shape what Arnold disparages – although Jackson traces a longer genealogy for the changing journalism – finding examples in the radical press of the 1830s along with features found in Sunday-only papers from the 1840s – as well as from the many chapbooks, almanacs and broadsheets churned out during these years.[7]

England's changing economy was another advantage for Newnes. He certainly benefited from the earlier removal of the stamp duty on newspapers in 1855, along with the contemporary expansion of literacy following the 1870 Education Act that outlawed child labour while mandating education for *all* children. These liberal changes helped fill new clerical and business jobs while generating more newspaper readers. At the same time, printing and publishing were substantially helped by the flow of new technologies – including the telegraph, telephone, high-speed rotary press as well as the monotype and linotype presses. Newnes embraced these changes along with tracking better ways to reproduce photographs and illustrations for his publications.

Tit-Bits was published on Thursdays for Saturday distribution – to coincide with many whose jobs had half-holidays on Saturdays. It is the kind of detail Newnes knew from his first jobs. He also realized that many more people were commuting – so he quickly made a canny deal to have W.H. Smith's railway

5 Gifford helps us here: "a tennis and five court – A building for court tennis (in which the side and end walls are in-bounds, as in squash) and for English handball, called 'fives'"; Don Gifford, *"Ulysses" Annotated: Notes for James Joyce's "Ulysses"*, 2nd ed. (Berkeley: University of California Press, 1988), 591.

6 Matthew Arnold, "Up to Easter", *Nineteenth Century* 21, no. 123 (1887): 638–39. A very different sort of "New Journalism" was promulgated by the American writer Tom Wolfe in the 1960s – which is not relevant here.

7 Jackson, *George Newnes*, 45–46.

bookstalls carry *Tit-Bits.* He then originated the paper's famous train-accident insurance policy: if you were killed in a train crash while carrying a *current* issue of *Tit-Bits*, your next of kin would be paid one hundred pounds. (But note that it had to be a current issue – nicely sustaining sales.) The policy was bannered on the paper's front page – and soon imitated, with slight differences, by other publishers. Newnes initially gave considerable attention to his paper, setting its amicable tone and non-judgmental voice, thereby creating a strong sense of community amongst its readers – a bit like today's online social networks.

The diverse array of short items, puzzles, contests, columns of inquiry and fiction made *Tit-Bits* able to offer something for everybody. Bloom got it right: "It's the ads and side features sell a weekly, not the stale news" (*U* 7.89–90). Nevertheless, I admit finding the paper's mulligatawny mix to be mind-numbing; however, it mimics well a wondering, wandering mind like Leopold Bloom's, albeit without his quirks or human appeal.

The front page of *Tit-Bits* alerted its readers: "One guinea per column is paid for original contributions to this paper" for both reportage and fiction. Occasionally grander prizes were offered. The 1883 *Tit-Bits* Villa competition for best story garnered over twenty-two thousand entries. Private William Mellish of the eighth Hussars was awarded a seven room semi-detached house (then known as a villa) in the Dulwich section of London.[8] Both the public and press became obsessed with the contest. Lord Salisbury (1830–1903) used the word "villa" – politically – remarking that many recent suburban voters were likely to switch to the Conservative Party, which Salisbury dubbed "Villa Toryism".[9] Salisbury served three times as Prime Minister while in strong opposition to Home Rule – explaining why he is dismissively referred to in "Aeolus":

---

8 Google images displays a *carte de visite* showing Mellish in front of the villa. Unhappily this image was auctioned on eBay before I started my research. It seems that Mellish's story had actually been written and published by someone else. When the real author found out he waggishly suggested an award of "a street", such as Piccadilly or Pall Mall. However, the original author and settlement both remain mysterious; Friedrichs, *The Life of Sir George Newnes, Bart*, 88.

9 Lord Salisbury first used the expression "Villa Toryism" in his letter of 25 June 1882 to Sir Stafford Northcote. The phrase quickly entered the political vocabulary; Peter Marsh, *The Discipline of Popular Government: Lord Salisbury's Domestic Strategy, 1881–1902* (Sussex: Harvester Press; Atlantic Highlands: Humanities Press, 1978), 63, n. 4. Marsh also explains how Gladstone was out-manoeuvred by Salisbury, who would only support the 1884 Third Reform Bill if the Liberals would agree to support Salisbury's 1885 Redistribution of Seats Act. These two bills were separate yet entangled. See also Herbert Van Thal, ed., *The Prime Ministers: from Sir Robert Walpole to Edward Heath* (New York: Stein and Day, 1975), and especially Alan Palmer on Lord Salisbury, 503–19.

LOST CAUSES
NOBLE MARQUESS IS MENTIONED

U 7.551–52

after which MacHugh comments, "We were always loyal to lost causes, ...We were never loyal to the successful. We serve them.... Material domination.... Lord Jesus? Lord Salisbury? A sofa in a westend club" (*U* 7.553–58). Joyce briskly melds two of Ireland's problems – effectively clubbing them both.

In 1889 *Tit-Bits* awarded one year's house rent for the best short story. In 1891 it offered one thousand pounds for the best serial, which was won by Grant Allen (1848–1899) for *What's Bred in the Bone*. Some trace Allen's title back to an old English proverb. The expression "what's bred in the bone" appears four times in *Ulysses*. It first surfaces in "Telemachus" as part of the ballad sung by Buck Mulligan – which actually was written by Oliver Gogarty (*U* 1.598). Later in "Nausicaa" the phrase is found again amidst Bloom's thoughts on the caprices of women (*U* 13.918) and in "Eumaeus" it makes two appearances, both in relation to the noble nature of Parnell's character (*U* 16.1338, 1520). Grant Allen's work cannot be pinned down to one genre; he explored science, social issues (especially in his 1895 *The Woman Who Did*) along with other novels, mysteries and science fiction, while continuing to write intermittently for Newnes. In "Cyclops", one of the interpolation – lists contains "The Woman Who Didn't" (*U* 12.186–87).

Bound volumes of *Tit-Bits* were published regularly, although ads were not included – which is a real loss to contemporary readers, since they provide such a rich window onto the period's problems, fads and culture. Where else could one learn about asbestos smoking pipes or "Cigars of Joy" for asthma and bronchitis? If you owned a pair of "Science-applied" suspenders from Crosstree Patent Adjusting Braces – your pants would always fit – even if you had put on weight. If those same trousers sprouted baggy-knees – the John Hamilton and Co.'s "portable trouser stretcher" would eliminate that problem. Various hygio-electric and electro-pathic belts offered relief from rheumatism. A person with literary interests yet tempted to dye their hair, would no doubt want to try the E. Griffiths Hughes brand – "TO DYE OR NOT TO DYE THAT IS THE QUESTION". If such a product caused you to cough – there was sure to be relief from Kemp's Whoopaline. Those upset about their safety pins rusting (and aren't we all) might be tempted to buy the exclusive safety pins made from German, non-corrosive silver, to assuage our distress.[10] I should add that bound volumes

10 I want to thank the Zurich James Joyce Foundation and Aida Yared for access to individual and bound copies of *Tit-Bits*. Aida Yared generously loaned me her cache of *Tit-Bits*, for which I am especially grateful.

of *Tit-Bits* included an index listing the current prize story winners, by name and location. It was good to see a fair number of women on the list, although overall more winners were men.[11]

In 1890 George Newnes and William T. Stead teamed up to publish the *Review of Reviews*; however, after a mere six months, Newnes asked Stead to buy him out, explaining his reasons in this letter to Stead:

> There is one kind of journalism which directs the affairs of nations; it makes and unmakes cabinets; it upsets governments, builds up Navies and does many other great things. It is magnificent. This is your journalism. There is another kind of journalism which has no such great ambitions. It is content to plod on, year after year, giving wholesome and harmless entertainment to crowds of hardworking people, craving for a little fun and amusement. It is quite humble and unpretentious. This is my journalism.[12]

However, Newnes did not include his uneasiness over Stead's growing involvement with spiritualism or with Stead's intention to publish a letter from socialist, theosophist, women's rights activist and supporter of Irish Home Rule Annie Besant.[13]

Newnes kept his *Review of Reviews* staff on the payroll while planning the *Strand Magazine*, which was launched in January 1891. This monthly was targeted at a more prosperous, tonier audience, featuring fiction, interviews and reportage along with many more photographs and artwork. Early promotions noted that Lord Tennyson had helped choose some of those to be interviewed. Later the magazine bragged that Beerbohm Tree, John Millais, Gladstone and Cardinal Manning had all been "most obliging".[14] Various ads in *The Strand* for stamp collections, fine art insurance and pianos were clearly aimed at those with money – including their ads for hair dye – and were more restrained than those found in *Tit-Bits*.

The Strand is still known today for publishing Sherlock Holmes.[15] The July 1891 issue included Conan Doyle's *A Scandal in Bohemia*, boosting sales

11 The last issue of *Tit-Bits* appeared on 18 July 1984. An attempted revival collapsed in 1989.

12 Jackson, *George Newnes*, 53.

13 Reginald Pound, *Mirror of the Century: The Strand Magazine, 1891–1950* (South Brunswick: A.S. Barnes, 1967), 29. The first edition of this book was published in 1966 as *The Strand Magazine, 1891–1950*.

14 Pound, *Mirror of the Century*, 34.

15 Several Sherlock Holmes stories had already appeared in other publications before their long run with *The Strand*.

considerably, so Newnes immediately acquired past and future copyright for these stories. The Sidney Paget drawings of Sherlock Holmes went on to fix our image of the detective for well over a century – in print, film and television. Only recently have there been real changes to that iconic look. Conan Doyle's 1910 interview with *Tit-Bits* offered some curious advice. He urged his audience to read good solid books; however readers were then encouraged to take notes, since he was convinced that reading without notes was like eating without digestion.

In "Eumaeus" as Bloom is trying to size up the red-bearded sailor we find him "Sherlockholmesing" the situation (*U* 16.831). In "Circe" part of the stage directions finds Bloom eating twelve dozen oysters (and their shells) before he is ordered to screw up his face to resemble a number of people – including Sherlock Holmes (*U* 15.1848–49). In "Ithaca" the catalogue of Bloom's books includes a copy of Conan Doyle's *The Stark-Munro Letters* (*U* 17.1375). After trying to read the book online, I now understand why Bloom's copy of the book is overdue at the library, since it wore me down didactically. (The Sherlock Holmes references in *Finnegans Wake* are for another day.)

The Strand attracted many other well-known writers, including Grant Allen, H.G. Wells, Rudyard Kipling, Agatha Christie, G.K. Chesterton, Dorothy Sayers, P.G. Wodehouse, Georges Simenon, Max Beerbohm, Winston Churchill, Somerset Maugham and Graham Greene. One of Queen Victoria's sketches appeared in the magazine although a cynic might suggest this was not solely on its artistic merits. The last issue of *The Strand* was published in 1950.

Newnes published an enormous number of other periodicals, focusing on children, sports, women's issues, the military and the Empire. He made an exception in 1893 with his *Westminster Gazette*, which was specifically intended to support the Liberal Party, thereby becoming his only politically focused paper. During these same years countless pamphlets, guides and books were churned out by Newnes Ltd. He really seems to have had an almost gambler-like compulsion to publish, especially since some of them were now losing money. His luck as a publisher was running out.

Early moving pictures caught Newnes' interest and money.[16] Initially he invested in the Kinesigraph (a camera for unperforated film), which didn't do well. In 1898 he invested in the motion picture studio American Mutoscope and Biograph Company and was later filmed in one of their features titled *Antarctic Expedition*, which he helped fund. By 1904 Dublin was also keeping up with the times by having two Mutoscope venues: the classier one

16 Stephen Herbert, Luke McKernan and individual contributors, "Who's Who of Victorian Cinema", accessed 6 December 2016, http://www.victorian-cinema.net/newnes.

was on Grafton Street, but the one Bloom patronized was close to Capel Street.[17] Bloom's memories in "Nausicaa" confirm this, "a dream of wellfilled hose. Where was that? Ah, yes. Mutoscope pictures in Capel street: for men only. Peeping Tom. Willy's hat and what the girls did with it. Do they snapshot those girls or is it all a fake? *Lingerie* does it" (*U* 13.793–96).[18]

Newnes also lost money investing in an oil-shale (!) project in New South Wales, in Peruvian rubber and in financing risky ideas, such as an Ever-Clean collar for men or a would-be alternative for pneumatic tires. His health began to decline from a combination of diabetes, alcohol and senility and he died in June 1910. His fortune was gone, leaving his son Frank to spend the better part of his life paying off his father's substantial debts. Although Newnes had no background as a writer or journalist, he "changed the landscape of British publishing".[19] The press empire he established – before its collapse – stemmed from his curiosity, energy and ambition. He was refreshingly direct about his talents, describing himself this way: "I am the average man. I don't have to put myself in his place. I am in his place. I know what he wants".[20] Such candor is rare.

Yet, he faced plenty of competition: within one year, there were twenty-two imitations of *Tit-Bits* along with a truck load of other new publications. T.P.O'Connor (1848–1929) was a journalist and publisher while serving as an MP in Parliament. His contentious Disraeli biography helped Gladstone win the election in 1880. O'Connor (sometimes dubbed "Tay Pay") began *The Star* in 1888 as a Liberal evening paper known for its political cartoons. Amidst the news-stand stack of papers in "Aeolus" Myles Crawford reminds his cronies that "Paddy Hooper worked Tay Pay who took him on to the *Star*" (*U* 7.687). Bloom mixes up the correct name of O'Connor's light entertaining weekly, M.A.P. (Mainly About People), which Bloom thinks is "Mainly all pictures" (*U* 7.97). Despite O'Connor's staunch support for Home Rule, he is sarcastically dealt with in "Cyclops": "Tay Pay's dinnerparty with perfidious Albion" (*U* 12.1387–88). O'Connor published the *Weekly Sun, The Sun* and *T.P.'s Weekly.*

17 Mullin explains that the venue Bloom must have gone to was on Parliament Street just south of the river from Capel Street; Katherine Mullin, *James Joyce, Sexuality and Social Purity* (Cambridge: Cambridge University Press, 2003), 146.

18 *Peeping Tom* (1901) and *What the Girls Did with Willy's Hat* (1897) were both Biograph films; single blurred photos from each film are on the cover page of *James Joyce Broadsheet* no. 49 (February 1998); Mullin, *James Joyce*, 147.

19 Margaret D. Stetz, "Publishing Industries and Practices", in *The Cambridge Companion to the Fin de Siècle*, ed. Gail Marshall (Cambridge: Cambridge University Press, 2007), 117.

20 Pound, *Mirror of the Century*, 25.

It was a surprise to learn that O'Connor also served as the first President of the British Board of Film Censors.[21]

Arthur Pearson (1866–1921) won a difficult *Tit-Bits* contest at the age of eighteen by correctly answering more of the questions than any of the other contestants. He immediately went to work for Newnes for almost six years, before leaving to publish *Pearson's Weekly* in 1890. In "Nausicaa" Gerty thinks, "Had her father only avoided the clutches of the demon drink, by taking the pledge or those powders the drink habit cured in Pearson's Weekly, she might now be rolling in her carriage, second to none" (*U* 13.290–92). During the 1890s, advertisers and publishers faced increased scrutiny for fraud and misrepresentation; Pearson was penalized for using his paper's entry fees for contest prize money. However, the charge did little to hurt his reputation or slow his publishing career.

Pearson's Magazine came out in 1896 – successfully aimed at a more educated audience. Pearson bought the *Morning Herald* in 1900, which merged into his London-based *Daily Express* later that year, becoming his most influential paper. Initially it startled its readers – having only news on its front page – with nary an ad. It was also the first paper in Britain to feature crossword puzzles. Two of the paper's editors are named in *Ulysses*.[22] However, the paper has no connection with today's *Daily Express* in England nor with Dublin's past *Daily Express*, which published twenty-one of Joyce's reviews and articles (some of which are very short), nor does it have any connection with the reviews written by Gabriel Conroy and Gallaher.

Pearson continued to acquire regional papers but lost his bid for the *London Times* to Alfred Harmsworth. He also published other periodicals and books before losing his sight in 1910. Consequently, he then sold his press holdings in order to concentrate on projects for the blind. By 1912 he published *Pearson's Easy Dictionary* in Braille; he also made special efforts to help the many soldiers who lost their sight during World War I. Pearson died in 1921 – following an accidental fall – for a bitter end to his doubly – productive life.

In "Aeolus" J.J.O'Molloy refers disparagingly to Gallaher's "Chapelizod boss, Harmsworth of the farthing press" (*U* 7.732–33). Alfred Harmsworth (1865–1922)

---

21 The following link includes a charming silent film showing O'Connor happily typing away: Robert Messenger, "ozTypewriter: The Wonderful World of Typewriters, 1714–2015", accessed 6 December 2016, http://oztypewriter.blogspot.ch/2013/09/rudyard-kipling-jmbarrie-talk-about.html.

22 Ralph D. Blumenfeld (*U* 7.688) and Ernest Victor Longworth (*U* 9.302): in both cases the editors are only given their last names.

was indeed born in Chapelizod, although his education and career were based in England. In his teens he started a school paper, but he soon switched to free-lancing for *Tit-Bits*, which published a number of his articles. In 1888 he started *Answers to Correspondents* – using the exact name of a column in *Tit-Bits* – which was soon shortened to *Answers*. It quickly matched the circulation of *Tit-Bits* – energizing Harmsworth to crank out – or buy – a wide range of publications. His 1890 *Comic Cuts* for kids pledged to be amusing without being vulgar. He took over the struggling *Evening News* before starting the *Daily Mail* in 1896 – which Lord Salisbury considered to have been written by office boys for office boys.[23]

Harmsworth's holdings continued to grow with the *Daily Mirror* in 1903, the *Observer* in 1905 and *The Times* of London in 1908 (outbidding Pearson). His company also acquired Canadian paper mills while promoting their publications widely. Soon, Harmsworth was overseeing the world's largest press conglomerate of the day. But, unlike Newnes, Harmsworth showed no reluctance in using his papers politically. During the First World War, he harshly attacked British military leadership – costing him a fair number of readers. After the war, he owned the *Times Literary Supplement* between 1920 and 1922. He died from a lingering staph infection in 1922 before antibiotics were available. In *Finnegans Wake*, Joyce nicely cobbles together three of the publishers we have just reviewed: "...with them newnesboys pearcin screaming off their armsworths" (*FW* 363.5–6).

Joyce's brother Stanislaus Joyce says that *Tit-Bits* "was the only one my father used to read for general culture", about which Eugene Sheehy tells us more:

> Joyce Senior apparently devoted a good deal of his spare time by studying the pictures in *Tit Bits* and *Answers* ... Joyce appeared to be entertained by this hobby of the old man. He told me that in the form he filled up, when seeking admission to the university, he described his father's occupation as 'going in for competitions'.[24]

To date, no such admission form has been found.

My Brother's Keeper continues with an equivocal account about a story Joyce apparently wrote:

23 Hamilton Fyfe, *Northcliffe: An Intimate Biography* (New York: Macmillan, 1930), 63.

24 Stanislaus Joyce, *My Brother's Keeper – James Joyce's Early Years* (New York: Viking Press, 1958), 92; Eugene Sheehy's remarks are found in *The Joyce We Knew: Memoirs of Joyce*, ed. Ulick O'Connor (1967; reprint Dingle: Brandon, 2004), 31.

> to the style of a weekly paper admired by Leopold Bloom, was to have been sent to *Titbits* as a joke and as an experiment in raising the wind. Not wanting to use his own name, he gave it to a young man of his acquaintance who rejoiced in the patronymic of MacGinty to send it in under that name. The last time I heard of the story, MacGinty was 'just going' to post it to *Titbits*. It takes so much out of one to put a manuscript in an addressed envelope with a brief covering letter![25]

The account continues with colourful details about the plot of this story – involving Russian anarchists, a masked ball, a woman in gypsy disguise called "the laughing witch", an assassination attempt, assorted arrests and an unlikely resolution. His brother adds – in contradiction – that Joyce's natural bent was for the plotless sketch. Jackson and Costello wonder if Joyce might have read an 1896 *Tit-Bits* story by John K. Leys titled "The Black Terror" before writing his story; they add that if Joyce's essay was in fact submitted, "it was James Joyce's first rejection, for it was never published".[26]

Confusing biographical details may stymie us but *Ulysses* readers know how comically Joyce stages the privy scene in "Calypso". While walking to the garden jakes, Bloom muses about manure, dung and cattle waste. But, before we continue with what then happens, it is time for a brisk historical look at the alternatives to toilet paper. Over the centuries an astonishing number of things have been used – including grass, moss, ferns, leaves, straw, hay, plant husks, corncobs, wood shavings, sea shells, rags, silk, wool, lace or just plain water.[27] However, by the seventh century the Chinese were using paper for cleansing. By the fourteenth century they were making a specific kind of paper for this purpose. As paper making spread from China through the Middle East to the West, many cultures used paper – once there was enough of it – especially from throwaways or scrap. Here endeth the lesson! And a return to Bloom:

> Asquat on the cuckstool he folded out his paper … No great hurry. Keep it a bit. Our prize titbit: *Matcham's Masterstroke*. Written by Mr Philip

25 Joyce, *My Brother's Keeper*, 91.

26 John Wyse Jackson and Peter Costello, *John Stanislaus Joyce: The Voluminous Life and Genius of James Joyce's Father* (London: Fourth Estate, 1997), 214.

27 Wikipedia and Google images provided some of this information. However, I used to make hand-made paper myself and learned some of paper's intriguing history. The online "Virtual Toilet Paper Museum" has pedestrian information about the product, but a more thorough exploration of the various holders for those rolls of toilet paper: "The Virtual Toilet Paper Museum", accessed 6 December 2016, https://web.archive.org/web/20150915034715/http://nobodys-perfect.com/vtpm/index.html.

> Beaufoy, Playgoers' Club, London. Payment at the rate of one guinea a column has been made to the writer ... He read on ... *Matcham often thinks of the masterstroke by which he won the laughing witch who now*. Begins and ends morally. *Hand in hand*. Smart ... he envied kindly Mr Beaufoy ... Might manage a sketch. By Mr and Mrs L.M. Bloom. Invent a story for some proverb. Which? ... He tore away half the prize story sharply and wiped himself with it.
>
> *U* 4.500–537

It has been known for some time that *Tit-Bits* published a number of stories by Beaufoy; however, recent sleuthing by John Simpson gives us more facts – most of which cannot be included here – except to say that Beaufoy also published under the name of Philip Beaufoy Barry.[28] The excerpt above mentions the "laughing witch" from Stanislaus's summary of Joyce's story. She is mentioned again in "Sirens" as Bloom tries to cover up what he is writing to Martha Clifford – along with another topic Bloom might write up for *Tit-Bits*: "Blot over the other so he can't read. There. Right. Idea prize titbit. Something detective read off blottingpad. Payment at the rate of guinea per col. Matcham often thinks the laughing witch" (*U* 11.901–3). Later in "Nausicaa" Bloom thinks about writing "*The Mystery Man on the Beach*, prize titbit story by Mr Leopold Bloom" (*U* 13.1060).

References to Beaufoy and writing a prize story keep surfacing in *Ulysses*. To give a few examples, "Circe" stages an extended scenario involving Bloom and Beaufoy, after Bloom brags that he is an author and journalist whose "collection of prize stories" is about to be published (*U* 15.802). Beaufoy confronts Bloom with a barrage of insults, noting that Bloom is "no born gentleman ... a plagiarist ... and a soapy sneak masquerading as a *littérateur*" (*U* 15.820–23). Bloom meekly mentions his doubts about the laughing witch, which Beaufoy ignores.

In "Eumaeus" Bloom's late-night thoughts return to Beaufoy and to prize-story writing:

> To improve the shining hour he wondered whether he might meet with anything approaching the same luck as Mr Philip Beaufoy if taken down in writing suppose he were to pen something out of the common groove

28 "Philip Beaufoy and the Philosopher's Tone", *James Joyce Online Notes*, accessed 6 December 2016, http://www.jjon.org/jioyce-s-people/beaufoy. Elisabetta d'Erme provides further details in her essay in this volume.

> (as he fully intended doing) at the rate of one guinea per column. *My Experiences*, let us say, *in a Cabman's Shelter*.
>
> *U* 16.1227–31

Somewhat later Bloom succumbs to another fantasy: "All kinds of Utopian plans were flashing through his (B's) busy brain, education (the genuine article), literature, journalism, prize titbits, up to date billing, concert tours in English watering resorts…" (*U* 16.1652–54).

"Ithaca" includes part of Bloom's "first piece of original verse" – written when he was eleven – and submitted to the *Shamrock*, a Dublin weekly:

> *An ambition to squint*
> *At my verses in print*
> *Makes me hope that for these you'll find room.*
> *If you so condescend*
> *Then please place at the end*
> *The name of yours truly, L. Bloom.*
>
> *U* 17.392–401

(I cannot help wondering how many eleven year olds today would know or use the word "condescend".) Richard Pigott (1828–1889) founded the *Shamrock* in 1866 as a "national weekly journal of Irish history, literature, arts, &c".[29] Excuse my lack of "hesitancy" in pointing out that Pigott certainly found his place in Irish history, having forged the Parnell letters, falsely linking Parnell to the Phoenix Park murders.

"Penelope" appears to be free of *Tit-Bits* since Molly recalls only two other papers. After she has mistakenly left one of her gloves in the D B C lavatory – distracted about Boylan – Bloom suggests she place an ad for the missing glove in *The Irish Times* (*U* 18.255), which Molly ignores. Her later newspaper memory is more chilling:

> youd never know what old beggar at the door for a crust with his long story might be a tramp and put his foot in the way to prevent me shutting it like that picture of that hardened criminal he was called in Lloyds Weekly news 20 years in jail then he comes out and murders an old woman for

29 Barbara Hayley, "A Reading and Thinking Nation: Periodicals as the Voice of Nineteenth-Century Ireland", in *300 Years of Irish Periodicals*, eds. Barbara Hayley and Enda McKay (Gigginstown: Lilliput Press, 1987), 44–48. A footnote adds that Pigott sold the *Shamrock* in 1879 to the Irish National Newspaper and Publishing Company – before his suicide.

> her money … I couldnt rest easy till I bolted all the doors and windows to make sure.
>
> *U* 18.989–95

Lloyd's Weekly Newspaper was a Sunday paper published in London between 1842 and 1931. I am curious that Molly is familiar with the paper, described by Gifford to be "conservative" but not "yellow".[30]

At least sixty-five different papers, periodicals and magazines are mentioned in *Ulysses* – easily proving Joyce's interest in the press. Both he and Sylvia Beach used press clipping services during their Paris years. His letters are filled with comments about or requests for various publications – especially those to family members and Frank Budgen. Nor should we forget his wide-ranging articles and reviews – particularly for Dublin's *Daily Express* (1891–1921) and Trieste's *Piccolo della Sera*. "Aeolus" is saturated with the world of newspapers – as is some of Bloom's working life – although I suspect he will probably never actually write up anything for *Tit-Bits*. Joyce's letter to George Antheil from January 1931 is of interest here: "I am quite content to go down to posterity as a scissors and paste man for that seems to me a harsh but not unjust description" (*Letters I* 297). I would suggest that there is no problem in seeing *Tit-Bits* as the epitome of a scissors and paste paper.

On the other hand, back in April 1907 – Joyce boasted to Stanislaus – "I may not be the Jesus Christ I once fondly imagined myself, but I think I must have a talent for journalism" (*JJII* 255). Fortunately for us Joyce did not get that exactly right.

30 Gifford, *"Ulysses" Annotated*, 625.

CHAPTER 2

Bloom, the Dandy, the Nymph and the Old Hag: *Tit-Bits* and *Photo Bits*, Reflections of the Victorian Press in James Joyce's *Ulysses*

Elisabetta d'Erme

Abstract

The two late Victorian penny weeklies, *Tit-Bits* and *Photo Bits*, play an important role in the narrative of James Joyce's *Ulysses*. An analysis of their peculiarities and the use Joyce makes of them, especially of the "Prize Tit-Bit" competition and the *Photo Bits* ads column, illustrates this. With particular focus on Leopold Bloom and his interest in these periodicals, both as an advertising canvasser and as a casual reader, *Tit-Bits* can be appreciated for the various ways Joyce reworked it into *Ulysses* in, for example, his treatment of the figure of the prize-winning writer Philip Beaufoy. *Photo Bits*, on the other hand, a periodical heavily illustrated with photographs and advertisements and amounting to what, in today's terms, may be described as a soft porn magazine, provided traits that resurface in the more erotically charged episodes like "Calypso", "Nausicaa", "Circe", "Ithaca" and "Penelope". We will see how, by opting for a style in which he assembled and recycled texts from the mass media like the periodicals, Joyce was able to transform advertising slogans into declarations of love, weather forecasts into acknowledgements of failure, prize stories into chances of social advancement, or penny weekly supplements into works of art.

Keywords

Ulysses – Victorian popular press – *Tit-Bits* – George Newnes – Philip Beaufoy – Penny weeklies – *Photo Bits* – advertising – competitions and prize games – style and memory

In this essay I will be discussing *Tit-Bits* and *Photo Bits*, two late Victorian penny weeklies that play an important role in the narrative of *Ulysses*. I'll analyse their peculiarities and the use that Joyce makes of these publications, especially the "Prize Tit-Bit" competition and the *Photo Bits* ads column. I will also focus on Leopold Bloom's interest in these periodicals as an advertising

 | DOI 10.1163/9789004359062_004

canvasser and as a casual reader. Furthermore, we will see how Joyce, opting for a style "à la *Tit-Bits*" in which he assembled and recycled text from the mass media, was able to transform slogans into love declarations, weather forecasts into acknowledgements of failure, prize stories into chances of social advancement, or penny weekly supplements into works of art.

The Old Hag's Heritage

My research at the Colindale Newspaper department of the British Library began under the conviction that James Joyce was a product of Victorian culture. He was in his late teens when Queen Victoria died on 22 January 1901, and besides his classical and Jesuit upbringing, he grew up reading all kinds of Victorian literature as well as typical Victorian newspapers and periodicals, from the *Daily Mail* to *Ally Sloper's Half-Holiday*.

Late Victorian Dublin, where Joyce lived until he was twenty-two, was a colonial city overwhelmed by British publications like *The Sun* or *The Illustrated London News* and popular weeklies, which were the new expressions of mass culture. Copies of *Tit-Bits* or *Answers* were typically found in Victorian homes and in Joyce's later dwellings in the north inner city of Dublin. The Victorian popular press provided him with important working material. He understood the newspaper business, its formats, advertising and its role as a mass medium. Joyce also decided to involve Leopold Bloom in newsprint and advertising, fields which at that time were considered to be lowbrow. However, Joyce's Dublin was also full of people involved in the publishing industry. Over eighty newspapers are listed in the 1906 *Thom's Directory*, from the *Freeman's Journal* to the *Irish Cyclist*.

In fact, under the reign of the "great squaw Victoria" (*U* 12.1525),[1] publishing had steadily gathered momentum thanks to the abolition of the "Taxes on Knowledge",[2] the invention of faster transport systems, important progress in telecommunication, as well as cheaper, faster and better ways of printing

1 There are two dozen references that Joyce makes to "old Vic" (*U* 12.1395) in *Ulysses*, like the "Old hag with the yellow teeth. *Vieille ogresse* with the *dents jaunes*" (*U* 3.232-33), the "old queen in a bathchair" (*U* 8.710), "the flatulent old bitch that's dead" (*U* 12.1392), or "the white chief woman, the great squaw Victoria" (*U* 12.1525).

2 Taxes on Knowledge: Advertisement duty (3 shillings and sixpence per ad) abolished in 1837, Stamp tax (compulsory penny newspaper stamp) abolished in 1855, Paper duty abolished 1861; see Leah Price, "Victorian Reading", in *The Cambridge History of Victorian Reading*, ed. Kate Flint (Cambridge: Cambridge University Press, 2012), 41.

and producing paper.[3] As a consequence of these innovations, newspapers, magazines and novels became available and affordable to all classes of society, even the poorest. The "Thumping. Thumping" "printingworks" (*U* 7.72, 33), the rotary printing presses and the linotypes, the telegraph and the telephone are topics which have been frequently discussed in connection with Joyce, as in Fritz Senn's chapter "Stephen *Telegraphos*".[4] Less discussed are references to the abolition of the "Taxes on Knowledge" or to the change from cotton-rags paper to wood-pulp paper. At the beginning of the nineteenth century two thirds of publishers' total outlay was spent on paper. In fact, during the Napoleonic Wars England suffered an acute paper shortage and, as supplies of cotton rags could not keep pace with the high demand, the price of paper doubled. After some experimentation with esparto and jute fibre, around 1870, wood-pulp paper was invented in Sweden and, by 1890, it was supplying the growing British newspaper industry with cheaper raw material. The drop in paper prices resulted in a drastic reduction of newspapers' costs. The more economical wood-pulp paper also fostered the birth of popular weeklies, enabling the printing industry to rethink layout, increase page numbers and give more space to illustrations and ads.

On 16 June 1904 in the "Lotus Eaters" episode, we find Joyce's Bloom "smelling freshprinted rag paper" (*U* 5.58) from a newly purchased copy of the *Freeman's Journal*, while, as we have seen, the switch from rag to wood-pulp paper had occurred at least 10 years before. Nonetheless, Joyce may be suggesting that Bloom is "remembering" an earlier moment of his life when he smelt freshly printed rag paper, and also hinting at the strong physical relationship (almost addict like) that Bloom has with his paper.

The effects of the abolition of the "Taxes on Knowledge" were also crucial for the Irish publishing industry, enabling the birth of a wide number of nationalist papers, such as the weekly *United Irishman* established by the founder of Sinn Fein, Arthur Griffith; or the *Irish Independent*, a paper quoted by Joyce in "Aeolus", "Wandering Rocks", "Sirens", "Ithaca" and much discussed by the Citizen in the "Cyclops" episode. It was founded by Charles Parnell shortly before his death in 1891 in order to compete with the anti-Parnellism of the *Freeman's Journal*, but the paper was chronically in financial trouble, and in 1900 it was bought by William Martin Murphy who merged it with the *Daily Nation*.

---

3 These include railways and steamboats, the electric telegraph and the laying of transoceanic telegraphic cables, high-speed rotary printing presses and new means of reproducing illustrations, the telephone, machines for typesetting such as linotypes and cheap wood-pulp paper.

4 Fritz Senn, *Ulyssean Close-ups* (Roma: Bulzoni Editore, 2007), 81–89.

In 1904, Murphy transformed the *Irish Daily Independent* into a stylish, gossipy, philo-imperial, reactionary gazette. In "Cyclops" the Citizen calls William Martin Murphy "the Bantry jobber" (*U* 12.237) and cries, "And look at this blasted rag, ...Look at this, ...*The Irish Independent*, if you please, founded by Parnell to be the workingman's friend" (*U* 12.219–21) and then he goes on to quote from the marriages column of the real *Irish Daily Independent* issue of 16 June 1904.

Murphy was not the only real "Gentleman of the press" (*U* 7.20) quoted in *Ulysses*, a book which teems with the names and deeds of a wide range of clever entrepreneurs who made the British publishing industry. I could talk about them all, but I will limit myself to George Newnes, the man who invented a weekly that was going to mark the history of mass culture: *Tit-Bits*.

Tit-Bits's Unique Formula

By 1900, in Great Britain the most popular penny weeklies were George Newnes's *Tit-Bits*, also called "the verdant one" because of its green cover, *Pearson's Weekly* with its pink cover, and Harmsworth's *Answers to Correspondents* with its orange cover. Together, they were selling over two million copies per week. Harmsworth's description of *Answers* could equally apply to the other two:

> We are a sort of Universal Information provider. Anyone who reads our paper for a year will be able to converse on many subjects on which he was entirely ignorant. He will have a good stock of anecdotes and jokes and will indeed be a pleasant companion.[5]

Indeed, these three penny weeklies were the perfect periodicals for men longing "to converse on many subjects" and to be "pleasant companions", like John Stanislaus Joyce or Leopold Bloom. These papers were not only avidly read by Joyce's father, but represented a longstanding presence in James Joyce's mental landscape. In "Calypso", "Sirens", "Nausicaa", "Circe", "Eumaeus" and "Ithaca" we find more than twenty references to the "verdant one", quoted as "Titbits": one word, only the initial letter capitalised, without hyphen.

Tit-Bits appeared on the publishing scene on 22 October 1881 in Manchester. George Newnes' original formula changed popular journalism and, adapting itself to the times, survived until 1984, becoming an integral part of British popular and cultural identity for more than a century. *Tit-Bits* can be seen as

5 W. Hamish Fraser, *The Coming of the Mass Market 1850–1914* (London: Macmillan, 1981), 73.

a product of the so called "March of Intellect", which was the definition used in satiric cartoons to describe the British working classes' struggle for cultural advancement.[6] Newnes saw readers from this milieu, from the lower-middle and upper-working classes, as the ideal target for his new enterprise.

Tit-Bits was essentially a miscellany paper: a 16 page patchwork with a bit of everything. As the title – *Tit-Bits from All the Most Interesting Books, Periodicals and Contributors in the World* – suggests, it was mostly a cut-and-paste bricolage of texts from existing publications plus readers' contributions. The "Answers to Correspondents" column was particularly successful because it offered the space for interactive dialogue between the publisher and the reader. By current standards, the range of knowledge *Tit-Bits* offered to its readers looks remarkably broad. Its synthetic patterns and its democratic openness made this magazine a precursor to modern TV formats based on the interactive participation of the audience, and to modern social-networks such as blogs or Facebook.

However, what made *Tit-Bits* so peculiar was that Newnes offered his readers not only a useful, pleasant paper, but the unique chance to become members of the interactive community of "loyal Tit-Bitites": a bond of fellowship aiming to "recreate a sort of pre-industrial social model of mutual responsibility".[7] Furthermore, Newnes's community was a secularized one, rather than a religious or political one and had no proselytizing strains.

Besides letters and competitions, readers were actively involved in the "making" of the magazine by means of their "original contributions". They were encouraged to enter a variety of competitions that offered money prizes for the best jokes, anecdotes, short stories, quizzes and "treasure hunts". The result was a broad range of styles used by hundreds of prize winners in their original stories, which were often mere imitations of bestselling authors of the times. Consequently *Tit-Bits* provided Joyce with a gallery of literary persiflage that he would have loved. In addition, it had its own distinctive quality in the language of advertising.

Tit-Bits offered its readers and contributors the creative freedom of an open text. It was this structure, with its many different voices, that Joyce developed in *Ulysses*'s community of speech, a treasure trove for a writer who had in mind

6 A selection of these has been digitized by the British Museum and is available at its web site accessed 6 December 2016: http://www.britishmuseum.org/research/collection_online/search.aspx?searchText=%22march+of+intellect%22.

7 Kate Jackson, "George Newnes and the 'Loyal Tit-Bitites': Editorial Identity and Textual Interaction in *Tit-Bits*", in *Nineteenth-Century Media and the Construction of Identities,* eds. Laurel Brake, Bill Bell and David Finkelstein (New York: Palgrave, 2000), 17.

to write a book where each chapter would have a different style, if not different styles within itself. The magazine's initial title, *Tit-Bits from All the Most Interesting Books, Periodicals and Newspapers in the World*, soon changed to *Tit-Bits from All the Most Interesting Books, Periodicals and Contributors in the World*, and from the 1930s onward it was *Tit-Bits for Great Fun and Splendid Prizes*.

Although it was designed for the masses, *Tit-Bits* captured the interest of intellectuals and writers from the very beginning, not least James Joyce who cherished reading it all his life.[8] Initially, the title of this penny weekly must have caught Joyce's interest: "Titbit" means a small piece of tasty food, or a small and particularly interesting item of gossip or information; and "tit" means tender, young girl, is slang for a woman's breast and (British informal) for a foolish person.[9]

The Tit-Bitites Community

Joyce's family may have been among the earliest members of the so called "Tit-Bitites" "discursive community". It would be hard to call James's father, John Stanislaus Joyce, a bookish man. One of the very few novels that he supposedly read was *The House by the Churchyard* by Joseph Sheridan Le Fanu. We also know that his most cherished readings were penny weeklies, most of all *Tit-Bits* and *Answers*. He used to spend a great deal of time taking part in competitions organized by these papers, hoping to win a "crisp five pound note" like Ben Dollard in "Sirens": "Decent soul. Bit addled now. Thinks he'll win in *Answers*, poets' picture puzzle. We hand you crisp five pound note" (*U* 11.1023–24).

John Wyse Jackson and Peter Costello report that Joyce told his friend Eugene Sheehy that, on his college application form under "occupation of father", he had put "going in for competitions".[10] Even if it was only a joke, that was what John Stanislaus Joyce used to do, trying to win cash prizes wherever possible.

8 Throughout the literature of the time, references to *Tit-Bits* are widely to be found, for example in Kipling's *The Finest Story in the World*, H.G. Wells's "*The First Men in the Moon*", or Orwell's "*Animal Farm*". In *New Grub Street*, George Gissing mocks journals like *Tit-Bits* in his description of the new periodical *Chit-Chat* (a thinly veiled analogue of *Tit-Bits*), whose articles were supposed to contain "bits of stories, bits of description, bits of scandal, bits of jokes, bits of statistic, bits of foolery" and were to be no longer than "two inches"; George Gissing, *New Grub Street* (London: Smith Elder, 1891), 232.

9 *OED Online*, accessed 6 December 2016, http://oed.com.

10 John Wyse Jackson and Peter Costello, *John Stanislaus Joyce: The Voluminous Life and Genius of James Joyce's Father* (New York: St. Martin's Press, 1998), 213.

This makes it more than likely that copies of *Tit-Bits* were to be found in Joyce's many dwellings in Dublin, from the middle-class ones of his early youth to the miserable ones in the north inner city of his early twenties. *Tit-Bits* was a steadfast presence in Joyce's homes where he grew up reading it, as highlighted by Joyce's brother Stanislaus in *My Brother's Keeper*: "'That *Titbits* paper' was the only one my father used to read for general culture"[11] and in Joyce's mind this penny weekly must have been closely associated with the figure of his father, the memory of his voice and the flow of jokes, anecdotes and stories he used to tell in Dublin pubs.

Tit-Bits provided John Stanislaus Joyce not only with a good stock of anecdotes and jokes but also with a good source of prize games, and "competitions" were precisely the means George Newnes used to gain the loyalty of his readers. In exchange he offered them a sort of complicity pact, sealed with valued prizes. Amongst the biggest prizes ever offered was a "*Tit-Bits* Villa" in 1883 for the best Christmas story (max. 3000 words), consisting of a seven-room freehold house, plus bath, scullery and cellar. The villa became for many years a sightseeing destination for hundreds of *Tit-Bits* readers and was widely referred to in the pages of the magazine for many years to come.[12] We may suppose that some recollections of those ads for the "*Tit-Bits* Villa" may have found their way into the description of "Bloom Cottage. Saint Leopold's. Flowerville" in "Ithaca" (*U* 17.1580), which might have resembled it closely, both suggesting a dream of domestic bliss.

What's New in "an old number of *Titbits*"?

If perception is interpreted as impressions occurring when "remembered" (sometimes many years later), then memory is nothing else than an active process that steadily produces new perceptions. How does this process work in regard to James Joyce's recollections of the popular press? A good example is the competition "Prize Tit-Bit for an Original Complete Story". In 1888 *Tit-Bits* published an advertisement inviting "litterateurs" to submit their stories to the paper and, a year later, the competition was first introduced. Each winning text, usually three to five columns long, was traditionally preceded by the following ritual formulation: "The following has been judged by the Arbitrators

11 Stanislaus Joyce, *My Brother's Keeper: James Joyce's Early Years*, ed. Richard Ellmann (London: Faber and Faber, 1958), 106.

12 Hulda Friederichs, *The Life of Sir George Newnes, Bart.* (London: Hodder and Stoughton, 1911), 87.

to be the best story sent in, and has therefore gained the prize. Payment at the rate of One Guinea per column has been sent to the author"; this was followed by the name and address of the lucky winner.

Some contributors were frequent "Prize Tit-Bit" winners, like Mr John J. Armstrong from Birmingham or Mr R.E. Young from Stoke Newington, but among them there is a name that catches the eye because of its exceptional frequency: Mr Philip Beaufoy. In fact, between January 1897 and December 1904, Mr Philip Beaufoy was the winner of the "Prize Tit-Bit for an Original Complete Story" competition an astonishing twenty-eight times.

Philip Beaufoy's identity has finally been established as that of Philip (Zaleg) Bergson (1871–1947).[13] Philip Beaufoy, also known as Philip Beaufoy Barry, beside being a compulsive "Prize Tit-Bit" writer and subsequently the "Winner of the George Newnes Gold Medal for Fiction", was a journalist, a writer of books for children and of a number of handbooks of practical hints, such as *How to Succeed as a Writer,*[14] *Sinners Down the Centuries*[15] or *The Secret Power: A Handbook to the Art of Living.*[16] Like his father, Michael Bergson,[17] Philip was a musician and he wrote the lyrics for his father's composition "Firelight Visions" for soprano or tenor in B flat. He had four brothers and four sisters. All this also means that Philip Beaufoy was none other than the brother of the artist and occultist Moina Mathers, wife of Samuel Liddell "MacGregor" Mathers, and of the Nobel prize-winning Henri-Louis Bergson, one of the leading philosophers of the early twentieth century, whose work played a major role in the creation

13 Information on Philip Beaufoy's identity has been divulged by John Simpson, who explains that the real identity of Philip Beaufoy was revealed in a legal notice published in the *London Gazette* and the (London) *Times* by his executors shortly after his death in 1947: "*Philip Bergson deceased. Pursuant to the Trustee Act 1925 All persons having claims against the ESTATE of PHILIP BERGSON, also known as PHILIP BEAUFOY also known as PHILIP BEAUFOY BARRY late of Heathfield Hotel Guildford Street W.C.1, formerly of 31 Regent Square, W.C.1, the Stage Guild, 9 Great Newport Street, W.C.2 and the O.P. Club, 3, King William Street, W.C.2. who died on the Nineteenth day of January 1947 are required to send particulars thereof in writing to the Trustee Department Barclays Bank Limited, 27, Regent Street, S.W.1.*", from *The Times*, 25 April 1947, p. 1; "Philip Beaufoy and the Philosopher's Tone", *James Joyce Online Notes*, accessed 6 December 2016, http://www.jjon.org/jioyce-s-people/beaufoy.

14 London: Allen & Unwin, 1927.

15 London: Jarrolds, 1929.

16 London: 1927.

17 Michael Bergson (Warsaw 1820 – London 1898) was a pianist and composer. A pupil of Chopin, he lived in Switzerland, France, Italy and England. He wrote operas, songs, pianoforte sketches, and the *Scena ed aria* for clarinet, played by military bands throughout the world.

of James Joyce's "stream of consciousness" technique.[18] It is unlikely that Joyce was aware of the real identity of a man whose name must have caught his attention while reading it in a late Victorian penny weekly. What I want to do is to examine how Joyce memorized and subsequently used in *Ulysses* a name and address that he had read in Dublin around 1900 in *Tit-Bits*.

The "Prize Tit-Bit" first appears near the end of the "Calypso" episode in a famous passage concerning Bloom's morning habits in the "jakes"[19] (*U* 4.494): "A paper. He liked to read at stool. Hope no ape comes knocking just as I'm. In the tabledrawer he found an old number of *Titbits*" (*U* 4.465–67). Then after a few lines:

> Asquat on the cuckstool he folded out his paper, turning its pages over on his bared knees. Something new and easy. No great hurry. Keep it a bit. Our prize titbit: *Matcham's Masterstroke*. Written by Mr Philip Beaufoy, Playgoers' Club, London. Payment at the rate of one guinea a column has been made to the writer. Three and a half. Three pounds three. Three pounds, thirteen and six.
>
> *U* 4.500–105

Leopold Bloom reads on and on, "seated calm above his own rising smells" (*U* 4.512–13). After finishing both his activities he envies "kindly Mr Beaufoy", wondering if he too could win a prize titbit for a "sketch" or a story signed by Mr and Mrs L.M. Bloom (*U* 4.516, 518). Eventually, after some afterthought: "He tore away half the prize story sharply and wiped himself with it" (*U* 4.537).

As a matter of fact, the "Prize Tit-Bit" for an "Original Complete Story" was of direct interest to James Joyce; it belonged to his storage of personal, subjective memories. Richard Ellmann reports Stanislaus Joyce's account that, while a student at Belvedere in 1893, Joyce wrote a story for *Tit-Bits* called "Matcham's Masterstroke" (*JJII* 50). The story, which was about a fake Russian diplomat, a Nihilist and a charming "laughing witch", was never published (maybe also because of its allusive title). Instead, in the 1 May 1897 issue, *Tit-Bits* published

18 Perusing Philip Bergson's literary production, one is compelled to think that he must have been a real source of embarrassment for his genial brother, which might also explain the decision to write under pseudonyms.

19 In using the noun "jakes" Joyce may have had in mind the Elizabethan wordplay between "a jakes" (for privy) and Ajax, the Homeric Greek warrior, a wordplay treasured by William Shakespeare in his only play with an Homeric background, *Troilus and Cressida*, in relation to the "blockish" character of the Ajax opposed to the "wise" Ulysses. It may be interesting to note that, in the 1930s, ajax became the brand of a popular toilet cleaning product.

a "Prize Tit-Bit" story based on a similar subject entitled "For Vera's Sake", for which: "Payment at the rate of one guinea per column has been sent to Mr. Philip Beaufoy, Playgoers' Club, Strand. W.C.". The young Joyce must have been understandably upset, but his "Matcham's Masterstroke" went on to become a private family joke and provided material for his master-piece.

Joyce was not the only writer who had a story rejected by the *Tit-Bits* arbitrators. Many writers of the time tried to win a "Prize Tit-Bit" without success. For example, Virginia Woolf's rejected *Tit-Bits* story was later to become the novel *The Voyage Out*. It's a pity that there are no *Tit-Bits* archives left, as they may have provided us with valuable information.[20]

The Story of an Obsession

From the moment Leopold Bloom locks himself into the jakes, reads Philip Beaufoy's story and uses it to wipe himself, "Prize Tit-Bit" becomes for him not only toilet paper but also the allegory of a successful life. In fact, Bloom sees winning a "Prize Tit-Bit"[21] as the answer to all the humiliations and defeats in the world, and not only for himself. For example, in "Eumaeus" he dashes through a brilliant possible future for Stephen Dedalus as well: "All kinds of Utopian plans were flashing through his (B's) busy brain, education (the genuine article), literature, journalism, prize titbits" (*U* 16.1652–53). Moreover, in "Sirens", we see Bloom writing a letter to Martha Clifford. After having used the blotting paper, he wonders: "Blot over the other so he can't read. There. Right. Idea prize titbit. Something detective read off blottingpad. Payment at the rate of guinea per col. Matcham often thinks the laughing witch" (*U* 11.901–3).

20 Vanessa Bell wrote this remembrance for a reading at the Memoir Club after Virginia Woolf's death: "I think it must have been a good deal later that she sent a short story to *Tit Bits*, keeping it a deadly secret from all but me. *Tit Bits* was our favourite weekly, which we used to buy together with 3d worth of Fry's Chocolate, taking both to Kensington Gardens to read and eat together, lying in the grass under the trees on summer afternoons. The story was refused – as far as I remember, it was a wildly romantic account of a young woman on a ship – and the secret kept till this day".

Vanessa Bell, "Notes on Virginia's Childhood", in *Interviews and Recollections*, ed. John Henry Stape (Iowa: University of Iowa Press, 1995), 8.

21 Bloom's desire to have a story published by *Tit-Bits* recalls "A Little Cloud" in *Dubliners* where Little Chandler also desires to see one of his unwritten poems published in a London paper, but for both it will remain an unrealised dream.

Later on, in "Nausicaa", after having met Gerty, Bloom is still obsessed with "Prize Tit-Bit": "*The Mystery Man on the Beach*, prize titbit story by Mr Leopold Bloom. Payment at the rate of one guinea per column" (*U* 13.1060–61). When asked his profession and trade in "Circe", Bloom declares himself to be an "author-journalist", who is "bringing out a collection of prize stories of which [he is] the inventor" (*U* 15.802–3). Finally, if we assume that, in "Eumaeus", the narrating voice is heavily co-edited by Bloom, we may read the episode (a pastiche of literary Victorian styles) as Poldy's own draft for a "Prize Tit-Bit original story". In fact, in the middle of the night, after the adventurous flight with Stephen from Bella Cohen's bordello to the cabman's shelter, Bloom thinks:

> To improve the shining hour he wondered whether he might meet with anything approaching the same luck as Mr Philip Beaufoy if taken down in writing suppose he were to pen something out of the common groove (as he fully intended doing) at the rate of one guinea per column. *My Experiences*, let us say, *in a Cabman's Shelter* (*U* 16.1227–31).

The "palefaced" Philip Beaufoy reappears, in dandy-like attire, in a long passage in "Circe" (*U* 15.814ff.) carrying "a large portfolio labelled *Matcham's Masterstrokes*" and accusing Bloom of being "A plagiarist. A soapy sneak masquerading as a *littérateur*" but also a "funny ass" and a "low cad". Beaufoy then produces from his portfolio a specimen of his "Prize Tit-Bit" story "disfigured by the hallmark of the beast", the "damning evidence" of Bloom's "moral rottenness" (*U* 15.842–45). Beaufoy is mentioned for the last time in "Ithaca" when Bloom is once more obsessed about "certain possibilities of financial, social, personal and sexual success" (*U* 17.650, 646–47).

The Dandy's Address

As we have already noticed, the formulaic incipit of "Prize Tit-Bit" contained the winner's name, surname and address. This information was supposed to be true to fact. Beaufoy's surname recalls references to a Huguenot ancestry and, in addition, *beau* evokes beauty, a companion or lover, a dandy or a fop, and *foy* a feast, a farewell gift or drink as well as faith or foyer. In Bloom's mind Beaufoy's name is sometimes also confused with that of Mrs Purefoy. So, it is a name that suggests a happy occurrence, an inviting foyer, but also the theatrical role of the buffo or "buffoon".

From his first winning story, published in January 1897, to his last, published in December 1904, Beaufoy kept giving slightly different addresses: "Playgoers'

Club, Strand, W.C." (in 1897) – "Playgoers' Club, Strand" (from 1898 to February 1901) – "Playgoers' Club, Strand, W.C." (August 1901) – "Playgoers' Club, Clement's Inn, W.C." (from October 1901 to December 1901) – "Playgoers' Club, Strand, W.C." (in June 1902) – "6, Clement's Inn, W.C." (from November 1902 to December 1904).[22] However, these original addresses differ slightly from the address given in "Calypso", in the story that Leopold reads in the jakes: "Playgoers' Club, London" (*U* 4.503).[23]

What catches the eye when reading the addresses is that almost all of them have the post code for the Western Central area of London. Here we can see how Joyce's "symbolic memory" works in regard to the perception of images or, in this case, of the abbreviation of the W.C. I would like to suggest that one of the reasons why Joyce may have decided to use Philip Beaufoy's name, among hundreds of other "Prize Tit-Bit" winners, lies in his address, a "portmanteau word" which he was able to link with a cluster of meanings.

Leopold Bloom chooses to read his paper in an outside toilet, in other words, in a W.C. – a Water Closet – and all the readers who are "watching" the scene are like members of a "Playgoers' Club" (people who go – frequently – to theatrical performances). In other words, Mr. Philip Beaufoy ushers the readers into the foyer of a voyeurs' club.

The semantic cluster expands even further. In fact, that "palefaced" "bachelor", as Bloom calls Beaufoy in "Circe" (*U* 15.814, 857), writes "Matcham's Masterstroke" stranded, as it were, in the W.C.: in other words, his writing could be the idle product of a furtive act performed in a privy.[24]

It is not the first time that Joyce made a joke about the Water Closet, either. As "wātāklāsāt" the W.C. is listed together with "tālāfānā, ālāvātār, hātākāldā" and "wātāklāsāt" among the "modern home comfort[s]" in the "Cyclops" episode (*U* 12.353–54), and Alessandro Francini Bruni wrote in his farcical portrayal of his friend that Joyce used to say that the English man "provvido e sesquipedale, fornisce al ventre turgido dell'umanità lo strumentario perfetto di un luogo comodo: il Water Closet".[25] Presumably, this is an obsession the

22 See appendix. David Pierce as been very helpful in helping me to find all of Philip Beaufoy's "Prize Tit-Bit" stories.

23 The "Titbits back number" that Bloom finds in the kitchen and that ends "in the bucket" (*U* 15.933–34) could have been that of January 1904 with the "Prize Tit-Bit story" *The Counsel for the Defence* by P. Beaufoy, 6, Clement's Inn, W.C.

24 With different arguments, a similar hypothesis is shared by Margot Gayle Backus in her book *Scandal Work: James Joyce, the New Journalism and the Home Rule Newspaper Wars* (Notre Dame: University of Notre Dame Press, 2013), 166–71.

25 Alessandro Francini Bruni, *Joyce intimo spogliato in piazza* (Trieste: La editoriale libraria, 1922), 31–32. In English, "The English, judiciously practical and ponderous, furnish the over-stuffed stomach of humanity with a perfect gadget – the water closet" (*JJII* 217).

English share with the Romans, as professor MacHugh explains in the "Aeolus" episode, "The Roman ... gazed about him in his toga and he said: *It is meet to be here. Let us construct a watercloset*" (*U* 7.491–95). As a young aspiring writer in Dublin, James Joyce must have been quite struck by the name and address of his rival Philip Beaufoy, so much so that he treasured both in his memory for decades, before making them synonymous with success years later in *Ulysses*.

"Mastermind" Quiz Show

For Joyce, "Prize Tit-Bit" was not the only appealing section of *Tit-Bits*. Besides the paper's general concept, there were other sections of *Tit-Bits* that caught his attention and subsequently shaped his recollections, such as the "Medical & Legal Advice", the "*Tit-Bits* Inquiry" and the "Competitions" columns.

In response to the great number of practical questions regarding legal or medical matters, George Newnes had launched the column "Medical & Legal Advice" which was written by professionals. We can find its wording in *Ulysses*, almost verbatim, in a passage of "Circe", where Jimmy Henry offers "Free medical and legal advice" (*U* 15.1629–32). On the other hand, the "Competitions" column challenged *Tit-Bits* readers with every kind of contest and prizes ranging from twenty guineas to a free holiday in Paris. You could win a "£20 Bank of England Note" for the highest number of anagrams you could make with the words of the poem "The Burial of John Moore" (by Charles Wolfe): "Slowly and sadly we laid him down";[26] or from Henry Wadsworth Longfellow's "The Village Blacksmith": "Toiling, – rejoicing, – sorrowing / Onward through life he goes".[27] These are poems that play with alliterations just as Joyce does at the end of "The Dead" or in many of his poems ("falling softly", "softly falling", "falling faintly", "faintly falling") or ("fading", "dissolving", "dwindling"). Bloom also shows a taste for anagrams and acrostics when, in "Ithaca", he plays with his own name (*U* 17.404–16).

Finally, the "*Tit-Bits* Inquiry" column featured a wide range of questions and answers from many scientific fields such as physics, botany, chemistry, astronomy, technology, etc. Competitors had three months to submit their answers and could win ten guineas. The kinds of questions were, for example, whether a lake of sulphuric acid exists, what the human body is made of, or whether the Bible is used for trading purposes.

Joyce may have had various sources of inspiration for the "question and answer" style of Ithaca: the catechism, new journalism interviews, police

26 *Tit-Bits* (20 January 1904).

27 *Tit-Bits* (13 February 1904).

interrogations or advertising slogans in the form of open questions, but we may include the possibility that this episode is also based on the "*Tit-Bits* Inquiry" column; at least in the case of questions such as, "What in water did Bloom … admire?" (*U* 17.183–84) or in the inquiry about Bloom's "demonstration" of "various constellations" (*U* 17.1040–41) or, even more so, in the case of its pseudo-scientific answers to questions like, "How was a glyphic comparison of the phonic symbols of both languages made in substantiation of the oral comparison?" (*U* 17.731–32).

It is difficult not to draw a comparison between the joy that a *Tit-Bits* reader must have experienced in solving these rebuses and quizzes (and maybe winning a prize) and the satisfaction Joyce readers experience when we are able to recognise and understand one of Joyce's wordplays, puzzles, complicated patterns or semantic clusters.

To sum up, however, what distinguished *Tit-Bits* was the idea to give an "Everyman or Noman" (*U* 17.2008) like Leopold Bloom a chance to contribute in the making of a magazine. Everyone was welcomed and encouraged to express themselves in writing "original" stories or in solving anagrams, inquiries or whatever George Newnes was inventing.

The Great War brought changes to *Tit-Bits* as it did to everything else in the world. The relationship between the reader and the editor became more anonymous. As its new title, *Tit-Bits for Great Fun and Splendid Prizes*, suggested, the reader was no longer the creative co-star that had made the paper unique during the previous forty years. "The Prize Tit-Bit for an Original Complete Story" disappeared and its place was taken by a new column of illustrated jokes named, significantly, "SMILE AWHILE and life's worth-while, because you smile".[28]

In the decades after the 1920s, even the traditionally light tone of *Tit-Bits* couldn't conceal the reality of a declining empire in search of certainties and a new identity. Nonetheless, James Joyce was still a faithful "Tit-Bitite". In fact, we still find references to *Tit-Bits* in his letter to Frank Budgen on 9 September 1937 (*Letters I* 396), which confirms that he was still reading and using *Tit-Bits* as a source of inspiration during the late 1930s. In this letter, Joyce refers to old numbers of *Tit-Bits* that Budgen had sent him and he writes that, eventually, he should become a subscriber to *Tit-Bits*.

What is more, Joyce may have had a special reason to be afraid of missing issues of his beloved paper during that summer of 1937. In fact, from 5 June the magazine began the serialization of a new "*Tit-Bits* Special Fiction Feature": the luridly illustrated "Vengeance Goes to Sea", written by an anonymous

28 *Tit-Bits* (3 January 1920).

SINBAD ... a name that awakens the memory of Leopold Bloom's late night friends that accompany him in the realm of sleep.

In spite of the same old green cover full of ads, *Tit-Bits* was no longer the peculiar Victorian penny weekly of the past that had provided Joyce with so many fertile memories but, nonetheless, even in the 1930s it was still an inspiring reading for him, full of curiosities and strange news.

Photo Bits

Another penny weekly that played a great role in Joyce's personal life and in the narrative of *Ulysses* was *Photo Bits: Up to date, Bright, Sketchy, Smart, Witty, Pictorial, Pithy, Original, Spicy*, as its title stated. It was launched in 1884 by W. Lucas with the title *Illustrated Tid-Bits*, renamed *Photo Bits* in 1898, and from 1916 it was called *Bits of Fun*. For its time, *Photo Bits* was a very original publication, classified as a "comic paper" in contemporary press directories, but in reality it was more of what could be termed a soft porn magazine. References to *Photo Bits* occur in "Calypso", "Nausicaa", "Circe", "Ithaca" and "Penelope".

In the editorial of its first number we read that it aimed "to be the cocktail of the press.... Sparkling 'Pick-me-up', pretty in appearance and reviving in effect".[29] It was a miscellany of slightly indecent photos, gossip from the stage, fashion and society news. It also included short stories, comic pieces, drawings and sketches of showgirls and stars from the music hall and the pantomime, jokes and competitions. All contributions were editorial.

The pictures published in *Photo Bits* were not explicitly pornographic or obscene but, like everything else in the paper, shared a cheeky and uninhibited flair that contributed to the paper's erotic allure. The majority of the photos showed women *en travesti*, of the tom-boyish type, wearing "French" bathing suits, trousers, military uniforms or dressed for a gala, in the style performed by the misses Bellingham, Barry and Talboys in "Circe". Often the subjects were photographed in provocative poses, smoking, jumping, dancing, fencing, pirouetting, in ways that would show their "lingerie", legs, bloomers and pants, similar to Gerty McDowell in "Nausicaa": "...and she leaned back" and "the garters were blue to match on account of the transparent and they all saw it" (*U* 13.715–17).

Standard features of *Photo Bits* were "The Belles of the Halls of Mirth and Song", "Bathing Beauties" and "Chorus Girls at the Seaside", images that recall Harry B. Norris's song "Seaside Girls", often quoted by Joyce, also in reference to Bloom's daughter, Milly. A group of girls on a shore is also a recurring theme

29 *Photo Bits* (9 July 1898).

of late Victorian ads – a fact that Bloom, as an advertising canvasser, was well aware of – and Gerty, Edy and Cissy fit perfectly into the frame: "The three girl friends were seated on the rocks, enjoying the evening scene and the air which was fresh but not too chilly" (*U* 13.9–10).

In *Photo Bits* there were also hints of fetishism and sadomasochism, which may in part explain Leopold's interest in the paper, or possibly Molly's distaste for it: "Im glad I burned the half of those old Freemans and Photo Bits leaving things like that lying about hes getting very careless and threw the rest of them up in the W C" (*U* 18.600–602).

Joyce's use of *Photo Bits* hints at some traits in Leopold's character and his sexual fantasies. The magazine also offered him a number of clichés which resurface in "Circe" and in characters like Gerty McDowell and Molly Bloom.

This kind of titillating men's magazine was the ideal target for those concerned about social "purity", and its editors often faced arrest and prosecution – a fact Joyce was well aware of. His steadfast interest in this spicy penny weekly is documented in his correspondence with Budgen of September and October 1920, when he was in Trieste working on the "Nausicaa" episode, and where he writes, "Thanks for letter and papers. The latter very useful, especially *Bits of Fun* of which send me any back numbers you can find" (*Letters I* 144); and a month later, "I perceive the editor of B of F (a Jew by his name) has been up before the beak and fined so whatever else in that way you send had better be enclosed in a copy of the *Christian Hero* or some such paper" (*Letters I* 148). Joyce also explained to Budgen in 1920 that "*Nausicaa* is written in a namby-pamby jammy marmalady drawersy (alto la!) style with effects of incense, mariolotry, masturbation, stewed cockles, painter's palette, chitchat, circumlocutions…" (*Letters I* 135), thus revealing how much he owed to this magazine.

A Nymph in My Bedroom!

This periodical was equally cherished by the lower strata of the late Victorian middle class, also because of the coloured reproductions of paintings which the paper offered "free gratis". The "Great Gift Pictures" offered by *Photo Bits* between 1898 and 1909 were colour reproductions of works painted by minor artists, of very low artistic value, printed on "cheap pink paper that smelt of rock oil" (*U* 15.3248) as the Nymph describes it in "Circe".[30] Bathing nymphs

30 "Three handsome works of art from the Paris Salon" came already with the Xmas issue of 1898, but only from 1902 till 1909 did it present "free gratis *Great Gift Pictures* at regular intervals without extra charge" as a supplement to the summer and Christmas issues and to special Salon issues.

were a recurring subject because it gave amateurs an excuse to paint naked women. A similar subject, Greek beauties draped in light peplums, was often used in Victorian ads, especially for soap and the like.

James Joyce must have treasured the memory of those "handsome works of art" seen in old issues of *Photo Bits* because, many years later, we find one of them in the pages of *Ulysses*. In "Calypso" we see Bloom wondering over a picture that hangs over his bed:

> *The Bath of the Nymph* over the bed. Given away with the Easter number of *Photo Bits*: splendid masterpiece in art colours. Tea before you put milk in. Not unlike her with her hair down: slimmer. Three and six I gave for the frame. She said it would look nice over the bed. Naked nymphs: Greece: and for instance all the people that lived then.
>
> *U* 4.369–73

Although a reproduction of a painting entitled "Bath of the Nymph" was never offered in an Easter number of *Photo Bits*, a December 1905 issue sported this ad:

> The twelve-colour plate is pronounced by the Press and Public alike to be A Superb Work of Art. Neatly framed, it is a handsome addition to any collection of pictures. Hung in a bedroom it has a warm, cosy effect. Hung anywhere, it cannot fail to delight the eye.

Once again Joyce gives us a lot of information here about Leopold Bloom's social position and aspirations, as Tess Marsh points out:

> To hang a *Photo Bits* supplement in one's bedroom was evidence, it would seem, of the most discerning taste. Joyce would have appreciated the double value of this inference in his description of Leopold and Molly; it sets them firmly in the lower middle class and lightly mocks the pretensions of that class.[31]

The Nymph Calypso, this allegory of "bad taste", reappears in "Circe" (*U* 15.3239ff.) in a sort of *tableau vivant*, where she accuses poor Leopold of having kissed her "in four places" (*U* 15.3264) and where, while addressing him as a mere "Mortal!", she describes perfectly the paper she came from:

---

31 Tess Marsh, "Is There More *to Photo Bits* Than Meets the Eye?" *James Joyce Quarterly* 30, no. 4 (1993): 882.

> Mortal! You found me in evil company, highkickers, coster picnicmakers, pugilists, popular generals, immoral panto boys in fleshtights and the nifty shimmy dancers, La Aurora and Karini, musical act, the hit of the century. I was hidden in cheap pink paper that smelt of rock oil. I was surrounded by the stale smut of clubmen, stories to disturb callow youth, ads for transparencies, truedup dice and bustpads, proprietary articles and why wear a truss with testimonial from ruptured gentleman. Useful hints to the married.... Rubber goods. Neverrip brand as supplied to the aristocracy. Corsets for men. I cure fits or money refunded. Unsolicited testimonials for Professor Waldmann's wonderful chest exuber. My bust developed four inches in three weeks, reports Mrs Gus Rublin with photo.
> *U* 15.3245–59

At the end of the "Circe" episode the real nature of the (revisited) Nymph is revealed when the plaster cast cracks and "a cloud of stench" (*U* 15.3469–70) emerges from it. The last image we have of the nymph is in the "Ithaca" episode, where she is referred to as the mythical goddess Odysseus refused to marry: "A nymph immortal, beauty, the bride of Noman" (*U* 17.2010–11).

Fateful Ads

As the Nymph points out, the last of the thirty-two pages of *Photo Bits* were full of all kinds of advertising, such as "personal-ads", pills against impotency or venereal diseases, condoms, pseudo-pornographic publications such as *Rosario, or the Female Monk* or *Flagellation & the Flagellants*, a 544 page volume with more than twenty photographs.

This is just the kind of merchandise that Bloom is browsing for in the baskets of a second-hand bookshop while looking for a novel to take to Molly: "Mr Bloom turned over idly pages of *The Awful Disclosures of Maria Monk*,[32] then of Aristotle's *Masterpiece*" (*U* 10.585–86). Memory plays funny jokes in Molly's mind when, in "Penelope", she wrongly refers to "Aristotle's *Masterpiece*" as the "Aristocrats Masterpiece": "like those babies in the Aristocrats Masterpiece he brought me" (*U* 18.1238–39).

While browsing among old issues of *Photo Bits* at the British Library, my attention was drawn to an ad for a quack remedy, so typical in Victorian times,

32 References to Maria Monk's "disclosures" appear also in "A Little Cloud", written in Trieste in 1906, a short story full of hints to the kind of doubtful literature regularly advertised in *Photo Bits*.

and to a peculiar coincidence. It is interesting that on 7 August 1909 Joyce wrote to Nora Barnacle "you made me a man" (*SL* 159), referring to their meeting on 16 June 1904, and that "made me a man" also recalls a recurring advertisement published by *Photo Bits* at the turn of the century. It is a popular advert for an American import product: the Ajax Tablets that appeared on the last pages of *Photo Bits* from September 1898 on:

> MADE ME A MAN. AJAX TABLETS positively cure all Nervous Diseases – Failing Memory, Impotency, Sleeplessness, &c., caused by Abuse or other excesses and indiscretions. They quickly and surely restore Lost Vitality in old or young, and fit a man for study, business, or marriage. Prevent Insanity and Consumption if taken in time. Their use shows Immediate Improvement, and effects a CURE where all others fail. Insist upon having the genuine Ajax Tablets. They have cured thousands and will cure you. We give a positive written guarantee to effect a cure in each case or money refunded. Price 2/9 per box, or six boxes (full treatment) for 14/. Mailed in plain wrapper upon receipt of price. *Circular free.* Ajax Remedy Co., B55, 114 Thrush St., Walworth, London, S.E.[33]

Let's go back to the autumn of 1898: Joyce had enrolled at University College, Dublin, and his best friends and colleagues were J.F. Byrne, Francis Skeffington and Vincent Cosgrave. *Photo Bits* was exactly the kind of magazine likely to be commented on among young male friends. A slogan like that cannot have failed to capture their attention.

I take the liberty to presume that the slogan "MADE ME A MAN" could have been in Joyce's mind when Nora first appeared in his life and that years later, declaring to Nora, "you made me a man", in a decisive moment of his life in the middle of a love crisis, Joyce may have chosen to entrust a message of great importance not to a song or a poem, but to a concise and condensed slogan from an advertisement for potency pills read a decade before in the popular weekly *Photo Bits*.

In a way it is what Gabriel Conroy does in the last pages of "The Dead", where his turmoil of sentiments is conveyed in a sentence that he remembers having read in that day's weather forecast in the evening newspaper: "Yes, the newspapers were right: snow was general all over Ireland" (*D* 15.1605–66) – a commonplace phrase, repeated by the mass-media on an uncommon and extraordinary, snowy day.

33 *Photo Bits* (10 September 1898).

Equally, it is what Leopold Bloom does in "Circe", where his uneasiness, his anxiety is conveyed through a sentence recollected from the now well-known Plumtree's Potted Meat jingle: "The home without potted meat is incomplete" (*U* 15.495–596). These slogans, recalled from newspapers, are transformed by Joyce, conferring on them not only a lyric aura, but also a multiplicity of symbolic meanings.

Conclusions

James Joyce was a mediator of the late Victorian popular memory. Recollections of mass market periodicals of that time provided him with invaluable working materials. Particularly useful for him was the inclusive, discursive, open-text structure of *Tit-Bits*, a paper he also associated with personal remembrances of his father.

Throughout his life Joyce was a "loyal Tit-Bitite" and (among many other things) it was in *Tit-Bits* that he found a name and address that he would eventually use in *Ulysses*: Mr. Philip Beaufoy, Playgoers' Club, London.

On the other hand, *Photo Bits* nourished his fantasies with clichés and images of nymphs and uninhibited women. Together, the two publications were influential in reconstructing and establishing the class and cultural milieu of the period through the main character of *Ulysses*, the Victorian Dubliner Leopold Bloom.

We could say, that if *Photo Bits* contributed to making James Joyce a man, *Tit-Bits*, also by rejecting his "original complete story" "Matcham's Masterstroke", may have contributed to making him a writer.

Appendix

List of Philip Beaufoy's twenty-eight "Prize Tit-Bit Original Complete Stories", published in *Tit-Bits* (1897–1904). Source: British Library.

02.01.1897 "My Last Card: A Baritone Story" – Mr. Philip Beaufoy, Playgoers' Club, Strand. W.C.

06.03.1897 "A Reading-Room Romance" – Mr. Philip Beaufoy, Playgoers' Club, Strand. W.C.[34]

34 This story is also published among the "Fifty Prize Stories from *Tit-Bits*" (London: George Newnes, 1908) but it is not signed like the others in the same collection.

10.04.1897 "Jack Langley's Over Coat" – Mr. Philip Beaufoy, Playgoers' Club, Strand. W.C.

01.05.1897 "For Vera's Sake" – Mr. Philip Beaufoy, Playgoers' Club, Strand. W.C.

19.06.1897 "The Jeweler's Mummy" – Mr. Philip Beaufoy, Playgoers Club, Strand, W.C.

05.03.1898 "A Cheque Mystery" – Mr. Philip Beaufoy, Playgoers Club, Strand.

02.04.1898 "On A Circular Saw: A Timekeeper's Story" – Mr. Philip Beaufoy, Playgoers' Club, Strand, W.C.

07.05.1898 "A Millionaire's Cheque: An Ex-Criminal's Story" – Mr. Philip Beaufoy, Playgoers' Club, Strand, W.C.

11.06.1898 "The Mablethorpe Mystery: A Detective Story" – Mr. P. Beaufoy, Playgoers' Club, Strand.

10.12.1898 "The Tell-Tale Semi-Colon – A Detective's Story" – Mr. P. Beaufoy, Playgoers' Club, Strand (also in *The Storyteller*, 1898, p. 213).

31.12.1898 "A Marble Bill Sykes – An Ex-Criminal's Story" – Mr. P. Beaufoy, Playgoers' Club, Strand.

21.01.1899 "A Lucky Loop" – Mr. P. Beaufoy, Playgoers' Club, Strand.

11.02.1899 "The Percy Street Pillar Box: An Ex-Criminal's Story" – Mr. P. Beaufoy, Playgoers' Club, Strand, W.C.

22.04.1899 "A Handshake with Death: An Anarchist Story" – Mr. P. Beaufoy, Playgoers' Club, Strand.

04.11.1899 "A Genuine Rembrandt: An Ex-Criminal's Story" – Mr. P. Beaufoy, Playgoers' Club, Strand.

23.12.1899 "Dick Darrell's Victoria Cross" – Mr. P. Beaufoy, Playgoers' Club, Strand (Five guinea Christmas Prize, no. 4).

10.03.1900 "The Reservist's Chum: An Incident of the Boer War" – Mr. P. Beaufoy, Playgoers' Club, Strand.

21.04.1900 "The Split Button: A Detective's Story" – Mr. P. Beaufoy, Playgoers' Club, Strand.

17.11.1900 "The Man and the Mesmerist: A Conjurer's Story" – Mr. Philip Beaufoy, Playgoers' Club, Strand.

09.02.1901 "The Finale of Act 2: An Actor's Story" – Mr. P. Beaufoy, Playgoers' Club, Strand.

17.08.1901 "Wilfrid Mason's Engagement: A Story of the Stage" – Mr. Philip Beaufoy, Playgoers' Club, Strand, W.C.

05.10.1901 "Dandy Dick's Device: An Ex-Criminal's Story" – Mr. P. Beaufoy, Playgoers' Club, Clement's Inn, W.C.

28.12.1901 "Billie Scott's Eva" – Five Guinea Christmas Prize N. 2 awarded to Mr. P. Beaufoy Playgoers' Club, Clement's Inn.

14.06.1902	"Dick Armstrong's Sacrifice" – Mr. Philip Beaufoy, Playgoers' Club, Strand, w.c.
01.11.1902	"A Stratagem That Failed" – Mr. P. Beaufoy, 6, Clement's Inn, w.c.
07.11.1903	"A Mysterious Post-Card" – Mr. P. Beaufoy, 6, Clement's Inn, w.c.
30.01.1904	"The Counsel for the Defence" – Mr. P. Beaufoy, 6, Clement's Inn, w.c.
31.12.1904	"Mr Renshaw's Typist" – Mr. P. Beaufoy, 6, Clement's Inn, w.c.

CHAPTER 3

Types of News Events

Fritz Senn

Abstract

James Joyce uses a technique that will here be referred to as "superimposition". A suitable instance to elucidate this is provided by "Aeolus". As the newspaper episode, it gathers the complete infrastructure of communication and transmission of news, but at the same time incorporates the notion of incomplete and erroneous information. The prime example is Miles Crawford's detailed, although hardly clear or even reliable, account of the report about the code used to encrypt the escape-route on which Skin-the-Goat supposedly drove the car for the Invincibles, that is, an advertisement superimposed on a map of Dublin. Technically the device hinges on a superimposition by which elements of one system of reference point to that of another – in this case, a prominent letter in an advertisement to a specific place on a map. This device can be considered one possible formula for the makeup of *Ulysses* as a whole: the book can be read as an arrangement of multiple overlays and stratifications in which everything tends to point towards something else. *Finnegans Wake* compounds the device even further.

Keywords

"Aeolus" – *Ulysses* – *Finnegans Wake* – General Slocum disaster – superimposition – stratification – code – Phoenix Park Murders – parallax

General Slocum

The probably biggest worldwide news event on 16 June 1904, apart from the Russian-Japanese War far away, was the General Slocum disaster of the previous day, when an excursion steamer caught fire in the New York East River, with heavy casualties, mainly children. It was reported in the Dublin newspapers and is echoed in a few of the characters' thoughts in *Ulysses*, obviously from what they had read in the papers. The catastrophe is a minor motive in the texture of the book; it does not, however, surface in "Hades", devoted to death, nor

 | DOI 10.1163/9789004359062_005

in "Aeolus", concerned with news. There is only one brief reference to an analogous occurrence: the lawyer J.J.O'Molloy asks jocularly, "Or was it you shot the lord lieutenant of Finland between you? You look as though you had done the deed. General Bobrikoff" (*U* 7.601–2). Nikolai Ivanovitch Bobrikoff, Governor General of Finland, had been assassinated in the morning of June 16 so that the news could have reached the editorial office in Dublin.

Ulysses uses the General Slocum tragedy in parallactic diversion. First it is Bloom, whose empathy with the blind stripling he has guided for a while makes him ponder:

> Where is the justice being born that way? All those women and children excursion beanfeast burned and drowned in New York. Holocaust. Karma they call that transmigration for sins you did in a past life the reincarnation met him pike hoses.
>
> *U* 8.1145–48

Bloom would have read the account in the *Freeman's Journal* he carries with him. As the innocent school children did not deserve such a fate, one possible explanation, briefly entertained but hardly believed in, would be the karma of theosophy and certain religions, the retribution for sins committed in earlier incarnations.

Next Father Conmee S.J. walking along North Strand Road takes fleeting notice:

> He passed Grogan's the Tobacconist against which newsboards leaned and told of a dreadful catastrophe in New York. In America those things were continually happening. Unfortunate people to die like that, unprepared. Still, an act of perfect contrition.
>
> *U* 10.88–92

The priest's reaction seems a trifle dismissive and even callous, with a condescending general blame on the place of the event, America (locality is foregrounded in the spatiality of "Wandering Rocks"). His concern for the innocent victims is that they were hurled into death "unprepared", without the benefit of requisite holy rites. In such unforeseen accidents an "act of contrition" may relieve the victims of their sins, according to dogmatic opinions; but even so the word "perfect" seems oddly out of place. It is just conceivable that Father Conmee's uncharitable attitude has something to do with his awareness that the women and children burnt or drowned were Lutherans, not Catholics. In actual fact, "such things" (about 1000 victims) were not "continually happening": in America; the General Slocum disaster was the greatest catastrophe in the history of New York up to that time.

For Thomas Kernan, merchant of tea, the accident serves as a topic for small talk in conversation with a client, the publican Mr Crimmins. Kernan remembers the dialogue with some pride:

> Terrible affair that *General Slocum* explosion. Terrible, terrible! A thousand casualties. And heartrending scenes. Men trampling down women and children. Most brutal thing. What do they say was the cause? Spontaneous combustion. Most scandalous revelation. Not a single lifeboat would float and the firehose all burst. What I can't understand is how the inspectors ever allowed a boat like that.... Now, you're talking straight, Mr Crimmins. You know why? Palm oil. Is that a fact? Without a doubt. Well now, look at that. And America they say is the land of the free. I thought we were bad here.
>
> I smiled at him. *America*, I said quietly, just like that. *What is it? The sweepings of every country including our own. Isn't that true?* That's a fact.
>
> *U* 10.725–35

Kernan sprinkles what he must have read as facts with speculation, with again a complacent side thrust at the place where such things occur, and its probable causes. His account depends on the *Freeman's Journal* or the *Irish Times* of 16 June 1904; they are, with minor changes, substantially identical and based on the reports of a news agency: "Press Association. Foreign Special". Both carry the headline "Women Trampled to Death", and "500 Lives Lost", but they also mention "thousand victims or more". The *Freeman's Journal* puts "Children Thrown over-board" into a headline. The paper's "heart-rending cries" become "heartrending scenes", a phrase that is in tune with Kernan's known taste (like "*trenchant rendering*" or "That touches a man's inmost heart", *U* 6.147, 670). Kernan seems to have his information from "No attempts were made to lower the lifeboats" and "Survivors allege that the life-belts were rotten and the fire-hose decayed". Again it is typical of "Wandering Rocks" to focus on places, whereas in "Lestrygonians" there was a minor association with something edible, "beanfeast".

Late in the night, in the Cabman's shelter, a copy of the *Evening Telegraph* is handed round. Its captions are a concise "New York disaster. Thousand lives lost" (*U* 16.1244), but no further attention is paid to it.

There is little doubt that Joyce had the *Freeman's Journal*, the *Irish Times* and the *Evening Telegraph* at his disposal. He used their information with a certain creative latitude and tampered with the sequence of information. Naturally the *Evening Telegraph*, being the latest edition, had the most updated account; it places "the death roll at 1,000". It ran both a report, "Appalling American Disaster", on page 4, and a general comment and leader, "The America Horror", on the second page. It starts by emphasizing the country: "It is just as well for us that we cannot adequately appreciate in all their horror such big disasters as occur in America, and the latest of which, reported last evening, must have sent a thrill around the world". This conforms with Kernan's speculation, though he could have had his views independently, maybe a stereotype reflex. The report specified, for example, "Thousand Lives Lost". Some items in the mind of Bloom and Kernan during the day could only have been picked out of that last account and so they are slightly anachronistic. The *Evening Telegraph* describes the event as "surely a holocaust", using a word that Bloom could not have seen in the morning's paper and which would hardly be part of his active vocabulary; at that time it was mainly Biblical (a complete burning, in the Catholic Douay version, where King James has "burnt sacrifice"). And it was only the *Evening Telegraph*'s speculation that substantiates Kernan's "spontaneous combustion", yet not as a fact but merely as a legal observation: "In order that the owners and crew may clear themselves of the charge of negligence they must show that there was spontaneous combustion in the storage room".

It does not appear that Joyce took scrupulous care of what Bloom, Conmee, or Kernan gleaned from which paper at which particular time of the day, nor does it matter in a work of (still mainly) fiction. In writing his work he remains the chief editor and decides what goes in where as long as there is a sense of veracity.

One question that was also raised but received only speculative answers at the Zurich Workshop on Newspapers was how Joyce, who undoubtedly needed the *Freeman's Journal*, the *Irish Times* and the *Evening Telegraph* for his composition, could obtain the actual copies when he had decided on 16 June 1904 as the actual date, either from Trieste or from war-time Zurich.

"old the news of the great big world" (*FW* 194.23)

The various portions of news from New York, not essentially different, but naturally more detailed in the evening, came via news agencies like Press Association, a modern form of dissemination. "Aeolus" is the first of the "OMNIUM GATHERUM" (as at *U* 7.604) episodes; it tends to assemble all variations of a particular topic in a dispersive way, such as, in "Aeolus", the transmission of news items. They can just be passed on orally, whether true or invented; *Ulysses* is suffused with rumours that may have little to do with realities. News can be sent by a messenger, a role which Stephen[1] assumes when he takes Mr. Deasy's letter first to the editor of the newspaper office and then to George Russell in the National Library. This unplanned deviation determines much of Stephen's itinerary during the rest of the day. Being a kind of *ad hoc* postman, he then ironically uses the postal service to send a telegram from a post office in "College Green" to "The Ship, lower Abbey street" (*U* 9.554), so as to avoid the appointment arranged with Buck Mulligan. As it happens, the person delivering the telegram from the post office would have to take a similar way to Stephen's own since the newspaper offices in Prince's Street were not far away from The Ship, Lower Abbey Street.

Personal news travelled as letters or postcards as they are frequent in *Ulysses*, where they are written, sent, read or carried. "Aeolus", with its location close to the General Post Office, naturally features the postal service and its recent possibility of telegrams for written messages. Analogously it also features the telephone for oral messages, that is to say almost instant messages. "Aeolus" accumulates the complete infrastructure of communication.

The chapter indirectly hints at the oldest and one of the slowest possible transmissions on record, a messenger on foot who had to run a distance of forty-two kilometers from Marathon to bring the tidings of a victorious battle to Athens, and paid for it with his life, thereby acquiring lasting fame. So it may be no coincidence that the battle is worked into "Aeolus" as a jocular comment on Dan Dawson's bombastic speech in the paper: "And Xenophon looked upon Marathon, Mr Dedalus said, looking again on the fireplace and to the window, and Marathon looked on the sea" (*U* 7.254–55). It is an elaboration of Lord Byron's "The mountains look on Marathon / And Marathon looks on the sea".[2] This line of poetry, which is merely a comment on the speech and was never meant to be truthful anyway, is factually wrong: the historian Xenophon has nothing to do with the battle. In fact the various antique accounts of just what happened do not agree; there are, for example, variants of the runner's name. The news as was current in antiquity was already divergent. The accounts, in other words, of an event are contradictory and not to be trusted. The tradition of incomplete, erroneous, or contradictory news goes far back into antiquity.

1 He in turn mentally transforms J.J.O'Molloy, who is about to quote a "polished period", into a "Messenger" (*U* 7.747–62). O'Molloy will quote a lawyer's eloquent admiration of a statue of Moses, and later on an imagined address delivered to the youthful Moses is the substance of a (remembered?) speech by John F. Taylor (*U* 7.793–869). Moses of course is an arch-messenger of consequential and permanent commands from on high.

2 Lord Byron, *Don Juan*, ed. Harold Bloom (New York: Chelsea House Publishers, 1987), Canto III, 86, 3.

Doubtful reports can affect a transmitter of news like the *Freeman's Journal* itself, as is borne out by its editor's proud boast of a smart piece of journalism, in a case of meta-news in "Aeolus".

"the smartest piece of journalism ever known" (*U* 7.631)

While Bloom is generally disregarded, in obvious contrast Stephen is greeted with respect and enthusiasm by the editor and his cronies and instantly invited to write something for the paper: "You can do it" and "Put us all into it, damn its soul" (*U* 7.617, 621). We know that Joyce ended up doing just this. The model held out is Ignatius Gallaher, whose unique exploit Myles Crawford recounts in considerable though far from clear detail. It dates more than twenty years back: "That was in eightyone, sixth of May, time of the invincibles, murder in the Phoenix park" (*U* 7.632–33). The murders took place on 6 May 1882, one year off,[3] so that Crawford at the outset is not reliably accurate.

According to him, the "*New York World* cabled for a special: .... Where it took place. Tim Kelly, or Kavanagh I mean. Joe Brady and the rest of them. Where Skin-the-Goat drove the car. Whole route, see?" (*U* 7.635–40). He lists some names of the Invincibles, who had perpetrated the murder, and their accomplices. After some digression the editor resumes the story of Ignatius Gallaher's clever device. "Inspiration of genius. Cabled right away" (*U* 7.651).

The genius consisted in a spatial coding. A specific advertisement is superimposed on a map of Dublin (both the ad and an identical map obviously being at hand at both ends of the transmission), so that a given letter in the advertisement points to an underlying spot in Dublin: "B is parkgate ... T is viceregal lodge. C is where the murder took place" (*U* 7.659–61). Such local information, incidentally, could have been conveyed without recourse to a device. But the focus is not on the actual spot of the murders (near the Viceregal Lodge, which was well-known), but on an escape path:

> F to P is the route Skin-the-Goat drove the car for an alibi, Inchicore, Roundtown, Windy Arbour, Palmerston Park, Ranelagh. F.A.B.P. ... X is Davy's publichouse in upper Leeson street.
>
> *U* 7.667–69

3 The *Reader's Edition of "Ulysses"*, which sets out to correct factual errors and existing names, substitutes "eighty-two"; Danis Rose, *A Reader's Edition of "Ulysses"* (London: Picador, 1997), 130. As has often been pointed out, however, it is unlikely that Joyce inadvertently put in the wrong year, an important one both in Irish history and in being his own birth year.

The impression created is that all of it took place right after the sensational atrocity, when the New York paper (which must have got wind of it through telegraphs) enquired after the route of Skin-the-Goat, who drove a getaway car. It has long been demonstrated that Crawford's account cannot be true. At the time of the murder and for months afterwards nobody had any clue as to who the murderers were, nor of their movements, except that a group calling themselves "the Invincibles" claimed responsibility. But what actually happened and the identity of the persons involved came out only months later in the trials, in February of 1883. By that time there was no longer any need for instant cables and cryptic devices, and certainly not for marginal details. The driver Fitzharris, nicknamed "Skin-the-Goat", played an absolutely minor part, driving only a decoy car (while the actual murderers were in Kavanagh's care). Accordingly he was not executed like the main perpetrators, but was released after serving a prison sentence so that he conceivably could still have lived in Dublin by 1904, where he may or may not have been identical with the keeper of the Cabman's shelter in "Eumaeus", the episode of doubtful identities and doubtful reports.

Crawford's recollection cannot accord with the actual facts. Something went wrong, at least in the chronology. At the same time something vaguely equivalent must to have occurred: "I saw it, the editor said proudly. I was present" (*U* 7.679). The question of historical truth already surfaced when Stephen reflected on Roman and general history: "And yet it was in some way if not as memory fabled it" (*U* 2.7–8). Facts tend to change in the telling. That reports in *Ulysses* are hardly ever quite on target will find its pervasive climaxes in "Eumaeus" (in *Finnegans Wake* the factual truth of any insinuation has ceased to be an issue).

By ironic coincidence, just when Crawford describes Gallagher's exploit, the telephone whirs in his office, with Bloom at the other end. If transatlantic telephone connections had been conveniently available at the time, 1882, any news could have passed through this channel instantly without recourse to coding. By 1904 technology allowed an instant exchange of information.

It would be revealing to learn what is hidden behind "Out of an advertisement. Gregor Grey made the design for it" (*U* 7.685–86) and what kind of role this hapax-legomenous character plays in the whole transaction. What, however, was Joyce's design behind the muddled mistake? He himself may have been misinformed (even so he would at least have been superstitiously aware of the year of his own birth). Is the implication perhaps that Crawford, who claims to have been a witness, is wrong about the annals of his own paper? The case is about news that concerns a newspaper, usually a disseminator of news.

"CLEVER, VERY" (*U* 7.674)

Whatever the factual basis of Gallaher's ingenious device, technically it hinges on the superimposition of a specific advertisement on a map of Dublin, as has been outlined above: a letter in an ad points to a location in Dublin – two birds with one stone. This is a device that also applies to *Ulysses* as an arrangement of multiple overlays and stratifications. A title with classical connotations is tacked on to a novel of quotidian events, so that mere trivialities can call up mythological echoes. Dublin trams or the postal system, for well-known examples, correspond to Homeric winds, which are found, as in the excerpts above, in "Windy Arbour" (*U* 7.668) or in terms like "inspiration" (*U* 7.651, 868) or "afflatus" (*U* 7.774).

By referring to the episode as "Aeolus" we are playing the game of superimposition, which most conspicuously manifests itself in Lenehan's riddle: it combines an opera, "The Rose of Castile", with modern transport, "rows of cast steel", by phonetic approximation. In fact the technique is spelled out expressly in Taylor's quoted speech: "*It seemed to me that I had been transported into a country far away from this country, into an age remote from this age, that I stood in ancient Egypt…*" (*U* 7.830–32). In this phrasing the usually spatial "transport" (implied in postal delivery) takes on the same temporal dimension that we also have in Joyce's title "Ulysses". In this way the Jewish people are compared to, superimposed on, the Irish, the Egyptian Empire is linked to the British one, Moses to Parnell (on another level to Bloom).

Dawson's speech, in English, but called "HIS NATIVE DORIC" (*U* 7.326), piles clichéd classical names on an idyllic Irish countryside: "*Neptune's blue domain*" (*U* 7.245) is the sea that was already described as "snotgreen" (*U* 1.78), a little brook is "*meandering*" (*U* 7.243) according to classical precedent. Trees have "*overarching leafage*" (*U* 7.247); in some loose way such decorative elements are overarching mundane reality, but "overarching" can easily be undercut by "*overarsing*" (*U* 7.253).

In fact the prevalent rhetorical figures or tropes are all instances of a figurative sense grafted on an ordinary one. Humans have hearts, as Bloom meditated on in the cemetery, but they can also be projected into cities: "IN THE HEART OF THE HIBERNIAN METROPOLIS" (*U* 7.1–2); not only does the city contain a figurative heart, a "metropolis" also contains a metaphorical Greek mother (*meter*). Metaphors are superimposition by nature.

A traditional divergence of real and figurative meanings is also embedded in the episode. The statue of Moses of a period is described as "horned" in accordance with tangible sculptural fact; Moses acquired his horns by sleight of translation of a Hebrew figure of speech; when, having spoken with the Lord, he descended from the mountain "the skin of his face shone" (Ex. 34:29–30). A Hebrew metaphor used physical horns, which are also a sign of power, for the symbolic rays, and the Latin Vulgate, either by misunderstanding or an implicit trust in figurative reading, turned this into "*cornuta esset facies sua*", "horned", which of course serves many of Joyce's purposes. So the chapter contains both the original sense, "*the light of inspiration shining in his countenance*" and the mistranslated "*horned*" (*U* 7.867–68, 768).

In "Aeolus" the subtitles in usually capital letters, or headlines, are superimposed on the body text, often in a straightforward way, or progressively in fanciful, wry elaboration. Every symbolic meaning, that is one reaching beyond its literal range, works on the principles of the same mechanism. Bloom's advertisement uses associations: the "HOUSE OF KEY(E)S" with "two crossed keys" (*U* 7.141–42) is reminiscent of the Vatican because St. Peter was given the "keys of the kingdom of heaven" (Mat.16:19). That the "House of Keys" happens to be the name of the autonomous parliament of the Isle of Man, adds a political, Irish, dimension: "the Manx parliament. Innuendo of home rule" (*U* 7.149–50). Crossed keys moreover can make readers think of the two main characters, both without keys, whose paths cross in the episode. So Bloom, "crossing his forefingers at the top", putting one above the other, is unwittingly signaling a prominent technique.

It is in the nature of comparisons that they superimpose: William Brayden, owner of the newspaper, looks like "Our Saviour" who in turn looks like "Mario the tenor" (*U* 7.49–58). Come to think of it, every quotation adds an external layer: When the editor, stretching "forth an arm amply", theatrically proclaims to Bloom "– Begone ... The world is before you" (*U* 7.434–35), he knowingly and mockingly calls up Adam and Eve's ejection from Paradise in nearly Milton's words.[4] On a trite scale Lenehan's type of forced jokes are in tune, "as we read in the first chapter of Guinness's" (*U* 7.497) pours beer on sacred scriptures. Lenehan also favours Latin or French grafted on ordinary English: "*Thanky vous*" (*U* 7.468) or "Muchibus thankibus" (*U* 7.780). In the same vein "*Joe Miller*" doubles as "joke" (*U* 7.582) and "M.A.P." suggests geographical maps but also abbreviates "Mainly all pictures" (*U* 7.97). All of these instances are "doubledeckers" (*U* 7.10).

A few homophones are already their own inherent superimposition, like "I", "eye", and "aye", particularly in "Cyclops". Potentially they always were, but Joyce managed to turn such coincidental facts into live actualities. At the end of "Circe" the apparition of Bloom's dead son Rudy filially hovers over unconscious

4 Milton, *Paradise Lost*, bk. 12, line 646.

Stephen Dedalus. "Oxen of the Sun" transforms present action into a sequence of literary historical recalls.

The simplest formula for the dynamism is that everything tends to point towards something else. A composition like *Ulysses* can be dissolved into a stockpile of layers grafted on realistic fictional events: on top of, or beneath, the well-known Homeric or a Shakespearean, a liturgical one, and countless others have been uncovered: Irish History, Fetishism, or Newspapers. The eighteen episodes foreground different layers and each episode moreover displays or hides a thematic overlay: wind in "Aeolus", music in "Sirens".

Finnegans Wake compounds the device to further extremes. In "these modes carrying us back to the superimposed claylayers of eocene and pleastoseen formation" the principle is also applied to the geological stratification (*FW* 165.25–26). *Finnegans Wake* of course consists, at every turn, of portmanteau superimpositions: If you put "Nausicaa" on top of, or underneath, "naughty calves" you get something like "Naughtsycalves" (*FW* 229.15) and, in this instance, a thumbnail of an episode in *Ulysses*, which, as it happens, contains both "Swell of her calf" and "naughty" (*U* 13.929, 1263, 1280).

All in all, Myles Crawford (or Ignatius Gallaher) may be wrong on facts but he directs attention to salient Joycean processes and devices. Gallaher's ploy, whatever it was and whenever it was put into action, relates the letters in a document, an advertisement, to locations on a map. This coincidentally can be considered one possible formula for the makeup of *Ulysses*: literature, consisting of the letters of the alphabet creatively arranged (Shakespeare, Homer, Beaufoy), combines with a particular city and specific places. The same ingredients surface when Bloom walks past St. Joseph's National School and hears, or (more likely) just imagines, in turn, first the alphabet: "Ahbeesee defeegee kelomen opeecue rustyouvee doubleyou", and then geography: "Inishturk. Inishark. Inishboffin. At their joggerfry" (*U* 4.137–39). The combination is again echoed in a fraction of Lenehan's career: he could hardly be kept "to school to learn his letters and the use of the globes" (*U* 14.555–56). Joyce's fiction is made up of a specific reality, Dublin at a certain time, and it is expressed by an arrangement of the letters of the alphabet that create the illusion of such reality.

CHAPTER 4

Newspapers, Print, Language: Steganography in Joyce

Jolanta Wawrzycka

Abstract

One novel way to approach James Joyce's writings is to read them steganographically. Steganography ("veiled writing") is the practice of hiding information from unintended eyes *in plain sight*; indeed it conceals the very fact that a message is being sent at all. This essay considers textual formations that draw attention to themselves *as* texts in *Ulysses* (such as the acrostic cipher, anagrams, the boustrophedonic cryptogram, acronyms) to reveal the significance of their materiality and their importance both as carriers of messages and as Joyce's experiments with steganographic methods. It posits that secret communication codes (like jargon code, cues, elements of Ogham and Bog Latin writing) deepen our understanding of Joyce's use of the veiling methods and of their functions as steganographic tests that engage the reader in pursuit of secrets buried in the text. Becoming aware of the steganographic aspects of Joyce's writing heightens our appreciation of how deliberate Joyce was in configuring *language events* as carriers of steganographically charged textual elements, as messages in plain sight about the rewards of attentive reading, one that involves detecting additional frame of reference (a code, a pattern) necessary to retrieve meanings behind his elaborate textual stratagems.

Keywords

Ulysses – print – steganography – cryptography – secret code – semagram – alphabets – boustrophedon – onomatopoeia – Ogham

At the beginning of May 1905, James Joyce wrote a long letter to his brother Stanislaus where he mentioned entering a contest:

> As you may have heard I am entering for a missing letter puzzle in 'Ideas'. There are to be 48 words in batches of six. As yet 42 words have appeared

 | DOI 10.1163/9789004359062_006

> and I have solved all. I am waiting for the last six. The prize is £250. I shall send you a sealed and registered letter containing a copy of my answers. You are *not* to open the letter but keep it carefully. In case I solve all or nearly all I shall also seal and register my letter to the paper so that if they do not give me a prize I can take an action against them.
>
> *Letters II* 88–89

A "missing letter puzzle" excited Joyce enough to enlist Stanislaus in the scheme to win the hefty sum of £250. But it was not to be: "owing to distance and time", Joyce's entry arrived "a day late" (*Letters II* 90) and his efforts were in vain. A letter puzzle contest is but one of many manifestations of Joyce's life-long fascination with all aspects of letters and lettering, riddling, printing and the graphic value of writing, all of which have made his works a happy hunting ground for scholars. Like Joyce's characters, letters, too, bob around Dublin: as alphabet and ads (H.E.L.Y'S, Kino's), as throwaways (Elijah), as correspondence (Deasy's letter to the editor, Milly's to Papli, Bold Hand's to Mrs Marion, Martha's to Henry, or Atty Dillon's "crossed letters"[1]), as press print (newspapers, books), as "misses in print" (L. Boom), as typesetters' and canvassers' tools (mangiD kcirtaP, House of Key(e)s), or as songs ("Kay ee double ell wy"). Some letters come with an attitude (K.M.A. / K.M.R.I.A; Martha's and Hester's x x x x x) and some with a challenge (U. p: up). The *materiality* of lettering demands the reader's attention often apart from semantics; its signification is frequently just that: the lettering-in-and-of-itself, the lettering to puzzle, to arrest the flow of narrative. I will address some of these aspects in two ways: by outlining Joyce's problematizing of press and press-ads as carriers of messages and by reading some of Joyce's experiments with lettering and language as *steganography*.

"bitched type" (*U* 16.1263)

Missing, transposed and otherwise "wronged" letters are a particular provenance of the "great daily organs" and such popular publications as *Tit-Bits*. The presence of newspapers in Joyce's works, whether by name or by misnomer ("*Freeman's General*" [*D* 1.234]), affirms their value as sources of information and of misinformation: on the one hand, the newspapers can be right about snow "all over Ireland" (*D* 15.1605–6); on the other, they place M'Intosh, the

1 See illustration 4.1 reproduced at the end of this essay.

Dedaluses and L. Boom at Dignam's funeral. Already in *Dubliners* Joyce's interest in newspapers and advertising is signalled by, for instance, M'Coy, who prefigures Bloom as "a canvasser for advertisements" (*D* 14.274), by Gabriel Conroy of *The Daily Express*, or by Ignatius Gallaher, who represents, rather ephemerally, the London Press. Both Conroy and Gallaher are connected to the press world in ways that recall Joyce's own early involvements. By the time Joyce was exchanging letters with Grant Richards about *Dubliners* and repeatedly blasting the "one-eyed printer" (*Letters II* 133) for his myopia, he had already rebelliously engaged in the self-publishing (with Sheehy-Skeffington) of a work rejected by *St. Stephen's* magazine. By the time he was writing *Ulysses* and *Finnegans Wake*, he was able to dismiss the press as, among others, "*Freeman's Urinal* and *Weekly Arsewipe*" (*U* 15.812), and as "...airs independence! ... freedman's chareman! ... the dully expressed!" (*FW* 500.14–16) and "The isles is Thymes. The ales is Penzance. Vehement Genral. Delhi expulsed" (*FW* 501.19–20).

Joyce's relationship with the publishing world is well-documented. His twin interests in the production of news (writing as fabrication, rhetorical material as fabric) and in the mechanical production of text (typesetting, arrangement of fonts, spacing, etc.) are reflected in his depiction of the "GENTLEMEN OF THE PRESS" (*U* 7.20) and in a rather reverent portrayal of Old Monks, the dayfather. And if Joyce, like Bloom, understands that "writing for the newspapers" is "the readiest channel" for a literary career (*U* 16.1154), he also indicts both the opportunism of the pressmen ("Funny the way those newspaper men veer about when they get wind of a new opening. Weathercocks" [*U* 7.308–9]) and the value of mechanical reproduction of the news ("Monkeydoodle the whole thing" [*U* 7.104]). For Bloom, it is "the ads and side features" that "sell a weekly, not the stale news in the official gazette" (*U* 7.89–90). That belief informs his wanderings in pursuit of the Keyes advertisement and explains, as we see in "Ithaca", why an advertisement "condensed in trilateral" symbols "K. 11" stimulates him "in his cogitations" (*U* 17.576–86): it represents "the infinite possibilities hitherto unexploited of the modern art of advertisement" (*U* 17.580–81) as well as Bloom's idea of a successful ad. Bloom counts his client's "two crossed keys" ad (U 7.142) among the best, on a par with "Kino's". There are bad ones ("Veribest" or "Uwantit" [*U* 17.593–94]), "damn bad" ones (the "horseshoe poster" with "cyclist doubled up like a cod in a pot" [*U* 5.551–52]) and the worst (Plumtree's potted meat).[2] Bloom's ambition to design "one sole unique

2 "Cod in a pot" echoes potted meat, canned sardines, pickled pork, and cannibals and connotes Dignam's coffin and obituary associations in "Lestrygonians". They all underscore Bloom's sensitivity to all aspects of advertising, from design to placement.

advertisement" that would arrest viewers through its simplicity and efficiency, so as to stand out among all the distractions and "the velocity of modern life" (*U* 17.1770–73), coalesces in his re-vision of the "College sports" ad which comes very close to that ideal, as Mark Osteen has demonstrated.[3] Ads, throwaways and flyers are central to Joyce's preoccupation with the material visuality of language, whose transactional power and agency of interpellation, commodification and subjectification become a cipher for a politics of consumerism and exchange.

"transliterated ... cryptogram" (*U* 17.1798–1800)

Joyce imparted his own interests in scripts and writing to "Stoom" and "Blephen" (*U* 17.549–51), who in "Ithaca" discuss the evolution of alphabets from complex hieroglyphs to simpler Greek and Roman scripts, a simplification that anticipated "modern stenography and telegraphic code in the cuneiform inscriptions (Semitic) and the virgular quinquecostate ogham writing (Celtic)" (*U* 17.772–73), culminating in telegraphs transmitting messages by the "dot and dash system" (*U* 17.1674). Bloom's and Stephen's engagement in a "glyphic comparison of the phonic symbols" (*U* 17.731) of Irish and Hebrew ("gee, eh, dee, em, simple and modified" and "ghimel, aleph, daleth and (in the absence of mem) a substituted qoph" [*U* 17.737–39]), plays into the ancient Irish and Judaic "reverence for the word and commitment to the power of text", as Ira Nadel pointed out in his discussion of Joyce's "Jewish typology".[4] Historically, both scripts share a relation to secrecy, magic and cryptography. Bloom the "Deceiver" (*U* 18.318) keeps the "transliterated name and address of the addresser of the 3 letters in reversed alphabetic boustrophedonic punctated quadrilinear cryptogram (vowels suppressed) N. IGS./WI. UU. OX/W. OKS. MH/Y. IM" (*U* 17.1798–1801) in his dresser, although we wonder, with John Gordon, why he would encrypt the name and the address he knows so well.[5] Courtesy of the "Ithaca" chapter's peculiar brand of omniscience, the encryption comes to

3 See Mark Osteen's discussion of Bloom's improvement in *The Economy of Ulysses: Making Both Ends Meet* (New York: Syracuse University Press, 1995), especially 138–41.

4 Ira Nadel, *Joyce and the Jews: Culture and Texts* (Gainesville: University Press of Florida, 1996), 121 (especially Chapter 3). Bloom, by explaining "arithmetical values" (*U* 17.739) of the letters, skirts around "Gematria", a tradition of "assigning numbers to letters", although his actual abilities to divine meaning from such combinations are wanting (2).

5 See John Gordon, *Joyce and Reality: The Empirical Strikes Back* (Syracuse: Syracuse University Press, 2004), 84.

us along with the cipher for its solution. Step one, reversing the alphabet, is a scheme known to the ancient Hebrews as Athbash[6] which is, in itself, a boustrophedon.[7] A form of Temurah, Atbash denotes a Kabbalistic belief that the rearrangement of letters, including anagrams of names (of which, below), holds spiritual significance, points to hidden meanings and reveals destinies.[8] The next two steps, boustrophedonic reading and replacement of dots with vowels, yield, as readers of *Ulysses* have come to accept, "Martha Clifford Dolphins *Barn*". However, as John Gordon points out (after Richard Henninge), we forgot to read "B.RN" boustrophedonically, in which case it becomes N.RB, a probable encryption for "Nora Barnacle".[9]

Steganography: "Good system for criminals" (*U* 8.324)

Unlike cryptography, defined as a method of secret writing (κρυπτός + γράφειν) designed to render messages visibly incomprehensible to a third party, *steganography* (στεγανός + γράφειν = "protected" or "covered writing") hides information from unintended eyes in plain sight. In some seventeenth century circles the two terms were used interchangeably to mean *ars occulte scribendi*,[10] but steganography is distinct in that it "conceal[s] the very fact that a message is being sent".[11]

Sources on steganography abound; numerous overviews make references to Herodotus, whose *Histories* records some of the earliest examples of how

6 David Kahn, *The Codebreakers: The Story of Secret Writing* (New York: Macmillan Publishing, 1967), especially 77–78. Friedrich L. Bauer, *Decrypted Secrets: Methods and Maxims of Cryptology*, fourth revised edition (Berlin: Springer-Verlag, 2007), 47.

7 Defined and discussed in Sangam MacDuff's essay in this collection. For another recent consideration of boustrophedon and codes see Scarlett Baron's "Joyce and the Rhythms of the Alphabet", in *New Quotatoes: Joycean Exegesis in the Digital Age*, eds. Ronan Crowley and Dirk Van Hulle, European Joyce Studies 25 (Leiden: Brill, 2016), esp. 34–36. Baron's study came out just as this volume was going into production, too late to be considered and integrated here.

8 Kahn, *The Codebreakers*, 92.

9 In *Joyce and Reality*, Gordon's discussion of the cryptogram in Chapter 6, "Henry's Flower" (especially 86–87), includes Richard Henninge's corrective solution of the cryptogram. While Gordon suggests that Molly's chance of "unpuzzling La Clifford's address" (86) are slim, the statement overlooks the fact that Molly has no access to the cipher: it is a metatextual message to the reader, steganographic in method thanks to the "unusual polysyllables" that *we*, unlike Molly, can solve because we can see them.

10 Bauer, *Decrypted Secrets*, 9.

11 Kahn, *The Codebreakers*, 513.

steganographic messages were sent.[12] The first book on steganography is the 1499 treatise written by the Benedictine abbot Johannes Trithemius (1462–1516) titled *Steganographia*, "a highly sophisticated system of cryptography".[13] Trithemius is also the author of *Polygraphiae libri sex* (*Polygraphy in Six Books*). Book One contains an encryption method called the *Ave Maria* cipher, where letters of the alphabet are arranged into "384 columns of Latin words, two columns per page".[14] They were used to construct ciphertexts that look like harmless prayers or litanies. Alberti's *cipher disc* (1470) and Trithemius's *tabula recta* (1508)[15] were among the more popular of a variety of cipher grilles. Although cipher grilles technically belong with cryptology, they also have a place in steganography, as I indicate below.

Technical and physical steganographic strategies include invisible inks, anamorphic pictures, hollow heels or boxes with double bottoms. But more pertinent to my discussion here is linguistic steganography of which there are two types: visibly and invisibly concealed secret writing.[16]

---

12 In one example, Herodotus describes sending a covered message by Histiæus who shaved off his most trusted slave's head and tattooed a message meant to incite a revolt against the Persians: covered by new hair, the message was protected from unintended recipients and the addressee recovered it by shaving the messenger's head. In another example, Herodotus reports that Demeratus, a Greek at the Persian court, was able to warn Sparta of an impending attack by Xerxes by removing the wax from a writing tablet, writing his message on the wood and covering it with a new layer of wax; Herodotus, *The Histories*, bk 5, trans. Aubrey De Selincourt, rev. John Marincola (London: Penguin, 2003). The full text is also available online, "Histories (Herodotus)", accessed 6 December 2016, http://en.wikipedia.org/wiki/Histories_(Herodotus).

13 Trithemius's *Steganographie: Ars per occultam scripturam animi sui voluntatem absentibus aperiendi certa* has been transcribed by Joseph H. Peterson and is available digitally: "Twilit Grotto: Archives of Western Esoterica", accessed 6 December 2016, http://www.esotericarchives.com/tritheim/stegano.htm. Peterson introduces *Steganographia* as Trithemius's "most notorious work. On the surface it is a system of angel magic, but within is a highly sophisticated system of cryptography". Circulated privately for a century, it was published posthumously in 1606. Illustration 4.2 reproduced at the end of this essay shows the title page of the 1621 printing; pages from the 1676 printing can be viewed at "H.E.R.M.E.S.' Antiquarian", accessed 6 December 2016, http://www.hermesantiquarian.h-e-r-m-e-s.org/Magical%20books/Trithemiussteganographie.htm.

14 Kahn, *The Codebreakers*, 133. For reproductions and discussions of the *Ave Maria* cipher see Kahn, 135, or Bauer, 17.

15 For reproductions and discussions of Alberti's *cipher disc* see Bauer, 52, or Kahn, 128; for Trithemius's *tabula recta*, see Bauer, 127, or Kahn, 136. Search engines will also fetch numerous images of the ciphers.

16 In my overview here I rely on Bauer's "Introductory Synopsis" chapter in *Decrypted Secrets*, 9–25.

First, in visibly concealed secret writing, a message is made to appear innocent in *textual semagrams* or in *visual semagrams*. In *textual semagrams*, letters are marked by, for instance, a barely perceptible lowering or spacing, by dots or dashes, by varied fonts, etc.[17] Kahn offers a neat modern example of a visual semagram: a picture with grass blades along riverbanks that conceal a message in Morse code.[18] Visual semagrams, that is, are decipherable only by those in the know. Bloom's design for the Keyes' advertisement – crossed keys as a visual allusion the House of Keys of the Manx parliament – shares some features of a semagram and acquires steganographic dimensions thanks to Bloom's stated objective to veil in plain view the "innuendo of home rule" (*U* 7.150), recognizable by, and flattering to, the summer visitors from the Isle of Man.

Second, in invisibly concealed secret writing, messages are represented by *open codes*, further subdivided into *masked* and *veiled* secret writing. Masked open code, such as jargon, uses cues and relies on substitution; it is metonymic in method, as are slang and cant.[19] Veiled open code relies on transposition and is produced with the aid of a concealment cipher such as grille and null cipher.

Among many textual semagrams in Joyce, we see, for instance, the crab[20] lettering of "mangiD kcirtaP" (*U* 7.206) that yields its secret only after readerly pause. Another semagram, "tālāfānā, ālāvātār, hātākāldā, wātāklāsāt" (*U* 12.354), recalls Sanskrit and shows, on one level, Joyce's playful engagement with visibly concealed secret writing – we have to pause in order to "uncover" the vowels "hidden" under the macrons. On another level, we see Joyce's satirical treatment (and a veiled metatextual note of dismissal) of theosophical preoccupations of the day. Letters marked with virgules in Molly's five-syllables

17 Some of the oldest known *visual semargams* are recorded in Aeneas Tacitus and include "an astragalos or knuckle bone" with holes representing letters of the alphabet: yarn was threaded through the holes to spell out a secret message. A tempting pun on yarn notwithstanding, this is just one of the many fascinating steganographic methods described in a treatise by Aeneas Tacitus, *How to Survive under Siege*. See Section 31.17–22, "Of Secret Messages", available online at "Demonax: Hellenic Library Beta", accessed 6 December 2016, http://demonax.info/doku.php?id=text:how_to_survive_under_siege#of_secret_messages.

18 Kahn, *The Codebreakers*, 523.

19 For a fascinating historical overview of secret uses of language see Daniel Heller-Roazen, "Principles of Cant", in *Dark Tongues: The Art of Rogues and Riddlers* (New York: Zone Books, 2013), Chapter 3.

20 In its simplest form, the message in a crab is "reversed word for word or in toto", as in "kool" for "look", "red rum" for "murder", etc.; Bauer, *Decrypted Secrets*, 93–94.

"symp~~h~~hathy … ne~~w~~wphew" ("I always make that mistake"; *U* 18.730), while not quite "virgular quinquecostate" of Ogham, are read here as a semagram of Molly's orthographical and pronunciation hiccups: "sym*f*athy" and "*new*phew" (the latter followed by a helpful cipher, "2 double yous" [*U* 18.730–31]). By doubling the *h* and the *w* in the two words, Joyce may be playing with one of the many steganographic methods of concealment, in this case the multiplication of letters or sounds. The *h* inserted into "sympathy" to produce the *f* sound is a calque of the *f* value of *ph* in "symphony", a word Molly would know. For what it is worth, the terms *sympathy* and *symphony* are adjacent in W.W. Skeat ("2 double yous") who also records that "the *ph* is a substitute for the older *v*, often written as *u*".[21] If Molly could not know this, her creator most likely did, judging from his alter-ego-Stephen's reading of Skeat "by the hour" (*SH* 26). Incidentally, a first rate philologist, W.W. Skeat was fond enough of cryptology to propose his own cipher.[22] He is also credited with the discovery of a steganogram of authorship of *The Testament of Love*, a work attributed to Chaucer but revealed by Skeat – thanks to an acrostic he found buried in the initials of various chapters – to have been written by Thomas Usk.[23] Joyce makes Bloom no stranger to acrostics, as I will discuss later, but he may also be playing with the concept of a steganogram of authorship when he contrives "Flower" to stand for "Bloom"; of note are Bloom's use of his "ha" (*U* 5.24) as a steganographic prop, which conceals the evidence of his secret correspondence, and the calling card of Henry Flower, whose "Greek ees" (*U* 11.860, 889) conceal Bloom's handwriting by acting as textual semagrams recognizable to Martha as letters peculiar to Henry.

"Code" (*U* 8.324)

Masked secret writing, or jargon code, has been used effectively by various social groups. Secret communication disguised as an open message relies on the premise that the participants in the exchange have agreed "as to the true meaning of seemingly harmless phrases".[24] Vagabonds, beggars and other disenfranchised groups relied on secret communication for centuries, which is why, as Bauer contends, "languages of the criminal underworld are of particular steganographic interest".[25] A cue, "a prearranged phrase or verse to mean a

21 Walter W. Skeat, *An Etymological Dictionary of the English Language*, new ed. (Oxford: Clarendon, 1910), 624.

22 Kahn, *The Codebreakers*, 765.

23 Kahn, *The Codebreakers*, 873.

24 Bauer, *Decrypted Secrets*, 13, *et passim*.

25 Bauer, *Decrypted Secrets*, 15.

particular message", is especially important to jargon-code: "linked to the time of transmission, the message serves as an alarm or acknowledgement".[26] In "Cyclops", as the narrator and Joe Hynes enter Barney Kiernan's, the cue "Stand and deliver" is met by Joe's assurance "Friends here" and the citizen's "Pass, friends" (*U* 12.129–31). The chapter is particularly rich in jargon and slang expressions that make up an open code system, retrievable and navigable by the initiated but veiled enough to exclude an outsider from fully participating in the patrons' "confab[s]" (*U* 12.119). In terms of cues, Bloom's stock with the pub patrons plummets (not that it was very high to begin with) when he ignores the cue to have a drink in favour of a cigar. One could plead Bloom's ignorance of pub customs, but his reflection in "Eumaeus" on the row created in the pub from the "bite from a sheep" (*U* 16.1640) gives Bloom away: he is quite in control of his conduct at Barney Kiernan's and his rejection of the myopic bigots' communication code is rather deliberate. Bloom is, after all, "a bit of an artist in his spare time" (*U* 16.1448–49).

But one man's cue is another man's old newspaper, as the phrase "I was going to throw it away" demonstrates (*U* 5.534, 537).[27] Paradoxically, that phrase also precipitates a number of cues that drive one of the narrative threads of *Ulysses* while also setting up a series of steganographic tests for readers. That is, what is hidden *from Bloom* in plain sight – the name of the horse to bet on in "Lotus Eaters", the whispers of men at Davy Byrne's (*U* 8.1023), or the meaning of gossip that fuels the rage against Bloom in "Cyclops" (*U* 12.1551) – is also initially hidden *from readers*. The difference is that whereas they remain forever unknowable to Bloom, Joyce grants omniscience to the readers whose laborious "Sherlockholmesing" (*U* 16.831) unveils secrets of his textual design.

Joyce also plays with jargon code. For instance, when Stephen asks his siblings about his parents' whereabouts, he hears the answer: "Goneboro toboro lookboro atboro aboro houseboro" (*P* IV.576). In terms of code, this jargon uses parasitic suffixing as null cipher for concealment. Lenehan's "Muchibus thankibus" (*U* 7.780) falls into that category as well, as it also recalls the so-called "tut Latin" jargon of schoolchildren who used to insert "-tut-" between all the syllables.[28] Joyce also experiments with non-jargon repetitions in such

26 Bauer, *Decrypted Secrets*, 17.

27 Similarly, a man's refusal of onions can be a woman's proof of impending infidelity: "Id know if he refused to eat the onions I know plenty of ways ask him to tuck down the collar of my blouse or touch him with my veil and gloves on going out" (*U* 18.188–90).

28 Bauer, *Decrypted Secrets*, 20–21. Bauer offers further examples that include a "stuttering" system that rendered "un fou" as "undreque foudreque" (recorded in 1670 in the city of Metz); or the Javanais language with "jave" for "je", "laveblavanc" for "le blanc" and "navon" for "non". These examples underscore the long tradition of using null ciphers in open code

"unspeeched" audibles as "ooeeehah", "wayawayawayawayaway" (*U* 3.403–4), "endlessnessnessness" (*U* 11.750) and "wavyavyeavyheavyeavyevyevyhair" (*U* 11.809); as onomatopoeias, they can be read in terms of steganographic veiling of sound as it travels through, and defines, *space/time*.[29]

"the abbreviation of his first name" (*U* 17.410)

Steganography also uses a null called *acrostic cipher* that can veil a message by following the rule of *the nth character after a particular character* (e.g. the third letter after a space, the first letter in each line, the second letter after punctuation, etc.). Bloom's 1888 Valentine Day's acrostic for Molly, "Poldy" (*U* 17.412–16), is a thinly veiled message of love and an invitation to pet-name intimacy; we can speculate that, eighteen years earlier, Bloom's steganographic message was, indeed, unveiled by teenage Molly. The acrostic "Poldy" appears right after "*Miss* Marion" (*U* 17.411) and there is a curious textual symmetry here with the very first appearance of "Poldy" in "Calypso" right after "*Mrs* Marion" (*U* 4.245) [emphases added]. While meeting Miss Marion spurred young Poldy to commit poetry, seeing "Mrs Marion" on the envelope mysteriously

veiling, including dummy syllables, such as in B talk in German (e.g. giving "Gabartebenlaubaubebe" for "Gartenlaube") and Cadogan talk in French (with "cadgadodgogadgan" for "cadogan") (21).

29 By suggesting that these particular onomatopoetic formations share a steganographic method of veiling, I mean to point to the fact that these alphabetic clusters appear as "meaningless" to a first-time reader but, once they are vocalised, their semantically inflected elements (way-; endless-) elongated by repetition (-awayaway-; -nessness-) unveil them as mimetic of sound reverberating through space and time. I read them as a subgroup of what Derek Attridge has termed "nonlexical onomatopoeia" (*Peculiar Language: Literature as Difference from the Renaissance to James Joyce* [London: Methuen, 1988], esp. 136–57). Attridge's discerning discussion of onomatopoeia in "Sirens" (e.g., Bloom's flatulence) centres on graphological, phonological, and morphological onomatopoeic conventions of rendering sounds (138–148, *passim*), and posits that our familiarity with these conventions helps us to understand nonlexical onomatopoeias as various sounds produced by human bodies, by animals and by objects ("Pprrpffrrppffff"; "Mrkgnao!"; "ee: cree"). Nonlexical onomatopoeias frequently rely on repetition of letters and Attridge addresses, among others, "different onomatopoeic tasks" of the letter "e" (144). However, repetitions in "endlessnessnessness" or "hissss" are for Attridge "instances that fall between the lexical and nonlexical categories, where the word is *deformed* for onomatopoeic purpose" (148; my emphasis). Needless to say, I do not see such words as deformed. Joyce's onomatopoeic purpose here is, in my view, to represent space/time through sound and, in my reading, his method is steganographic (as also discussed further in this essay).

quickens-slows older Poldy's heart (*U* 4.244) before we even know who the "she" of "Mn" (*U* 4.57) is. Such symmetries abound in Joyce's texts. As early as *Dubliners*, the chiasmic appearance of the word "general" in "The Sisters" and "The Dead" (both in the context of *newspapers*) anticipates the rhetoricity of Joycean language that will draw from, among other things, the "high falutin stuff" (*U* 7.260) of the newspapers. Indeed, the rhetoricity (and the noise) of the world of the "GENTLEMEN OF THE PRESS" in "Aeolus" is aptly foregrounded in the onomatopoeic chiasmus of Guinness barrels that Bloom passes on his way to the *Freeman's Journal*.[30] The chiasmic snow narrative that frames Gabriel-the-press-man's reverie is another example of how deliberate Joyce was in his configuration of *language events* as carriers of steganographically charged textual elements: messages in plain sight about the rewards of careful, attentive – Senn's hypolectic[31] – reading, one that involves detecting an additional frame of reference (e.g. a code, a pattern).

Bloom's acrostic appears in the vicinity of one of the oldest methods of concealment through permutation, anagrams. The four anagrams, "Ellpodbomool / Molldopeloob / Bollopedoom / Old Ollebo, M.P." (*U* 17.406–9) are steganographic in their potential purpose: ungraceful as they are, they could serve Bloom's need for a pseudonym. Joyce also uses other permutation methods, such as portmanteaux in "Stoom" and "Blephen" (*U* 17.549, 551) and "Siopold" (*U* 11.752) or metathesis in Lenehan's "clamn dever" (*U* 7.695). If anagrams and portmanteaux are traditionally steganographic, Lenehan's metathesis appears to be but an exercise in sophistry.[32] Other letter-manipulation-related steganographic methods include suppression of letters to mark as well as mask a message, as is the case with "vowels suppressed" (*U* 17.1800) in Martha Clifford cryptogram or in "L-n-h-n and M-ll-g-n" (*U* 12.542) where the *correct* vowels insert themselves into the dash-designated gaps as soon as consonants are vocalized. Joyce's play on vowel suppression may be a not-so-veiled nod to the

30 "Grossbooted draymen rolled barrels dullthudding out of Prince's stores and bumped them up on the brewery float. On the brewery float bumped dullthudding barrels rolled by grossbooted draymen out of Prince's stores" (*U* 7.21–24).

31 Fritz Senn, *Inductive Scrutinies* (Dublin: The Lilliput Press, 1995), 227, *et passim*.

32 Lenehan's verbal flatulence is further illustrated by his many rhetorically vacuous outbursts, like palindrome "Madam, I'm Adam. And Able was I ere I saw Elba" (*U* 7.683) and hysteron-proteron "Clever ... Very" (*U* 7.675). In terms of steganography, they could be classified as *crabs*. But since Lenehan's use of these devices (and of his limerick, riddle or Gallicisms) does not seem to carry any messages, they are devoid of steganographic purpose, unlike such sub-category of crab (note 20) as the reversed lettering in semagram "mangiD kcirtaP" (*U* 7.206) that actually veils a name.

Hebrew consonantal alphabet where the absence of vowels does not fully veil the message. Vowels under macrons in mock Sanskrit quoted earlier also insert themselves accurately and, notably, only one corresponds to the sound of "a".

Another veiling strategy, the acronym, hides the meaning of the entity it stands for; we see this in the list of clergymen with their post-nominal letters (*U* 12.927–38), or in Bloom's preoccupation with Russell's identity: "A.E.: what does that mean? Initials perhaps. Albert Edward, Arthur Edmund, Alphonsus Eb Ed El Esquire" (*U* 8.527–29). Acronyms, whether for *nomina sacra*, such as I.N.R.I, I.H.S. (*U* 5.372), or D.V. (*U* 10.69, 150), or ones familiar to Dubliners, like D.B.C. (*U* 8.510, 10.1058), are jargon-like and, to the uninitiated, yield their secrets only after some scrutiny.

"ogham writing (Celtic)" (*U* 17.773)

In *The Secret Languages of Ireland*, R.A.S. Macalister discusses in depth various Ogham writing systems and lists the following examples from Calder's study of *Scholar's Primer* which presents a list of names for letters:[33]

> Linn-ogam ('River-pool Ogham'), an alphabetical list of rivers…
> Dinn-ogam ('Fortress Ogham'), a similar alphabetical list of famous fortresses.
> En-ogam ('Bird Ogham'), as Bittern, Lark, Falcon, etc.
> Dath-ogam ('Colour Ogham'), as Blue, Lake, Flaxen, etc.
> Cell-ogam ('Church Ogham'), an alphabetical list of famous churches…
> Rig-ogam ('King Ogham'), an alphabetical list of kings.
> Ndem-ogam ('Saint Ogham'), a list of saints.
> Dan-ogam ('Craft Ogham'), a list of arts and occupations.
> Biad-ogam ('Food Ogham'), a list of foods.
> Lus-ogam ('Herb Ogham'), a list of plants.

The examples above cast a new light on Joyce's catalogues. My former engagement with this topic centred around the western medieval traditions of

33 R.A. Stewart Macalister, *The Secret Languages of Ireland* (Cambridge: Cambridge University Press, 1937), 42. Joyce worked with this book and used it for *Finnegans Wake*, as discussed by Adaline Glasheen in *Newslitter* no. 10 (1963): 1–3 (and confirmed by Clive Hart in a footnote to their text). Though it was published 15 years after *Ulysses*, Joyce would have been familiar with the material that Macalister discusses and systematizes in his still remarkable book.

enumeration and I read Joyce's lists and catalogues in terms of their synathroesmic qualities,[34] as *tropes* that operate on a figurative, hyperbolic level; I called them *catalements*, that is, the elements or units *in* (but not necessarily bearing *on*) the narrative structure whose effects can be epiphanic.[35] Considering lists also in terms of Ogham codes deepens my understanding of lists *as ciphers*, a salient feature in "Cyclops"[36] and "Ithaca", though none of them are alphabetical. Significantly, one of the lists in "Cyclops" appears to be a Cell-Ogham: it enumerates the ancient "seats of learning" (*U* 12.1448, *et passim*) and comes preceded by a reference to "Solomon of Droma and Manus Tomaltach og MacDonogh, authors of the Book of Ballymote" (*U* 12.1439–40). *The Book of Ballymote*, in addition to historical and genealogical information, contains methods for deciphering various systems of Ogham inscriptions. For Kahn,

> the most delightful thing about these systems is *their names*, the most charming in cryptology, which have been bestowed with all the Irish flair for poetry, blarney, and wit. There is, for an example, a system called "the ogham that bewildered Bres" [Ogam romesc Bres[37]], in which *the*

---

34 In rhetoric, *synathroesmus* (Gr. συναθροισμός, collection) refers to accumulation by enumeration, especially of dissimilar things; J.A. Cuddon, *A Dictionary of Literary Terms and Literary Theory*, 5th ed. (Malden: Blackwell Publishing, 2012), 703.

35 By considering catalogues in terms of *res* (signifieds) and *nomina* (signifiers), and evoking discussions by John Kidd, Northrop Frye, A. Walton Litz and Lorraine Weir, I proposed that catalogues, "with their non-beauteous manifestation as 'alphybettyformed verbage' (*FW* 183.13), fall outside of Joyce's Thomistic aesthetic criteria that required *integritas, consonantia* and *claritas* for beauty to be apprehended. In texts, catalogues and lists halt the spatial-temporal flow of narrative as they dwell upon their own enumerative process by taking space (on page) and time (to read), and they solicit two kinds of responses: either the readers skip over the lists (unlikely to *miss* anything relevant to the plot), or they read laboriously through catalogues (unlikely to *gain* anything relevant to the plot)"; see Jolanta Wawrzycka, "Traditions of Enumeration and Catalogues in Joyce", *Analele Universității "Constantin Brâncuşi" din Târgu Jiu, Seria Litere şi Ştiinţe Sociale*, 2 (2009): 79–80, "Academia", accessed 6 December 2016, http://www.academia.edu/518024/Traditions_of_Enumeration_and_Catalogues_in_Joyce._TRADIŢII_DE_ENUMERARE_ŞI_CATALOGARE_LA_JOYCE.

36 For a comprehensive study of lists in "Cyclops", see Marianna Gula, *A Tale of a Pub: Re-Reading the "Cyclops" Episode of James Joyce's "Ulysses" in the Context of Irish Cultural Nationalism* (Debrecen: DU Press, 2012).

37 Macalister, *The Secret Languages of Ireland*, 46.

> *name of the letter stands for the letter*, as if one were to encipher *who* as *DOUBLE-YOU AITCH OH* [emphasis added].[38]

Kahn explains that a message concealed in this manner was given to the ancient hero Bres on his way to a battle; as he tried to read it, his confusion was bad enough to cost him victory.

We share in this sort of confusion in "Hades" where the "Ogam romesc Bres"-like device appears twice in Bloom's thoughts: as an echo of the music hall song played by the street organ, "Kay ee double ell wy" (*U* 6.374), and again when Bloom loses sight of the man in the macintosh: "Kay ee double ell. Become invisible" (*U* 6.900). There are several levels of steganographic layering here: initially, the word-like letterings are puzzling to *the reader*, though vocalisation helps to recognize them as letters of the alphabet; the discovery that they refer to a name in a song deepens their meaning. In addition, we share *Bloom's* perplexity at the disappearance of the man in the macintosh as he wonders whether anybody has, indeed seen him. Like the song's "Kelly", covered under the letters "Kay ee double ell wy", the man in the macintosh is covered by the letters "m-a-c-i-n-t-o-s-h". Both men are initially "invisible" to us though both are *textually* present, spelled out. Steganographically, they are hidden in plain sight, signifiers to unveil.

Another phrase reminiscent of the "Ogam romesc Bres" appears in "Aeolus": "the unpar one *ar* alleled embarra two *ars* is it? double *ess* ment of a harassed pedlar while gauging au the symmetry with a *y* of a peeled pear under a cemetery wall" (*U* 7.167–69, emphasis added). But whereas "Ogam romesc Bres" is a cipher where every letter is spelled one by one,[39] the figure above recalls Bog-Latin, where "only one or two letters of each word are called by their names".[40] The steganographic method here veils a process of spelling-while-thinking (something Molly does too – "2 double yous" [*U* 18.730–31]) and accentuates Joyce's fondness for "ogham writing (Celtic)" (*U* 17.773).

Joyce's method of re-presenting Bloom's thinking is in most cases steganographic in nature: objects and thoughts present themselves to Bloom but, initially, they are far from clear to readers. Many pages separate "Pen…" from "Penrose" (*U* 8.178 and 8.1114); Molly's "istsbeg" (*U* 18.876) requires a pause to disconnect – *ists* from *mists, beg* – from *began* to make sense of the new union, even if we do not know that it is a line from a song. Song phrases, incidentally, are another constant in Bloom's and Molly's train of thought. They are

38 Kahn, *The Codebreakers*, 88.

39 Macalister, *The Secret Languages of Ireland*, 46, 91.

40 Macalister, *The Secret Languages of Ireland*, 91, note 1.

frequently invisible to the uninitiated readers yet they are integral to Joyce's presentation of the couple's memory triggers. Bloom's mnemonic device for recalling a telephone number is, arguably, also steganographic: "Better phone him up first. Number? Yes. Same as Citron's house. Twentyeight. Twentyeight double four" (*U* 7.219–20), later changed to: "Twentyeight. No. Twenty. Double four, yes" (*U* 7.385). Although the number might not have been a mystery to Joyce's early readers, some hundred years later our conundrum is this: if Citron's house number is 28, is the telephone number 28 as well? Or is it three-digit 244? Or four-digit 2844 or 2044? A strong case for one of the latter comes from Crawford who speaks to the "telephone receiver nozzle" in "Circe": "Hello, seventyseven eightfour" (*U* 15.809–11). Though both three and four digit numbers appear to have been in use, if we dismiss 244, the two remaining possibilities leave us none the wiser about Bloom's (re)call.[41]

"Sss. Dth, dth, dth!" (*U* 8.373)

From the standpoint of printing, many onomatopoeic elements, as noted earlier, can also be seen as steganographic in method, as enigmas to be unveiled, through vocalisation: sixfold repetition of "sllt" (*U* 7.174, *et passim*), the "whisper" of creaking doors: "ee: cree" (*U* 7.50) or "Cockcarracarra" (*U* 11.1048), the whistle of the night train (*U* 18.874) or the growling and barking of the dog, "rrrssstt awokwokawok" (*U* 18.813), the lacquey's bell's "barang" (*U* 10.282), the bells of George's church (*U* 4.546–48), the cuckoo clock (*U* 15.1133–35), the musical sounds and notations in "Sirens" and very many others. For Bloom, "everything speaks in its own way" (*U* 7.177), including his own behind in dialogue with the passing tram (and Robert Emmet's last words), "Prrprr ... Fff! Oo. Rrpr ... Tram kran kran kran ... Krandlkrankran ... *Let my epitaph be.* Kraaaaaa. *Written. I have.* Pprrpffrrppffff. *Done*" (*U* 11.1286–94). Molly, too, triggered by

41 Terence Killeen confirms that the ads in *Thom's Directory* for 1904 list four-digit phone numbers, though I also located an image of the 1904 *Corporation Diary* page (Dublin City Archives) that lists two three-digit numbers for Mansion House at Dawson Street. Having spotted a few three-digit phone numbers in a later *Thom's*, Terence wrote: "It's interesting how Bloom's method of recalling the telephone number has to be revised. ...Ironically, the 'real' Citron, according to Vivien Igoe's book [*The Real People of Joyce's 'Ulysses': A Biographical Guide* (Dublin: University College Dublin Press, 2016), 55], lived in 17 St Kevin's Parade, so that's no help". He argues that Bloom's use of "Citron's address as a mnemonic for recalling the phone number", including the readjustment of 28 to 20, remains "a complicated transaction" but that "it appears he is thinking in four-digit terms, either 2844 or 2044". Private correspondence, July 2016.

the song "Winds that Blow from the South", is timing the sound of her behind to the muffling whistle of the passing train while intoning "Love's Old Sweet Song": "piano quietly sweeeee theres that train far away pianissimo eeeee one more tsong" (*U* 18.907–8). The steganographic nature of these non-standard (non-semantic) lexes demands readerly investment that eventually yields the secrets of Joyce's textual stratagems in his configuration of language events as carriers of steganographically charged textual elements.

Bloom's onomatopoeic "Sss. Dth, dth, dth!" (*U* 8.373) is of interest because it straddles onomatopoeia and ellipsis-cum-euphemism. The context helps us translate these letter units into "Poor Mrs Purefoy". Martha Clifford's euphemistic ellipsis, "that word" (*U* 5.246), and Molly's "all those words" in Bloom's letters (*U* 18.318–19) have been discussed before, but only John Gordon has addressed them steganographically by proposing that "that word", "written up with a picture of a womans" that Molly "*couldnt* find anywhere" (*U* 18.325–27), is there, "*in plain sight*: just take '*couldnt*', and subtract 'old'" (emphasis added).[42] The appearance of "that word" in the context of the "old woman's" earlier in "Calypso" (*U* 4.227) creates yet another of those chiasmic correspondences, this time between the two "Molly" chapters of *Ulysses*. That the euphemism for the unmentionables can be steganographic is further exemplified by Molly's critique of her doctor's tortured "where you sit down" (*U* 18.110) and by Josie's "and did you wash possible" (*U* 18.205): the euphemisms veil two of Joyce's "four cardinal points" noted in a letter to Frank Budgen in 1921 on which, we remember, the "Penelope" chapter "turns like the huge earth ball" (*Letters I* 170).

"clandestine correspondence" (*U* 17.2251)

In his letter writing business, Bloom uses a number of steganographic concealments, both physical and linguistic. As I indicated earlier, Bloom's "ha" is a steganographic prop that houses the marker of his "clandestine correspondence" (*U* 17.2251), the calling card. The card mediates his communication carried out in plain sight and serves as metonymy for both Bloom's disguised identity and the exchange in the "language of flowers" (*U* 5.261), itself a cipher for a variety of emotions to be expressed nonverbally. As used by Mr Flower, the language of flowers is tinted with "that word", a cipher for a no-nonsense sexual come-on

42 Gordon, *Joyce and Reality*, 86.

that, as we learn from Molly (*U* 18.318–28) had worked at least once in the past. It may have worked again with Martha: she "answered anyhow" (*U* 5.65).

Both Molly and Richie Goulding see "Bloom" in the act of writing to Martha, though he is "Henry Flower Esq" in those instances (*U* 5.62). Caught by Molly in the act of writing, he covers his letter with a "blottingpaper" (*U* 18.49); seen by Richie writing a reply, he double-covers it with a lie (*U* 11.887–89) and with an "unfurled ... *Freeman*" (*U* 11.859). In this context, Bloom is a cipher of deceit who, tellingly, suspects that Gerty's name "might be false ... like my name" and Martha's "address Dolphin's barn a blind" (*U* 13.945–46), the same blind he uses to plea "guiltless" at being "wrongfully accused" by his "brother Henry" ("He is my double. He lives in number 2 Dolphin's Barn") (*U* 15.1769–71). Bloom's identity is further refracted into a cipher of "otherness" as a "Jew", though he is an uncircumcised thrice-baptized Christian born to an English mother. Kenner reminded us some time ago that "most readers never realise that Bloom by Jewish standards isn't Jewish",[43] to which we may add that Molly, "jewess looking after [her] mother" (*U* 18.1184–85), *is*.

These "correspondences" – very much *there* in the text – are initially concealed from the newcomers to *Ulysses*. But the status of a seasoned reader does not guarantee omniscience. As much as is known about Bloom's thoughts and doings in the course of the day, some of Joyce's objective, often numerical "facts" about Bloom, *do not* add up. Bloom's physical features, for one, are presented parallactically throughout the novel and are difficult to assess, as pointed out by, among others, Robert Adams and Hugh Kenner.[44] Bloom's birthday is also in question,[45] as is Joyce's math calculating the relation between Stephen and Bloom's respective ages in "Ithaca". For Adams, they are not "simply parodic" errors, but Joyce's arithmetical "mistakes", with "a kind of bumbling logic behind the whole thing".[46] The mistakes, however, are typical of Joyce's *Bloom* and consistent with Bloom's "defective mnemotechnic" (*U* 17.766) concerning scientific facts about, for instance, parallax or fundamental laws of physics about floating and falling bodies ("It's a law something like that" [*U* 5.41–42]).[47] Bloom's forgetting to move the house key into the right trouser

---

43 Hugh Kenner, *Ulysses*, rev. ed. (Baltimore: The Johns Hopkins University Press, 1987), 152.

44 See discussion in Robert M. Adams, *Surface and Symbol* (New York: Oxford University Press, 1962), 184; and in Hugh Kenner, *Ulysses*, 164–65.

45 Kenner, *Ulysses*, 152; Don Gifford, *"Ulysses" Annotated: Notes for James Joyce's "Ulysses"*, 2nd ed. (Berkeley: University of California Press, 1988), note on *U* 16.608.

46 Adams, *Surface and Symbol*, 183.

47 Other critics have also considered Joyce's practice of co-opting error in writing. See, for example, Patrick McCarthy, *Ulysses: Portals of Discovery* (Boston: Twayne, 1990), esp. 36–51. For exploration of the "aesthetic of error" in Joyce and the value of "misreadings", see

pocket ("doubly irritat[ing]" given that "he remembered that he had reminded himself twice not to forget" [*U* 17.77–79]), or his not picking up Molly's lotion, add to the psychological verisimilitude. Integral to the Joyce text, the errors, when read as steganographic devices, serve as readerly portals of discovery of the B.RN/NR.B nature mentioned earlier, already present in Eliza's "*Freeman's General*" (*D* 1.234). That is, hyper-textuality of the Joyce text as a whole is not unlike hyper-textuality of steganographic veiled writing: our eyes may glide over the text's recognizable signposts but, unless our brains "click", many of them will yield no message. To take it a step further, such elements as foreign phrases, or references to historical or literary events and figures, to popular culture, theatre, newspapers, advertising, etcetera, can be seen as *meta*-steganographic messages planted by Joyce. They keep us busy deciphering them and, as we fact- or myth-check, read and re-read, they deepen our understanding of Joyce's grand design. Adducing Joyce's correspondence to the text can open up a reading that acquires steganographic dimensions as well: long ago, for example, Fritz Senn identified numerous passages from Joyce's letters to Nora and Martha Fleischmann in "Nausicaa".[48] The letters (and the archives), in addition to helping scholars unveil Joyce's textual messages, have also confirmed Joyce's propensity for recycling his own writings, along with everything he had ever read: it is all there, in plain sight, subject to steganographic probes that engage and reward Joyce's insomniac readers happy to pursue the "puzzle [to] find the meat" (*U* 8.750–51),[49] or to locate that still elusive "missing letter puzzle" that captivated Joyce in 1905.

Tim Conley, *Joyces Mistakes* (Toronto: University of Toronto Press, 2003). Finally, for more recent studies that cover a range of Joycean lapses, misappropriations and slippages, see *Errears and Erroriboose: Joyce and Error*, ed. Matthew Creasy, European Joyce Studies 20 (Amsterdam: Rodopi, 2011).

48 These can be found among the holdings of the Zurich James Joyce Foundation, which contain numerous binders created over the decades by Fritz Senn, packed with textual clips, drawings, photographs and other archival materials pertinent to *Ulysses* (but also all other works), all meticulously arranged episode by episode and line-referenced. I had the opportunity to work with these documents on several occasions, including the pages from Joyce's letters to Nora cross-referenced by Senn with line numbers from "Nausica". For one of the critical applications of letters as meta-textual tools see Senn's "Nausica" chapter in *James Joyce's "Ulysses": Critical Essays*, ed. Clive Heart and David Hayman (Berkeley: University of California Press, 1974), 277–311.

49 Aida Yared's website "Joyce Images" features a steganographic puzzle postcard that accompanies Joyce's line, "Puzzle find the meat": "Lestrygonians", accessed 6 December 2016, http://joyceimages.com/episode/8/?page=15.

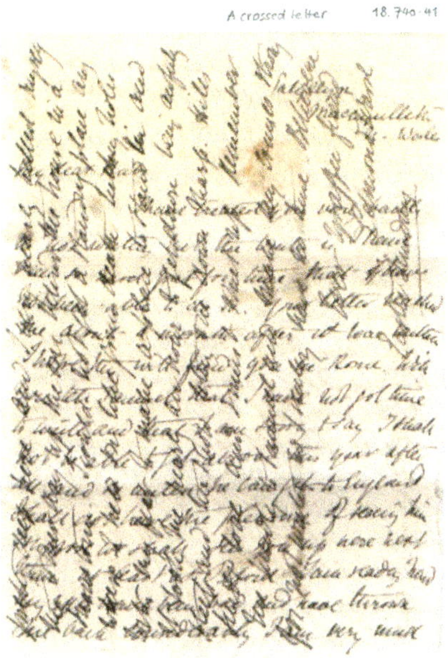

ILLUSTRATION 4.1
Sample of a "crossed" letter[50]

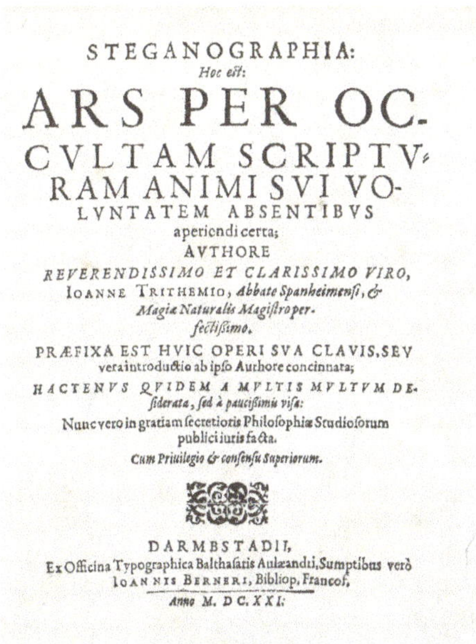

STEGANOGRAPHIA:
Hoc est:
ARS PER OC-
CVLTAM SCRIPTV-
RAM ANIMI SVI VO-
LVNTATEM ABSENTIBVS
aperiendi certa;
AVTHORE
REVERENDISSIMO ET CLARISSIMO VIRO,
IOANNE TRITHEMIO, *Abbate Spanheimensi, &*
Magiæ Naturalis Magistro per-
fectissimo.
PRÆFIXA EST HVIC OPERI SVA CLAVIS, SEV
vera introductio ab ipso Authore concinnata;
HACTENVS QVIDEM A MVLTIS MVLTVM DE-
siderata, sed à paucissimis visa:
Nunc vero in gratiam secretioris Philosophiæ Studiosorum
publici iuris facta.
Cum Privilegio & consensu Superiorum.

DARMBSTADII,
Ex Officina Typographica Balthasaris Aulæandri, Sumptibus verò
IOANNIS BERNERI, Bibliop. Francof.
Anno M. DC. XXI.

ILLUSTRATION 4.2
Title page of the 1621 printing of Trithemius's Steganographia
COURTESY OF H.E.R.M.E.S' ANTIQUARIAN.

50 *The Victorian Web*, accessed 6 December 2016, http://www.victorianweb.org/history/letters/rome.html. This image may be used without prior permission for any scholarly or educational purpose. Reproduction courtesy of Fritz Senn and Zurich James Joyce Foundation holdings.

Acknowledgements

I wish to acknowledge Dean Kate Hawkins and Chair Rosemary Guruswamy of Radford University for grants that funded Zurich Workshop travel, research and the writing of this essay, and Stephanie Nelson at Boston University for her attentive comments on an earlier draft.

CHAPTER 5

Classified Advertising in Joyce

David Spurr

Abstract

The classified ad is used and re-appropriated by James Joyce in *Ulysses* and *Finnegans Wake* in a number of ways. It appears in the form of Bloom's ad searching for a "smart lady typist" in "Lestrygonians" – resurfacing in a rewritten form in the "Shem the Penman" episode of *Finnegans Wake*. It features as the imaginary ad offering £5 for an imaginary runaway Bloom in "Ithaca", and in a passage in HCE's boastful speech, which bears resemblance to the language of the rooms-to-let ad of newspapers. The purpose classified ads serve in *Ulysses* ranges from functioning as an investment to providing a mode of concealment and alibi for illicit private communication. Operating as a means of negotiation between the private and the public sphere, adhering to a certain notion of respectability is key, but it also provides a particular language which can be re-used and re-appropriated, for example for erotic ends. The treatment the classified ad receives in Joyce diverts it from its original function of communication about goods and services; it becomes a minor form of fiction in itself, as well as a vehicle for parody and the return of the repressed.

Keywords

Ulysses – *Finnegans Wake* – classified ad – respectability – secrecy – *désoeuvrement* – Rowntree

Classified advertising may be defined as the form of communication, originally printed in newspapers, consisting of brief personal messages from individuals seeking an exchange of goods or services from other individuals. Classified ads are grouped together by categories such as employment opportunities, missing objects or persons and rooms to let, all of which appear in Joyce's fiction. The classified advertisement is nearly as old as the newspaper itself, the first classifieds having appeared in the early seventeenth century, such as the one selling "a young dromedary camel" or the one "looking for a travelling companion to

 | DOI 10.1163/9789004359062_007

go to Italy in two weeks", both in *La Feuille du Bureau d'adresses*, published in Paris from 1633 to 1651.[1]

The *Evening Telegraph* "pink edition" for 16 June 1904, the one that Leopold Bloom and Stephen Dedalus read at the cabman's shelter in *Ulysses*, carries several ads for "apartments vacant":

> Couple of respectable young Girls or Men can have comfortable double-bedded room, breakfast and tea; terms very moderate ... 1 Camden Row, Camden street.
>
> Lodgings; wanted three respectable young Men to share nice airy front room; terms, with attendance and washing, 10s ... Address 1 Valleymount Park, Kilmainham.
>
> Respectable lodgings for young men; terms moderate. Apply at 1a James's Place, Lower Baggot Street.

The key word here is "respectable". It is a word to which Joyce will have frequent recourse insofar as it designates the status to which the private individuals of Joyce's universe, from Martha Clifford to HCE, often lay dubious claim. Implying both the moral character and the social status of a person, respectability is situated at the intersection between the private and public spheres. As such, it is perfectly adapted to the classified advertisement, where the private individual represents his or her needs before the public. Joyce makes liberal use of the discourse of the classified ad precisely because his fiction is designed to explore the interpenetration of the private and public spheres in the modern world, where individual consciousness is invaded by mass media, and private desire becomes public scandal.

A good example of this often perilous overlap between the private and the public is the ad which Bloom has placed in the *Irish Times*: "Wanted, smart lady typist to aid gentleman in literary work" (*U* 8.326–27). Before commenting on the ad itself, let us consider the paper in which it is printed. The choice of the *Irish Times* rather than, for example, the *Freeman's Journal* is strategic. A Protestant Unionist paper familiarly called "The Old Lady of d'Olier Street", the *Times* had what would today be called a superior demographic in comparison to the

1 Howard M. Solomon, *Public Welfare, Science and Propaganda in Seventeenth Century France: Innovations of Théophraste Renaudot* (Princeton: Princeton University Press, 1973), 54 as quoted in M.C. Barrès-Baker, "An Introduction to the Early History of Newspaper Advertising", in *Brent Museum and Archive Occasional Publications*, no. 2 (London: Brent Council, 2011), 9. Also accessed 6 December 2016 at, http://www.brent.gov.uk/media/387509/Newspaper_advertising_article_2011.pdf.

Freeman's Journal. As the paper of social standing it was more in keeping with Bloom's claim to be a "gentleman" engaged in literary work. According to Bloom's own professional analysis, the *Times* also has better distribution and market penetration. He has already received 44 responses to his ad, and while walking past the *Times* building he reflects that there might be more waiting for him inside. "Best paper by long chalks for a small ad. Got the provinces now. Cook and general, exc. cuisine, housemaid kept. Wanted live man for spirit counter. Resp. girl (R.C.)[2] wishes to hear of post in fruit or pork shop" (*U* 8.334–36). In the same episode, the form of the classified ad fixes itself so firmly in Bloom's mind that even his passing observations take form in the language of classifieds. The sight of "a drowsing loafer lounged in heavy thought" against John Long's pub in Dawson Street thus provokes the following thought: "Handy man wants job. Small wages. Will eat anything" (*U* 8.1067–68). In such cases the classified ad becomes a way of seeing, of literally classifying experience.

Bloom's appeal for a "smart" lady typist has an ambiguity that might have given pause to prospective applicants for the position. As today, in 1904 "smart" had the alternate meanings of "clever" and "stylish", suggesting that the literary gentleman in question could be interested as much in the physical person of his typist as in her secretarial skills.[3] This ambiguity is in keeping with the bold imposture of the ad, the illicit nature of which is compounded by the secret and somewhat *louche* correspondence it occasions between "Henry Flower" and Martha Clifford, whose real name is Peggy Griffin, if we are to believe her confession in the "Circe" episode (*U* 15.765–66). In addition to seeking a straightforward exchange of goods or services, the classified ad can also serve as a code, a means of concealment, an alibi for the satisfaction of less than respectable desires: "Good system for criminals. Code" (*U* 8.324).

Given that the wording of Bloom's ad is code for an invitation to a secret erotic exchange, the simple Martha Clifford has understood it better than Lizzie Twigg, whose response to the same ad reveals an overly literal interpretation: "My literary efforts have had the good fortune to meet with the approval of the eminent poet A.E. (Mr Geo. Russell)" (*U* 8.331–32). This letter constitutes a rare and improbable point of contact between Bloom and the world of the Irish literary revival; it is the reason why, later in the same episode, Bloom speculates that the "listening woman" he sees in the company of Russell is the same Lizzie Twigg, "coming from the vegetarian" (*U* 8.534). Bloom's judgment is not flattering: "Her stockings are loose over her ankles. I detest that: so tasteless. Those literary etherial people they are all. Dreamy, cloudy, symbolistic"

2 Respectable girl, Roman Catholic.

3 "Smart", *OED Online*, accessed 6 December 2016, http://oed.com.

(*U* 8.542–43). When it comes to her reply to Bloom's ad, the joke here is that the "literary" Lizzie Twigg – "No time to do her hair drinking sloppy tea with a book of poetry" (*U* 8.332–33) – is less skilled at reading between the lines than the unschooled but more instinctive Martha. Lizzie is "smart" neither in the fashionable sense nor that of cleverness. Martha, on the other hand, has a talent for writing letters which, in their authentic soft-porn style, move Bloom to the "weak joy" of sensual reverie (*U* 5.268). The erotic charge of these letters is a literary accomplishment in itself, deriving from the balanced tension between bold flirtation – "I will punish you … you naughty boy" (*U* 5.251–52) – and the pretence of respectability: "a girl of good family like me, respectable character" (*U* 5.269–70).

The question of Martha's respectability resurfaces in "Circe", where, holding a copy of the *Irish Times* in her hand and pointing at Bloom, she calls in a tone of reproach, "Clear my name", and accuses him of "breach of promise" (*U* 15.752–65). It is then for Bloom himself, facing a jury, to protest, "I am a respectable married man, without a stain on my character" (*U* 15.776–77). We have seen how in the real classified ads published in Joyce's time the issue of respectability is omnipresent as a condition of the arrangements proposed: respectable lodgings offered for respectable "young girls or men", etc. The medium of the classified ad is obsessed with respectability in its discourse precisely because of the opportunities it offers for disreputable behaviour, a paradox that Joyce exploits in a treatment that exposes the hypocrisy of conventional respectability. Whereas this theme is treated sombrely in *Dubliners*, for example in the scene from "The Boarding House" where Mrs Mooney demands reparation for "the loss of her daughter's honour" (*D* 7.21), it becomes a comic motif in *Ulysses* and *Finnegans Wake*.

The paper that Bloom both works for and reads is not the *Irish Times* but the *Freeman's Journal*. A copy of this paper, one of the objects that Bloom carries throughout the day, serves as a material means of concealment for the correspondence that ensues from his ad in the *Irish Times*. In the "Lotus Eaters" episode, after collecting Martha Clifford's letter from the Westland Row Post Office, he transfers it from his pocket to the folded *Freeman's Journal* he is carrying, before reading the letter and destroying the envelope near the timber yard in Cumberland Street. In "Sirens", Bloom uses the same newspaper to conceal the letter he is writing in reply to Martha, while pretending to answer an ad for a town traveller. In order to satisfy the inquiring gaze of Richie Goulding, a fellow diner at the Ormond Hotel, he murmurs, "best references" while as Henry Flower he writes, "it will excite me" (*U* 11.888). This active performance of the epistolary charade compounds the system of disguises: by pretending to answer an ad in his own name, Bloom disguises the epistolary performance of "Henry Flower" in writing a letter which disguises its authorship by Leopold Bloom. If Bloom's ad in the gentlemanly *Irish Times* is a public cover for a clandestine liaison, the humbler *Freeman's Journal* serves literally to cover the written production of this literary-erotic masquerade.[4]

In the "Ithaca" episode we learn that Martha's letters are kept in a locked drawer at Bloom's home. On the envelopes containing the letters her return address is written in code, presumably the same code Bloom uses for his return address in letters to her. Does Bloom suppose that a letter with a return address obviously written in code would excite less suspicion than one from "Martha Clifford"? In any case, the use of code is in keeping with his earlier acknowledgment that his classified ad was a kind of code, while Martha's letters, coded and locked away, have now become "classified" in the bureaucratic sense. The subterfuge of the original ad has necessitated a whole system of secrecy extending to the storage of the letters as well as to the act of writing required to answer them. In the drawer, Martha's letters are stored with a press cutting from the English weekly *Modern Society* on the subject of "corporal chastisement in girls' schools" (*U* 17.1801–3). The subject of the press cutting resonates with a principal theme of the exchange between Martha and Bloom:

> Martha: "Remember if you do not I will punish you". (*U* 5.251–52)
> Bloom: "How will you pun? You punish me?" (*U* 11.890–91)

We note a curious constellation of the following terms: advertising, the press, secrecy, punishment. These terms are connected by a system of desire which apparently depends on the precarious status of respectability, the uneasy conjunction of public and private. An advertising man in his private fantasies as well as by profession, Bloom through his classified ad goes public with his private desires, albeit in disguise. At the same time he secretly appropriates public information (the press cutting on girls' chastisement) to his most intimate sphere as represented by the locked drawer. A similar transgression of the boundary between public and private takes place in "Circe", where Bloom's obscene letters to ladies of social distinction are exposed in court. There, his response to the threat of punishment is to say, "I love the danger" (*U* 15.1086). Everything takes place as if Bloom's desire took the form of this

4 The scene in the Ormond parallels one remembered by Molly in which Bloom "was scribbling something a letter when I came into the front room to show him Dignams death in the paper as if something told me and he covered it up with the blottingpaper pretending to be thinking about business" (*U* 18.47–49).

transgression between private and public, a desire only heightened by the danger of punishment.

In Joyce's day as in our own, classified ads made it possible for people to imagine themselves as other than they were. Even if his initial aim were merely to receive letters from "smart" ladies, Bloom had to imagine himself as a literary gentleman with the means and productivity to hire a private secretary. To this fantasy of another, more glorious existence, the "Ithaca" chapter adds Bloom's fantasy of "departure" from his world, again rendered in terms of a classified ad:

> What public advertisement would divulge the occultation of the departed?
> £5 reward, lost, stolen or strayed from his residence 7 Eccles street, missing gent about 40, answering to the name of Bloom, Leopold (Poldy), height 5 ft 9½ inches, full build, olive complexion, may have since grown a beard, when last seen was wearing a black suit. Above sum will be paid for information leading to his discovery.
>
> *U* 17.2000–2005

The question is strangely put, not least in the paradoxical sense of "divulge the occultation", meaning roughly "reveal the concealment". The question supposes that the purpose of the ad is primarily to declare Bloom's disappearance rather than to seek information leading to his discovery. Since the question concerns Bloom's early-morning meditations, we can assume that both question and answer reflect Bloom's speculative version of the ad that Molly would place in the event of his absence. Rather than seeking Bloom's discovery and return, would Molly be just as interested in making known his departure in order to advertise her newfound freedom? Such an intention would be most unlike Homer's Penelope, as in fact Molly mostly is unlike her. In any case, the form of the classified ad provides another opportunity for literary ventriloquism: Bloom puts himself in Molly's place and writes "in her name", to the point of using the nickname (Poldy) by which she alone knows him. The language of the ad is that more often used in seeking the return of a lost dog or cat, "lost, stolen, or strayed", suggesting Bloom's domestic status as a kind of pet, on the level of the "pussens" he addresses in his opening speech at *U* 4.24. The physical description is straightforward, except that we might expect Molly to know Bloom's age more precisely than "about 40". However, the most interesting feature of the ad is the £5 reward it offers for information leading to Bloom's discovery. We may assume that this represents Bloom's estimation of either the amount Molly would be able to pay for his return, or the amount she would be willing to pay. In the latter case, it is his estimation of her estimation of his value to her. It is not a particularly generous sum. According to the budget outlined at *U* 17.1455, £5 represents a little more than two days' daily expenses in Bloom's own modest way of life. The form of the classified ad thus has ambivalent consequences for Bloom's fantasy of departure: it allows him to imagine his absence as a kind of freedom, but also to imagine the precise and limited interest that his absence would occasion in the lives of others.

Before exploring the role of classified advertising in *Finnegans Wake*, let us recapitulate some of the observations of its treatment in *Ulysses*. First, classified advertising is presented as a profitable product of the publishing industry, with its own forms of capital, investment and return. Bloom observes that the investment in classifieds by James Carlisle, managing director of the *Irish Times*, has returned a dividend of six and one-half percent (*U* 8.337). The going rate for classified ads was 27 words for sixpence,[5] and Bloom's ad at only 10 words is well within that limit. For this investment he has had the handsome return of 44 letters from females eager to assist him, essentially supporting his fantasy of being a literary gentleman. These letters constitute an impressive capital on which to draw should he tire of the correspondence with Martha, a process which has already begun, to judge by his efforts at writing a new letter to her: "Bore this" (*U* 11.863).

Second, we have seen the manner in which the classified ad bridges the separation between the private and public spheres, along with the possibilities for the fulfilment of desire as well as the dangers occasioned by this passage. In the discourse of the ad, the code of "respectability" functions as the name for the moral and social condition reflecting the intersection of public and private. Third, we have seen how the classified ad can serve as a mode of concealment, as a public alibi for illicit private communication. And finally, we have seen how the language of classified advertising is subject to subversion, deviation and re-appropriation in various ways, especially for erotic ends. In a larger sense, the relation between literary work and erotic experience is not without relevance to Joyce's own work. There is in Joyce's writing the suggestion that literature is the written form of desire; it is writing both as desire itself and desire's object. Martha's letters, which embody her desire in language, are thus an object of desire as well as of interpretation, as if they constituted some minor, everyday form of literary expression contained within the more exceptional form of *Ulysses*. The achievement of *Ulysses* is not thus to express some

5 Ian Gunn and Alistair McCleery, eds., *Evening Telegraph: Dublin, Thursday, June 16, 1904* (Edinburgh: Split Pea Press, 1990). I am grateful to the Zurich James Joyce Foundation for supplying me with a copy of this edition.

higher desire, but to convey the common matter of human desire in an original and monumental form.

Given the possibilities of the classified ad for going public with private fantasies, it is not surprising to find it used in *Finnegans Wake*, where one of the principal motifs is precisely the "partial exposure" (*FW* 34.26–27) of HCE's "private parts" to public view and comment. The scandal created by this incident also brings into view another partial exposure, that of the ladies' undergarments presumably made visible when the two maidservants or "gown and pinners" enter the rushy hollow in Phoenix Park to answer the call of nature – a "ripe occasion to provoke" the ungentlemanly behaviour of HCE, according to the narrator of Chapter I.2 (*FW* 34.18–29). The respective accounts of the incident given by the two young ladies are here described as "published combinations of silkinlaine testimonies" (*FW* 34.22–23), where "combinations" refers both to joined testimonies and to underwear. To this is added the intriguing suggestion that the ladies' published testimony can somehow be clothed in the silk and *laine* fabric of their intimate lingerie.

The volatile combination of indecent exposure, ladies' underclothing and publication reappears in a parenthetical paragraph written in the form of a classified ad in the "Shem the Penman" chapter (*FW* I.7):

> Jymes wishes to hear from wearers of abandoned female costumes, gratefully received, wadmel jumper, rather full pair of culottes and onthergarmenteries, to start city life together. His jymes is out of job, would sit and write. He has lately commited one of the then commandments but she will now assist … Also got the boot. He appreciates it. Copies. ABORTISEMENT.
>
> *FW* 181.27–33

This ad, placed by an alter-ego of James Joyce himself, is a more elaborate version of the one Bloom has placed in the *Irish Times*, this time exposing everything repressed in the original. The language of the ad extends the fetishisation of female undergarments introduced in the trial scene of "Circe", where Mrs Bellingham testifies that Bloom "eulogised glowingly my other hidden treasures in priceless lace which, he said, he could conjure up" (*U* 15.1052–54). It also suggests the real nature of Bloom's interest in a "smart", i.e. smartly dressed lady typist. In contrast to the relative restraint of Bloom's ad, Jymes's abandons itself to the rich fantasy of female clothing, particularly clothes themselves abandoned, i.e. cast off after prolonged contact with the female body, though curiously re-worn by those to whom the ad is addressed. In his 1927 essay on "Fetishism", Freud speculates that the male fetishisation of objects closely associated with the female body functions as "a substitute for the woman's (the mother's) penis that the little boy once believed in and … does not want to give up" because her lack of a penis produces in him the fear of castration.[6] Whatever the reason for this substitution, the fetish functions both for Freud and for Joyce as both metaphor and metonymy: it stands metaphorically for the absent sexual organ, on the condition that, metonymically, it be in close contact with the female body. The logic of the fetish thus reproduces that of the language of "Shem the Penman", whose principal figure is both a metaphor for Joyce and a fantastically metonymic extension of his own writerly identity. It might be said in general that *Finnegans Wake* is the fetishisation of language in which the indistinguishable nature of metaphor and metonymy is the condition of desire.

If, as I propose, Jymes's "abortisement" is a rewriting of Bloom's, its second part, expressing the desire to "sit and write", echoes the ambitions of the gentleman engaged in "literary work", while the affirmation that "she will now assist" seems to fulfil that gentleman's search for a lady typist to assist him. Jymes has lately "commited one of the then commandments", which implies both that he has followed the commandment and committed a sin *against* it, though it is difficult to say which commandment has either been particularly followed or violated. Perhaps that is the point – that the Ten Commandments, eight of which take the form of interdiction, assume the inherent guilt of mankind even as they define the life of piety, so that to act according to them is both to "commit" them and to commit against them. In this respect Jymes has something of Bloom's sense of guilt in placing the ad, evidence of which we have already witnessed in the furtive manner of his collecting and responding to Martha's letters. But in *Finnegans Wake* the Ten Commandments have become the "then commandments", relegated to a past from which Jymes may now be free: free of the logic of sin and piety, free to write precisely because out of a job. The *Wake* is in this sense the writing of *désoeuvrement*, of creative idleness and undoing, as Bloom dreams of writing to Martha: "let everything rip. Forget…. Tell her: more and more: all" (*U* 5.293–99). With respect to Bloom's ad, Jymes's is the return of the repressed. In this respect it bears the same relation to the former ad that *Finnegans Wake* bears to *Ulysses*.

In the *Wake*, the most extended *tour de force* concerning the form of the classified ad occurs in III.3, originally published as *Haveth Childers Everywhere* (1930). This passage, a single sentence extending from 543.14 to 545.14, occurs in the context of a boastful speech by HCE about his colonial exploits – "I sent my boundary to Botany Bay and I ran up a score and four of mes while the Yanks were huckling the Empire" (*FW* 543.4–6) – followed by an invitation to

6 Sigmund Freud, "Fetishism", in *The Standard Edition of the Complete Psychological Works of Sigmund Freud*, trans. and ed. James Strachey, vol. 21 (London: Hogarth Press, 1978), 152–53.

emigration extended to the indigent, overcrowded population of the British Isles, i.e. to "all who have received tickets" (*FW* 543.21–22). The catalogue of those addressed in this speech functions as a double parody. On one hand, it serves as a satirical version of B. Seebohm Rowntree's *Poverty: A Study of Town Life*, an early sociological study of housing conditions among the poor in York.[7] On the other hand, the description of these conditions, as transformed by Joyce, bears a curious resemblance to the language of the rooms-to-let or "apartments vacant" section of newspapers like the *Evening Telegraph* (cited above), especially in their obsession with "respectability". Whereas Rowntree's study takes the form of the starkest realism, the classified ads do their best to put a good face on things. Joyce does neither, instead producing his own darkly comic language: "respectable in every way, harmless imbecile supposingly weakminded, a sausage every Sunday, has a staff of eight servants, outlook marred by ne'er-do-wells using the laneway" (*FW* 544. 27–30).

Rowntree's study includes a "classification of families" according to income and other general living conditions, often including their degree of "respectability". This work may have been of interest to Joyce because the population it studies is largely made up of Irish immigrants who, having fled the conditions of famine in their native land, settled in York in the late 1840s, only to become the underclass of their adopted city. In an otherwise fairly objective study of material living conditions, Rowntree's comments on the respectability of his subjects leaves this quality undefined, as in the following notes:[8]

> On the family of a widowed joiner: "Four boys, one girl. Seems respectable. Girl at home since mother's death".
>
> On the family of the keeper of a lodging-house: "Daughters married, respectable. House dirty and untidy".
>
> On a widow who keeps a lodger: "Disreputable old woman, ill; ought to be in Workhouse. Hawks when able … House very dirty, probably used as a house of ill-fame. Gets parish relief".
>
> On a bricklayer's household: "Respectable, looks well-to-do compared with many. House clean and tidy".

Rowntree assumes that his readers know what respectability is. For those who may not, the *Oxford English Dictionary* defines "respectable" persons as "having a good or fair standing in society, either because of status or (esp. in later use)

7 B. Seebohm Rowntree, *Poverty: A Study of Town Life* (London: Macmillan, 1901).

8 All notes are taken from Rowntree, *Poverty*, 17.

through being regarded as having a good character, a reputation for honesty or decency, etc."[9]

The question of respectability has bearing on Joyce's life and work in several ways. In *Ulysses*, it occurs exclusively in ironic contexts, as in Simon Dedalus' characterization of his in-laws: "De boys up in de hayloft. The drunken little costdrawer and his brother, the cornet player. Highly respectable gondoliers" (*U* 3.65–67). Stephen reflects ruefully, "Houses of decay, mine, his and all" (*U* 3.105), implicitly acknowledging that his own family is just barely respectable. In *Finnegans Wake* II.3, the dreary place awaiting a culpable HCE is, in John Gordon's reading,[10] what Irish ill-wishers have predicted for the emigrant Joyce: a habitation "auspicably suspectable but in expectancy of respectableness … three bedrooms upastairs, of which one with fireplace (aspectable), with greenhouse[11] in prospect (particularly perspectable)" (*FW* 362.23–35).

Like Jymes's "abortised" version of Bloom's ad in I.7, Joyce produces an abortive version of Rowntree's survey that serves as a return of the repressed for the language of room-to-let ads in the Dublin newspapers. Here are examples of Rowntree's notes, followed by Joyce's adaptation of them in *Finnegans Wake*:

> Rowntree: "Young son wants situation, just out of prison". (17)
> *FW*: "wageearner freshly shaven from prison" (543.27)
>
> Rowntree: "dangerous to life and limb to enter the doors" (19)
> *FW*: "floor dangerous for unaccompanied old clergymen" (544.14–15)
>
> Rowntree: "man 'has not had his boots on' for twelve months" (33)
> *FW*: "man has not had boots off for twelve months" (544.18)
>
> Rowntree: "house shares one closet with two others, and one water-tap with seven others" (37)
> *FW*: "shares same closet with fourteen similar cottages and an illfamed lodginghouse" (545.2–3)
>
> Rowntree: "slovenly wife" (50), "one adult entered with a jug" (319)
> *FW*: "slovenly wife active with the jug" (543.34)

9 "Respectable", *OED Online*, accessed 6 December 2016, http://oed.com.

10 John Gordon, *Finnegans Wake: A Plot Summary* (Syracuse: Syracuse University Press, 1986), 210.

11 In Dublin slang, a public toilet.

Rowntree's survey makes truly depressing reading, and Joyce does not miss the parallels between some of the households described and the one in which he grew up. Among Joyce's adaptations of Rowntree we encounter the family where "eldest son will not serve but peruses Big-man-up-in-the-Sky scraps" (FW 543.29–30), an allusion to Stephen in *A Portrait of the Artist as a Young Man*,[12] and thus indirectly to Joyce's own youthful aspirations. However, Joyce avoids the Victorian discourse of bourgeois respectability found both in well-meaning sociological studies and in the advertisements in Dublin newspapers. Rather, his parodic version of this discourse establishes a comic distance from his own origins, while subjecting the notion of respectability to merciless satire. In the space of 61 lines Joyce plays on every degree of this moral and social quality, respectively: "respectable", "more than respectable", "quasi respectable", "particularly respectable", "partly respectable", "most respectable", "thoroughly respectable", "outwardly respectable", "eminently respectable", "respectable in every way", "the pink of respectability", "more respectable than some", "respectability unsuccessfully aimed at", "as respectable as respectable can respectably be" (FW 543.23–545.12). The force of multiple repetition and declension serves to reveal the fetishistic nature of this notion in public discourse.

The various classified ads we have surveyed in the preceding pages might be reclassified according to their different functions in Joyce's fiction. Bloom's ad for a lady typist is a spurious one placed under a false name. In its modest way it is Bloom's own little work of fiction, generating a correspondence with the use of fictional names representing fictional characters, with Bloom as "literary gentleman" and Martha "doing the indignant: a girl of good family like me, respectable character" (U 5.269–70). In the "Ithaca" episode, Molly's ad for the missing Bloom is imaginary rather than being strictly false. It assists Bloom in his fantasy of departure, being all the more necessary to that fantasy in that his departure is unlikely to be realized. It is thus a fiction which compensates for the impossibility of departure. The discourse of classified advertising we have encountered in *Finnegans Wake* functions both as parody and as a return of the repressed, where the chaotic habitations of private lives emerge from darkness and are exposed to public view. In each of these cases, Joyce diverts the advertisement from its official function as a straightforward communication concerning goods and services. The discourse of the classified ad is thus made subject to the treatment Joyce reserves for every other form of conventional discourse: its subversion and re-appropriation for his own literary purposes.

---

12 "I will not serve that in which I no longer believe whether it call itself my home, my fatherland or my church" (P V.2575–57).

CHAPTER 6

"But Who Was Gerty?" Intertextuality and the Advertising Language of "Nausicaa"

Matthew Hayward

Abstract

The critical tendency has been to treat the "Nausicaa" episode of *Ulysses* naturalistically, interpreting Gerty as James Joyce's portrait of a young woman whose personality is conditioned by the commercialised texts that surround her. From the early 1990s, with a growing interest in advertising and consumer culture in *Ulysses*, critics went further still, finding Gerty to be modelled upon a "real" historical type – the deluded, fashion-attentive young woman of the early twentieth century. Yet a reconsideration of the style of the "Nausicaa" episode in the context of contemporary women's advertisements shows the chapter to be more thoroughly intertextual than has been recognised. Moving away from naturalistic conceptions of Gerty towards a more intertextual approach allows a reading of Joyce's parody as aimed not at the putative female consumer, nor at the culture within which she consumes, but at a certain advertising style, which was male-defined but attempted to project a language and sensibility onto the female subject.

Keywords

"Nausicaa" – *Ulysses* – advertising – language – intertextuality – style – parody – consumerism – *Lady's Pictorial* – commodity culture

Almost from the start, Gerty MacDowell has been interpreted as a young woman whose personality is a "product" of the commercialised texts that surround her. Hugh Kenner describes the first part of "Nausicaa" as "the section shaped by the mind of a Victorian lady novelist", Gerty a woman "whose mind has been shaped by such minds".[1] Karen Lawrence describes her in more or less the same terms: "What Joyce presents in the first half of 'Nausicaa' is the indirect

1 Hugh Kenner, "The Rhetoric of Silence", *James Joyce Quarterly* 14, no. 4 (Summer 1977): 382.

 | DOI 10.1163/9789004359062_008

monologue of Gerty MacDowell, translated into a language appropriate to her; he parodies her sentimental mind by parodying the second-rate fiction that has nurtured it".[2] Suzette Henke is more sympathetic, both towards Gerty as a character and towards Joyce's intentions: "The poignant, satirical jest of 'Nausicaa' is directed less against Gerty than against the manipulative society of which she is a product". Yet "a product" Gerty remains, her mind still "shaped by the clichéd rhetoric of fashion magazines".[3]

Thomas Richards's chapter in *The Commodity Culture of Victorian England* broke new ground, tracing the intertextual origins of Gerty's character in some detail, both to Maria Cummins's *The Lamplighter*,[4] and especially to the advertising figure of the "seaside girl".[5] However, despite this new attentiveness to the chapter's intertextual origins, Richards ultimately presents "Nausicaa" as a naturalistic depiction of a "real" early-twentieth-century female consumer. His broad argument, that "advertisers sucked consumers, especially women, into the vortex of a master–slave dialectic", still rests upon the conventional valuation of Gerty MacDowell as a young woman disfigured and debilitated by her consumerism, a valuation evident even in as sympathetic a reader as Henke, whose description Richards's certainly resembles: "Gerty has been sucked into a whirlpool of commercial fantasy".[6]

Richards finds Gerty to be all but helpless in the face of a dominant consumerism: she is a "generalized and impoverished" consumer, "shaped" – that word again – "by the developing forms of commodity culture".[7] For Garry Leonard, who has written the only full length study of Joyce's engagement with this

---

2 Karen Lawrence, *The Odyssey of Style in "Ulysses"* (Princeton: Princeton University Press, 1981), 120.

3 Suzette Henke, "Gerty MacDowell: Joyce's Sentimental Heroine", in *Women in Joyce*, ed. Suzette Henke and Elaine Unkeless (Urbana: University of Illinois Press, 1982), 134–35. Henke's point is made slightly differently by Kimberly Devlin, who takes it that the "episode's irony" is "aimed not so much at Gerty … but rather at the absurd romance exemplar she unsuccessfully tries to imitate"; Kimberly Devlin, "The Romance Heroine Exposed: 'Nausicaa' and 'The Lamplighter'", *James Joyce Quarterly* 22, no. 4 (1985): 393.

4 Maria Cummins, *The Lamplighter* (Boston: John P. Jewett, 1854).

5 Thomas Richards, *The Commodity Culture of Victorian England: Advertising and Spectacle, 1851–1914* (Stanford: Stanford University Press, 1990), 205–48. See also Garry Leonard, *Advertising and Commodity Culture in Joyce* (Gainesville: University Press of Florida, 1998), 98–143; Andrew Gibson, *Joyce's Revenge: History, Politics, and Aesthetics in "Ulysses"* (Oxford: Oxford University Press, 2002), 127–49; Katherine Mullin, *James Joyce, Sexuality and Social Purity* (Cambridge: Cambridge University Press, 2003), 140–70.

6 Richards, *Commodity Culture*, 7; Henke, "Gerty MacDowell", 135.

7 Richards, *Commodity Culture*, 211.

commodity culture, Gerty's response is more deliberate: her commodified self is "a desperate and crafty tactic for survival and not … the vain pursuit of a simpleminded girl".[8] Yet whether Gerty is knowingly or unknowingly manipulated, we find here the same assumption that Joyce is depicting a realistic figure who has either been shaped by, or shapes herself according to, the dictates of consumerism. Indeed, the naturalistic reading of Gerty is perfected by Richards and Leonard, because they reify the character into a psychological and historical case study. Richards is frank in his claim that "in cultural history Joyce's narrative of Gerty MacDowell ought to occupy a position similar to Freud's narrative of Dora"; Leonard extrapolates from the experience of Gerty and Bloom to the experience of "the consumer in the modern marketplace".[9]

The naturalistic, character-based readings of "Nausicaa" – whether they take the narrative intention to be the mockery of Gerty herself, as with Kenner and Lawrence, or whether they take it to be a broader cultural complaint, as with Henke, Richards and Leonard – all presuppose that Gerty is modelled upon a "real" historical type: the deluded, fashion-attentive young woman of the early twentieth century. Yet with the style of "Nausicaa" foregrounded as it is, the chapter is manifestly intertextual: it is parody proper, "a composition in which the characteristic style and themes of a particular author or genre are satirized by being applied to inappropriate or unlikely subjects, or are otherwise exaggerated for comic effect".[10] By definition, therefore, the parodic style of the chapter demands that it be read against other texts. This essay sets out to do just that, ultimately returning to the language of women's advertisements in the early decades of the twentieth century to show that the chapter is more thoroughly (if diffusely) intertextual than has been recognised.

It begins, however, by outlining some of the problems with the received assumption that Joyce uses Gerty MacDowell to present his critique of the female consumer. Gerty is frequently read as the embodiment of passive consumerism – a reading that hinges on conventional gendered distinctions between active male and passive female modes of consumption.[11] This essay looks more carefully at the way in which her character reflects her consumerism, and finds her not to be so different from Joyce's male characters as has been supposed. It goes on to reconsider what Joyce famously described to Frank Budgen as the "namby-pamby jammy marmalady drawersy (alto là!)

8 Leonard, *Advertising*, 134.

9 Richards, *Commodity Culture*, 210; Leonard, *Advertising*, 114.

10 "Parody", *OED Online*, accessed 6 December 2016, http://oed.com.

11 For a discussion of these conventional distinctions, see Rachel Bowlby, *Shopping with Freud* (London: Routledge, 1993), 18–34.

style" (*Letters I* 135) of the first half of the chapter, particularly its syntax, and shows that while the peculiar use of conjunctions and punctuation are likely intended to denote femininity, they are not in any essential way connected to her consumerism. Where the style can be related to consumerism, however, is in the employment of the loose but nevertheless identifiable lexicon of female-oriented advertisements from the early decades of the twentieth century. Concluding by moving away from naturalistic conceptions of Gerty towards a more intertextual reading, this essay resists the conventional interpretation of the "Nausicaa" episode as a critique of the young, consuming female. It argues that Joyce's satire is aimed not at the putative female consumer, nor exactly at the culture within which she consumes, but (far more playfully) at a certain advertising style, which – like "Nausicaa" itself – was male-defined, and yet attempted to project a language and sensibility onto the female subject.

The Projected Mirage: Gendering Consumerism

If "Nausicaa" has generally been read as a critique of the debilitating effects of consumerism, the minor premise has been that this debilitation is gendered. Richards notes that advertisers in the early twentieth century "were just beginning to explore the possibility of reaching women, who (it was assumed) would prove especially vulnerable to emotional appeals in the tonic tones of the domestic novel".[12] He argues that this feminine vulnerability is exposed in the "Nausicaa" episode through the penetrating gaze of Leopold Bloom: "Only under Bloom's watchful eye do we fully recognize Gerty as a preconditioned receptacle of false needs". The male's is the neutral perspective in this formation, the female's the distorted. While "Bloom's consciousness has undeniably been invaded and whittled down by the technology of advertisement", the male retains a critical discernment of the female's "thoroughly reified response to life".[13]

The first thing to say about this interpretation is that while Gerty's part of the narrative is no doubt limited, so too is Bloom's. In the Linati schema, Joyce gives the sense or meaning of the "Nausicaa" chapter as "The Projected Mirage", and it is not necessary to invoke his alleged comment that Gerty's exhibition "all took place in Bloom's imagination" to understand this key: it fits the

12 Richards, *Commodity Culture*, 214.

13 Richards, *Commodity Culture*, 238.

structure of the narrative.[14] The eversion of perspective that occurs in line 771, when the move from Gerty's vision of Bloom to Bloom's vision of Gerty is complete, ensures that the reader does not miss the importance of position and projection in this chapter. One of the comic effects of this perspectival shift is its exposure of the hopeless inaccuracy of the many appellations that each character attaches to the other. Gerty's perception is exaggerative: her "gentleman in black" (*U* 13.349) – "the image of the photo she had of Martin Harvey, the matinée idol" (*U* 13.416–17), "a man of inflexible honour to his fingertips" (*U* 13.694) – turns out to be the masturbator Bloom. Bloom's perception of Gerty, on the other hand, is reductive: the character whose hopes and vulnerabilities have been presented through nearly eight hundred lines of evaded insecurities is reduced by Bloom to a "hot little devil" (*U* 13.776), "that little limping devil" (*U* 13.851–52), a "little wretch" (*U* 13.1102), and, finally, simply "that female" (*U* 13.1253). Both perspectives are distorted, one by inflation, the other by reduction, perhaps fulfilling the "technic" that Joyce apparently intended for the chapter, "tumescence: detumescence".[15] Neither is neutral.

The second point to make is that consumerism is not, across the novel, presented as a particularly feminine activity. We read that "undies … were Gerty's chief care" (*U* 13.171), yet Bloom's commitment to their consumption is by this stage already well established. When he is swayed by the clothing on display in the windows of Brown Thomas, Bloom thinks to himself that the "sunwarm silk" is "all for a woman" (*U* 8.634). Yet it is he who considers the purchase – "could buy one of those silk petticoats for Molly" (*U* 8.1061) – and if Gerty spent a whole afternoon "hunting to match that chenille" (*U* 13.158), Bloom too is careful to ensure that the silk petticoat matches the other clothes that he has bought Molly: "colour of her new garters" (*U* 8.1061–62). Indeed, Bloom is still lingering over his lingerie several hours later, as he passes the Ormond Quay Hotel: "If I net five guineas with those ads. The violet silk petticoats" (*U* 11.189–90).

Of course, Bloom may buy these items for the enjoyment of seeing Molly "take them all off" (*U* 13.799) – or at least envisaging her taking them off for Boylan – justifying Leonard's basic argument that we are witnessing "a world where 'femininity' is male-defined". Leonard is right too that Gerty's self-adornment is for the sake of the "male gaze she dreams of attracting";[16]

---

14 First mentioned in the "Linati schema", in Richard Ellmann, *Ulysses on the Liffey* (London: Faber, 1974), 187; Arthur Power, *Conversations with James Joyce*, ed. Clive Hart (Dublin: Millington, 1974), 32.

15 Stuart Gilbert, *James Joyce's "Ulysses": A Study*, rev. ed. (London: Faber, 1952), 272.

16 Leonard, *Advertising*, 111, 109.

the narrator says as much: "something told her to put on the transparent stockings thinking Reggy Wylie might be out" (*U* 13.426–27). It is also fair to say that Gerty is presented as having internalised these standards of femininity, as we see in her judgments of other women. The Gerty-narrator repeatedly compares her appearance with that of other females, as with the inward sneer at Cissy Caffrey for her "insignificant" stockings "that had neither shape nor form" (*U* 13.503) – a criticism that quickly slides into social judgment: "she did look a streel tugging the two kids along with the flimsy blouse she bought only a fortnight before like a rag on her back and a bit of her petticoat hanging like a caricature" (*U* 13.506–9).

Leonard relates this judgmental aspect of Gerty's character to the situation of women in 1904 Dublin: it is a "strategy of increasingly desperate shrewdness whereby she hopes to decisively defeat other women in terms of her appearance".[17] Bloom too sees it in gendered terms, taking sartorial competitiveness to be a characteristic trait of "sister souls": "Picking holes in each other's appearance. You're looking splendid .... Showing their teeth at one another" (*U* 13.817–19). He has in mind here Molly and her friend Josie Breen, yet it is Bloom himself that we have seen "picking holes" in Mrs Breen's appearance during their earlier meeting:

> Same blue serge dress she had two years ago, the nap bleaching. Seen its best days. Wispish hair over her ears. And that dowdy toque: three old grapes to take the harm out of it. Shabby genteel. She used to be a tasty dresser.
>
> *U* 8.265–68

It is particularly significant that Bloom projects these observations onto a female passerby: "See the eye that woman gave her, passing. Cruel. The unfair sex" (*U* 8.269). That this is an act of projection is confirmed when Mrs Breen resurfaces in the "Circe" episode, and Bloom's earlier appraisal of her dress is linked directly to the catty dialogue he had imagined between her and Molly. The imaginary conversation between the two women that he had rehearsed in "Nausicaa" – "how are you at all? What have you been doing with yourself? Kiss and delighted to, kiss, to see you .... You're looking splendid" (*U* 13.816–18) – is precisely enacted in "Circe" by Bloom himself: "How do you do? It's ages since I. You're looking splendid" (*U* 15.399–400). What Bloom takes to be a female mode of consumption – one expanded by Leonard into a historical case study – is shown by Joyce to mask a similar tendency in the male character.

17 Leonard, *Advertising*, 115.

It could be countered that by attributing this stereotype of "feminine" competitive consumption to his male protagonist, Joyce means only to indicate an apparently feminine trait in Bloom, thus reinforcing rather than challenging that stereotype. It is in the "Circe" episode that Bloom is most literally feminised, first as "a finished example of the new womanly man" (*U* 15.1798–99) and eventually simply as a "good girly" (*U* 15.2884). However, while Bloom's concern with clothing and appearance has been clear from the earliest chapters – "Nice soft tweed Ned Lambert has in that suit. Tinge of purple .... Hello. It's dyed" (*U* 6.828–31) – he shares this trait with some of the most stereotypically masculine characters, from Blazes Boylan, the "spruce figure" (*U* 6.199) with his trademark "straw hat", "tan shoes" and "turnedup trousers" (*U* 8.1168), to Simon Dedalus, who we see wrangling with Ben Dollard over his tired getup:

> — Hold that fellow with the bad trousers ....
> Mr Dedalus eyed with cold wandering scorn various points of Ben Dollard's figure ....
> — That's a pretty garment, isn't it, for a summer's day?
> — Why, God eternally curse your soul, Ben Dollard growled furiously, I threw out more clothes in my time than you ever saw.
>
> *U* 10.905–12

Since these other male characters are generally described from the outside rather than within, we do not witness any mental connection between the appearance of clothing and the conditions of its purchase – a connection that tends to characterise Gerty's and Bloom's reflections. Still, there are occasional hints that these other characters are not so different in this respect either, such as the brief interior monologue given to Tom Kernan in "Wandering Rocks":

> Mr Kernan halted and preened himself before the sloping mirror .... Stylish coat, beyond a doubt. Scott of Dawson street. Well worth the half sovereign I gave Neary for it. Never built under three guineas. Fits me down to the ground .... John Mulligan, the manager of the Hibernian bank, gave me a very sharp eye yesterday on Carlisle bridge.
>
> *U* 10.742–47

Leonard may be right that Gerty's sartorial competitiveness indicates her adherence to the dictates of advertisements. But this is not presented as an exclusively female response, and the very assumption that this competitiveness is a particularly feminine trait is shown by Joyce to be a stereotype defined and projected by men, even as their own practices belie the distinction.

Gerty obviously seems overly credible in her acceptance of the claims of patent medicine advertisements, especially compared with Bloom's more cynical comments: "All breadcrumbs they are. About six hundred per cent profit" (*U* 6.61–62). But in a fuller sense, in the configuration of her social judgments of herself and others along consumerist lines, she does not seem to differ greatly from the other characters in the novel.

Gerty's Grammar: Consumerism, Gender and Style

The structure of Gerty's consumerism, then, cannot straightforwardly be attributed to her gender. However, it is the style of the "Nausicaa" episode that is most commonly taken to indicate the peculiar nature of her consumerist entrapment. Richards argues that it is "by leaving out conjunctions (or by using the wrong ones)" that Gerty's slack grasp of her mediated world is exposed:

> Gerty's syntax … is her own: presumably Bloom would not construct a sentence in which alabaster has fingers, "queen of ointments" has no article, "though" introduces a non sequitur, and "either" is left dangling.[18]

Yet this stylistic assumption too might be reconsidered. As far as the syntax goes, Richards's comparison mostly holds. For Bloom's interior monologue, Joyce tends to separate short clauses into new sentences using full stops. He often uses a subordinating conjunction to add a clause to an already closed sentence, and while this would make these conjunctions technically incorrect, they are suitable for their purpose: to modify or to add to one thought with another, in an approximation of the sequential but subjectively connected structure of thought. Since co-ordinating conjunctions function correctly at the start of a sentence, their meaning is hardly affected by Joyce's separation of Bloom's clauses. And if it is allowed that a dependent clause may follow a full stop in Bloom's diction, subordinating conjunctions are also generally used accurately.

In Gerty's narrative, on the other hand, conjunctions – particularly subordinating conjunctions – are used capriciously. In the passage that introduces Gerty to the chapter, "though" is used in almost every sentence, almost always incorrectly (*U* 13.79–92). "Because" is even more unruly:

> She was wearing the blue for luck … her own colour and lucky too for a bride to have a bit of blue somewhere on her *because* the green she wore

18 Richards, *Commodity Culture*, 215, 217.

> that day week brought grief *because* his father brought him in to study for the intermediate exhibition and *because* she thought perhaps he might be out *because* when she was dressing that morning she nearly slipped up ...
>
> *U* 13.179–84; emphases added

The syntax is so muddled that it is easy to ignore the word's proper function as a subordinating conjunction unless you separate the clauses, and if there exists a causal connection between them, it is so tortuously expressed that it cannot be followed without considerable rearrangement. "Because" thus comes to function as a co-ordinating conjunction, simply connecting separate phrases. Indeed, the use of "because" in the first half of "Nausicaa" is so wayward that it becomes recognisable as a characteristic linguistic signature. Towards the end of the final paragraph of the chapter, it is the free usage of this word that alerts us to Gerty's brief re-entry into what we have up to this point been reading as Bloom's narrative:

> Mr Bloom with open mouth, his left boot sanded sideways, leaned, breathed .... The clock on the mantelpiece in the priest's house cooed where Canon O'Hanlon and Father Conroy and the reverend John Hughes S.J. were taking tea ... *because* it was a little canarybird that came out of its little house to tell the time that Gerty MacDowell noticed the time she was there *because* she was as quick as anything about a thing like that ...
>
> *U* 13.1286–1301; emphases added

The disordered syntax of Gerty's narrative is taken by Richards to reflect her experience of consumerism: with her inaccurate conjunctions, "manufactured objects ... hover free, mediating Gerty's relationship to her world via a veil of commodities with which she finally lives in symbiosis".[19] However, it is worth making the obvious point that the irregular syntax foreshadows Joyce's more extended use of this technique in "Penelope", where Molly uses conjunctions in much the same way. Indeed, there is another strikingly Penelopean characteristic in the transitional passage between Gerty and Bloom quoted above, although Richards does not observe it. Bloom's heavily punctuated diction ends at the point at which he presumably dozes: "A bat flew. Here. There. Here. Far in the grey a bell chimed. Mr Bloom with open mouth, his left boot sanded sideways, leaned, breathed. Just for a few" (*U* 13.1286–88). Gerty's effusions follow, and from this point on there is a conspicuous absence of punctuation.

19 Richards, *Commodity Culture*, 217.

Muddled conjunctions, eschewed punctuation: if these linguistic features distinguish Gerty's narrative from Bloom's, they also bring the "Nausicaa" chapter closer to "Penelope" than has often been recognised. It is thus hard to avoid the suspicion that they are intended by Joyce to be, at least in part, mimetic of what he conceived as feminine expression, as indicated elsewhere by his oft-quoted comment to his brother Stanislaus from October 1906 – "Do you notice how women when they write disregard stops and capital letters?" (*Letters II* 173) – or by his overuse of the conjunction "but" in the free indirect discourse that introduces Lily at the start of "The Dead": "But Lily seldom made a mistake in the orders .... But the only thing they would not stand was back answers" (*D* 15.38–41).[20] However, if the stylistic elements shared by Gerty and Molly are gendered, sexist even, it does not necessarily follow that this style has been devised to represent the female response to consumerism. Richards suggests that the free syntax of Gerty's narrative indicates her entrapment within an alienating consumer culture: Joyce's "bringing together of the linguistic components of the commodity [fluidity of relations] creates a web of connection from which Gerty MacDowell cannot be freed".[21] Yet if the "linguistic components" were the effect of Gerty's consumerism, we would expect it to hold for Joyce's other female consumers – and it does not. Fritz Senn has pointed out that Miss Dunne, Blazes Boylan's typist, stands as "an earlier mild prefiguration of Gerty MacDowell",[22] and the comparison is helpful here, since she is one of the few minor female characters represented through interior monologue:

> Then she stared at the large poster of Marie Kendall, charming soubrette .... Mustard hair and dauby cheeks. She's not nicelooking, is she? The way she's holding up her bit of a skirt. Wonder will that fellow be at the band tonight. If I could get that dressmaker to make a concertina skirt like Susy Nagle's. They kick out grand. Shannon and all the boatclub swells never took his eyes off her.
>
> *U* 10.380–86

Here we have the same attention to advertisements, the same pleased contemplation of shopping and consumption, and the same careful scrutiny of both

20 Joyce explicitly associated the conjunction "because" with women at the time he was constructing the "Penelope" episode. In a 1921 letter to Budgen explaining the chapter's structure, he maps "*because*" to "the female breasts", as one of the "four cardinal points" of the "huge earth ball" that figures woman (*Letters I* 170).

21 Richards, *Commodity Culture*, 217–18.

22 Fritz Senn, "Nausicaa", in *James Joyce's "Ulysses": Critical Essays*, ed. Clive Hart and David Hayman (Berkeley: University of California Press, 1974), 282.

the dress of other women, and the male responses to that dress. And yet the style of the interior monologue is far closer to Bloom's than to Gerty's: short, regularly stopped clauses; lopped personal pronouns; the proper use of a relatively small number of conjunctions. If the internalisation of the "linguistic components of the commodity" in "Nausicaa" indeed represents a "miniature version of a new interconnectedness of commodity with human culture operative in Irish society", we should surely expect the same pattern to appear in a character like Miss Dunne; after all, while Richards awards the honour to Dilly Dedalus, it is Miss Dunne who might accurately be described as "in age and class Gerty's nearest rival in *Ulysses*".[23] Likewise with Miss Douce and Miss Kennedy of the "Sirens" episode. Although their interior monologues are minimal – Miss Douce's "flower in his coat: who gave him?" or Miss Kennedy's "flower, wonder who gave" (*U* 11.366, 380–81) – these passages are carefully punctuated, sharing none of Gerty's linguistic features. And finally, in a similar contemplation of Boylan's attire, the "blond girl in Thornton's" (*U* 10.299) demonstrates the same sartorial attentiveness that we have seen to be a major component of Joyce's depiction of consumerism, but none of the lax syntax that Richards takes to be its stylistic signifier: "got up regardless, with his tie a bit crooked" (*U* 10.330–31).

Intertextuality and the Language of the Women's Advertisements

If these elements of Gerty's narrative cannot be explained as linguistic reflections of her consumerism, that is not to say that the chapter does not engage quite carefully with a consumerist language. Gerty's narrative includes many fragments of particular advertisements, obviously with the direct mention of brand names such as "iron jelloids" (*U* 13.84), but in unlikely phrases too: when we find that Procter and Gamble's immensely successful Ivory brand soap was heavily advertised from the late-nineteenth century as "$99\frac{44}{100}$% PURE", the "ivorylike purity" of Gerty's face begins to seem more material than "spiritual" (*U* 13.87–88). What has not been fully recognised is that even the most banal language of the first half of the "Nausicaa" episode carries an intertextual burden, reflecting the vocabulary used in contemporary advertisements directed at female consumers. In 1902, an American advertising guidebook claimed that "men are reached by a strong swift style – a style the reflex of their business life – a style that does not lose itself in a maze of details and wanderings into fashionable features – a style sententious, business-like, pleasant and at times

23 Richards, *Commodity Culture*, 217, 239.

a trifle humorous".[24] In 1928, another guidebook studied women's magazine advertisements to find what language appeals most to female consumers, and found there a "softer, more delicate, and often more suggestive terminology".[25] In the years between, this terminology had become ubiquitous in the advertisements printed in the women's magazines.

A glance through the *Lady's Pictorial* – the magazine upon whose sartorial advice Gerty MacDowell places so much stock (*U* 13.151) – demonstrates the linguistic codification of women's advertising in the early decades of the twentieth century. The issue for 4 January 1919, the first of the year in which Joyce began writing "Nausicaa", gives a clear sense of the kind of language that male advertisers were using to appeal to female consumers. To pick an example more or less at random, an advertisement for the London drapers Stagg and Mantle includes four short captions for four images: "smart", "fascinating", and two lots of "attractive".[26] These are among the "bywords" or "watchwords" found by Carl A. Naether to be "omnipresent … in the sentences and paragraphs of copy written for firms using space in women's magazines", and the list of words he presents as "more or less common to all advertising" for "toiletries and feminine attire" gives an accurate picture of the *Lady's Pictorial* for 1919.[27] In the columns headed "THE SEASON OF SALES", attributed to the fashion writer Mrs Florence Roberts ("Butterfly"), but evidently sponsored by the companies the column promotes, almost every sentence confirms Naether's list.[28] He describes the "omnipresent 'smart'" as "striking in point of frequency of use and variety of reference", and says "without fear of being exaggerative" that it "is indeed rare" to find an advertisement for women's clothing which does not contain "smart" or "smartness".[29] His description certainly holds for 1919: "smart" is by far the most commonly used word in these columns, appearing in one form or another fifteen times across the three pages; an advertisement for Dickins and Jones in the same issue uses "smart" or "smartly" in three of its six picture

24 J. Angus MacDonald, *Successful Advertising: How to Accomplish It* (1902), quoted in Ellen Gruber Garvey, *The Adman in the Parlor: Magazines and the Gendering of Consumer Culture, 1880s to 1910s* (New York: Oxford University Press, 1996), 178.

25 Carl A. Naether, *Advertising to Women* (New York: Prentice Hall, 1928), 27.

26 *Lady's Pictorial* (4 January 1919): ix.

27 Naether, *Advertising to Women*, 87, 77.

28 *Lady's Pictorial*, 4 January 1919, 18–20. The fact that the issue contains display advertisements for each of the companies "Butterfly" recommends strongly suggests that the column consists of "puffs" for paying advertisers. Garvey provides evidence to show that "puffing" was as typical of women's magazines as it was of newspapers in the late-nineteenth century; Garvey, *The Adman in the Parlor*, 94–95.

29 Naether, *Advertising to Women*, 77, 78.

captions, showing just how well-worn is the "smart vee" of Gerty's blouse (*U* 13.152).[30] Naether's other "common advertising bywords" follow in Butterfly's columns, with some fifty instances of "charming", "beautiful", "delightful", "fascinating", "lovely", "attractive", "graceful", "wonderful" and the "commonplace 'exquisite'".[31]

To focus on this particular issue is, of course, in some sense arbitrary. Although Joyce's letters show that he frequently requisitioned newspapers and magazines from Dublin, especially from his aunt, Josephine Murray, we do not know exactly which issues or even which titles Joyce drew upon for the "Nausicaa" episode. It is a surprising fact that while the style of "Nausicaa" is commonly assumed to be based, at least in part, upon the women's magazines to which the chapter refers – *Lady's Pictorial* and *The Princess's Novelettes* – very few critics have paid attention to the content of these periodicals. As far as I am aware, only Andrew Gibson has attempted to read "Nausicaa" at length against the particular titles that form the chapter's background, and he identifies a number of "extremely specific details" that Joyce has drawn into the figure of Gerty MacDowell.[32] Gibson shows that "the Lady's Pictorial for 11 June 1904 has a number of connections with *Ulysses*",[33] but he is careful not to explicitly claim it as a direct source, for there is no evidence to suggest that Joyce read or drew upon this issue. References to the Mirus bazaar and the Alake of Abeokuta – the connections Gibson notes – were extremely prominent in the Irish and British press in June 1904, and there are no details exclusive to the *Lady's Pictorial* accounts to identify this periodical as a source.[34] In fact, many of the features Gibson identifies in issues contemporary to the novel's 1904 setting can be found in the issues from 1919, the year in which Joyce commented in a letter to Budgen that he had sketched his "notation of flappers' atrocities" (*Letters I* 132) to begin working on the "Nausicaa" chapter. For example, Gibson points out that "even Gerty's moments of superstition … may stem less from her 'Irishness' than from English magazines".[35]

30 *Lady's Pictorial* (4 January 1919): vii.

31 Naether, *Advertising to Women*, 77, 82, 84.

32 Gibson, *Joyce's Revenge*, 138. Others have found incidental connections, e.g. R. Brandon Kershner, *The Culture of Joyce's "Ulysses"* (New York: Palgrave Macmillan, 2010), 88, 96.

33 Gibson, *Joyce's Revenge*, 132.

34 The Mirus bazaar had a near-constant presence in the Irish press in June 1904; Phillip F. Herring has documented Joyce's use of *The Times* for 14–15 June 1904 in his descriptions of the Alake of Abeokuta. See Phillip F. Herring, *Joyce's Notes and Early Drafts for "Ulysses": Selections from the Buffalo Collection* (Charlottesville: University Press of Virginia, 1977), 139–40.

35 Gibson, *Joyce's Revenge*, 138.

He instances stories and advertisements from 1904 issues of *The Princess's Novelettes*, but there are equally suggestive examples in the 1919 *Lady's Pictorial*. A weekly column entitled "THE MAGIC OF SELF-HELP" featured a section in which one "O Hashnu Hara" – whose unlikely Indo-Irish name registers the popular English stereotyping of the Irish as both mystical, and racially other – would reply to readers' letters, briefly addressing their comments and advising them which days and colours would prove lucky for them. In January 1919, O Hashnu Hara replied to a Dublin reader, giving her lucky colours and advising that her "best day, as a rule, will be Thursday".[36] This could well have provided Joyce with material for Gerty: Thursday is her lucky day "for wealth" (*U* 13.119), and she is "wearing the blue for luck, hoping against hope, her own colour" (*U* 13.179–80). There are other suggestive items in the 1919 issues of the *Lady's Pictorial*, such as the advertisements for Iron Jelloids – the pills that had done Gerty "a world of good much better than the Widow Welch's female pills" (*U* 13.85–86) – advertised on the front page of every fourth issue, "devoid of all the usual drawbacks of Iron Tonics".[37] And it would be reasonable to argue that if Joyce indeed drew upon these titles, he is more likely to have had access to recent issues when he began the "Nausicaa" episode in Trieste towards the end of 1919 (*Letters I* 132); after all, we know that he furnished material for the chapter from other contemporary advertisements at this time.[38]

Yet to privilege 1919 issues over 1904 issues, however more likely they may seem, would be to miss the essential continuity of the women's magazines in the first decades of the twentieth century – in their content, perhaps, but especially in their use of a general "feminised" language. The vocabulary that Naether identifies in 1928, with reference to the American magazines *Vogue, Ladies' Home Journal*, and *Good Housekeeping*, is substantially the same as the vocabulary of the English *Lady's Pictorial* in 1919. It is also substantially the language of the "Nausicaa" episode, and – to a lesser extent and with a crucially different application – "Penelope". This claim is best demonstrated by cross-checking the "watchwords" listed above against a concordance for *Ulysses*, but a few examples establish the pattern. "Beauty" is a favourite word of Molly,

36 *Lady's Pictorial* (25 January 1919): 112.

37 *Lady's Pictorial* (4 January 1919).

38 For example, "Eyebrowleine" (*U* 13.111) was advertised from around 1916 and recorded by Joyce in his "Nausicaa" notesheets between September 1919 and February 1920. See Harald Beck, "Eyebrow Line", *James Joyce Online Notes*, accessed 6 December 2016, http://jjon.org/joyce-s-environs/eyebrow-line, and also Sabrina Alonso's essay in this volume. Kershner also finds the tone of the eyebrowleine passage to be anachronistic when read against an issue of the 1904 *Princess's Novelettes*, and includes some interesting observations on Joyce's "double chronological focus"; Kershner, *The Culture of Joyce's "Ulysses"*, 96.

with nine of the novel's forty-nine usages given to her, but in Molly's parlance it rarely denotes "personal attractiveness" in any degree, only twice being used to describe particular people (Mrs Galbraith and Lily Langtry; *U* 18.477, 484) and otherwise used variously in an idiomatic sense ("that other beauty Burke"; *U* 18.964–65), aesthetic sense ("theres real beauty and poetry for you"; *U* 18.1351), or abstract sense ("the woman is beauty"; *U* 18.559).[39] The noun is used only once for Gerty, but the adverb form "beautifully" is strongly concentrated in the "Nausicaa" chapter, with three of the novel's four instances appearing in Gerty's narrative. The fourth comes in "Penelope", and again, Molly's usage is non-personal (describing the moon; *U* 18.1336), whereas in "Nausicaa" it is used to describe Gerty's appearance: her throat is "so slim, so flawless, so beautifully moulded" (*U* 13.582–83), and she has "graceful beautifully shaped legs" (*U* 13.698). This is a typical pattern. Such stereotypically "feminine" language is used far more often in the chapters that operate with an explicitly feminised narrative, as we might expect. But whereas their usages in Molly's monologue are various in application, in Gerty's narrative they take on the two fundamental conditions that Naether finds common to all female-oriented advertising language: the promise of an attractive appearance is connected, directly or indirectly, to an advertised commodity.

The pattern is even clearer with the adjective. Nine of the thirty-eight usages of the word "beautiful" occur in the narratives of Gerty and Molly, showing a definite concentration: nearly a quarter, in sections that make up less than a tenth of the total narrative of *Ulysses*. Once again, Molly's use of the adjective is varied in application, from the appearance of Byron (*U* 18.209–10), to the female genitals (*U* 18.542), to the lyrics of a song (*U* 18.1340), to the countryside (*U* 18.1560). In "Nausicaa", by contrast, the word is directly attributed to the headline of an advertisement – "you have a beautiful face but your nose?" (*U* 13.114)[40] – and is elsewhere used primarily to describe Gerty's appearance: she is "pronounced beautiful by all who knew her" (*U* 13.81–82), and she has "beautiful eyes" (*U* 13.106). And sure enough, this description of Gerty's physical appearance quickly slides into an attribution of her attractiveness to her consumption of commodities: "It was Madame Vera Verity, directress of the Woman Beautiful page of the Princess Novelette, who had first advised her to try eyebrowleine" (*U* 13.109–11). The beauty of Gerty's eyes apparently depends upon her adherence to an advertisement in a women's magazine. (An editorial

39 The other time the word is given a personal application in "Penelope" is in quotation, as Molly recalls the English soldier Gardner's term of endearment for her: "my Irish beauty" (*U* 18.392).

40 For an illustration of this advertisement see Sabrina Alonso's essay in this volume.

recommendation of a named commodity would almost certainly have been a "puff" paid for by the manufacturer of eyebrowleine, or "par", as Bloom describes it in "Aeolus", *U* 7.157.) Just as the specific advertised commodity has been adopted by Gerty the consumer, so the language of the column has been lifted into the narrative that describes her: Gerty's obedience to "the Woman Beautiful" has brought the woman "beautiful eyes".

The pattern that emerges when working from this list of key advertising terms shows that within the "Nausicaa" episode, words that at first sight seem to be drawn from a neutral if uninspiring lexicon – beautiful, lovely, graceful, attractive, delicate, exquisite, perfect, radiant, wonderful, delightful, fascinating, entrancing, smart – are in fact drawn from a specific register, the exhausted diction of advertisements designed for women. Four of the twelve usages of "delicate" occur in "Nausicaa" and "Penelope", and the three in "Nausicaa" all describe Gerty's appearance: "her delicate hands" (*U* 13.98), her "telltale flush, delicate as the faintest rosebloom" (*U* 13.120), a "delicate pink" in "her pretty cheek" (*U* 13.360–61). A quarter of the twenty uses of "perfect" in *Ulysses* occur in these two chapters, with two of the four instances in "Nausicaa" describing Gerty's appearance: her mouth is "Greekly perfect" (*U* 13.89), and "her well-turned ankle displayed its perfect proportions" (*U* 13.168–69). This last comes as part of the extensive inventory of Gerty's commodities, as does the noun form of the word (one of only three examples in the novel): "a navy threequarter skirt cut to the stride showed off her slim graceful figure to perfection" (*U* 13.154–55). "Radiant" is used to describe Gerty's hair: "a radiant little vision" (*U* 13.511), and "wonderful" is used in the same connection: "Gerty's crowning glory was her wealth of wonderful hair" (*U* 13.115–16). "Delightful" occurs seven times in the novel, once in "Nausicaa" and once in "Penelope": "what did they say they give a delightful figure line" (*U* 18.448).

That Molly's usage is a quotation, from an advertisement for "one of those kidfitting corsets ... advertised cheap in the Gentlewoman" (*U* 18.446–47), confirms the provenance of the vocabulary we are dealing with here. These "feminised" advertising watchwords are strongly concentrated in "Nausicaa" and "Penelope", the chapters based explicitly upon female subjects. But as the *Gentlewoman* example shows, they are used quite differently in the two chapters. When Molly uses the word in a consumerist context, it is in quotation, and when other female-oriented advertising watchwords are concentrated in the "Penelope" chapter, they are given a range of contexts, meanings and applications. These words seem to be used simply (and not obviously ironically) as examples of what Joyce takes to be "feminine language". In "Nausicaa", by contrast, the advertising language found in the *Lady's Pictorial* and other women's magazines is almost always used to describe the female appearance, commodities, or both.

It is this difference that shows how cautious we must be of conflating interpretations of the style of the first half of the "Nausicaa" episode – more thoroughly intertextual even than the parodies of the previous chapter – with interpretations of its central character. Tracing the lexicon of "Nausicaa" to contemporary women's advertisements might seem merely to confirm the traditional reading of Gerty's character as a helpless female consumer, contained by the language that expresses her. Yet it is just this form of expression that indicates the thoroughly intertextual nature of the "Nausicaa" episode: not only are the specific claims and brand names of female-oriented advertisements drawn into the narrative, as has long been seen, but so too is the more general language used within these advertisements. With such an intertextual burden, it seems wilful to persist in interpreting the chapter as a critique of the young, female, Irish consumer, drawn into the novel from "real life". To follow the stylistic imperative so obviously laid out by Joyce, the chapter is surely parodic, invoking the male-defined, consumerist vision of "femininity" that was in no small part invented by the advertiser. Perhaps here, at last, we can see the relevance of Joyce's "Projected Mirage" key. R. Brandon Kershner has argued that Cissy Caffrey appears in "Circe" as "a paradigmatic figure, not a naturalistic one".[41] The same may be said of her friend Gerty, who exists through the style of the "Nausicaa" episode as a figure drawn from the consumerist spectacle of women's magazines – perhaps, though not necessarily, a direct projection of the spectator Bloom.

This intertextual reading brings "Nausicaa" closer in line with the other late episodes of *Ulysses* than has usually been recognised. It does not necessarily discredit psychological interpretations of character, nor deny that Joyce includes a wealth of realistic local detail in his portrayal of Gerty MacDowell: as with other late episodes, the "Nausicaa" narrative functions simultaneously in multiple significatory dimensions. However, a properly intertextual approach does require that the earlier, naturalistic accounts be reframed. For example, Gibson has drawn attention to the frequent narrative slips into the vernacular in Gerty's narrative, which he takes to indicate her resistance to the "imported, genteel idioms" of the British Empire – an "alien idiom" that "collapses, and can no longer be sustained".[42] This reading is unusually sensitive to the subtle changes of register within the first half of the "Nausicaa" episode, but

41 Kershner, *The Culture of Joyce's "Ulysses"*, 205.

42 Gibson, *Joyce's Revenge*, 147.

it continues to anchor the narrative in Gerty's imagined psychology, and thus continues to allow the received assumption that Gerty is an example of Joyce's tendency to naturalism – his portrait of a young woman whose personality, like that of his earlier heroine Eveline, is fundamentally constructed by her social environment, in this case the language of the advertisements. It seems to me that Gibson's acute observation could be reframed. Such naturalistic slips – the "little, rude tongues of language" that "stick out constantly at the magazine style"[43] – may be read as the hints of a "real" character, who is all but occluded by the male-defined projection that provides the impetus of the first half of the "Nausicaa" episode. Bloom presumably observes a "real" woman on Sandymount Strand. But he observes her in truly commodified terms, garnered from the contemporary register of women's advertisements – a register that was itself dreamed up and projected by men.

43 Gibson, *Joyce's Revenge*, 147.

CHAPTER 7

Advertising in *Ulysses*

Sabrina Alonso

Abstract

James Joyce's use of advertising in *Ulysses* can be studied by looking at some of its most prominent advertisements and at the way in which they are perceived by Bloom. In addition, reading their occurrence against the background of the notes that Joyce took on the issue of advertising adds another intriguing aspect. Starting from the premise that it is a characteristic of Joyce's prose that almost any passage would do to illustrate a principle and that any component can lend itself to highlight typical features of the whole book, the question that will be addressed is to what extent this is true of Joyce's use of advertising and what its consequences are for our understanding of the book as a whole.

Keywords

Ulysses – advertising – James Joyce's notebooks – Howard Bridgewater – historical advertising

This essay discusses *Ulysses* from the perspective of Joyce's use of advertising. Of the many instances of advertisements that feature in the book I will pick the most prominent and examine the manner in which they are filtered through Bloom's perception. At the same time, I will read them against the background of the notes that Joyce took on the issue of advertising. Starting from the premise that it is a characteristic of Joyce's prose "that almost any passage would do to illustrate a principle" and that any component can lend itself to highlight typical features of the whole book,[1] the question I will address is to what extent this is true of Joyce's use of advertising and if this has consequences for our understanding of the book as a whole.

1 Fritz Senn, *Nicht Nur Nichts Gegen Joyce; Joyce Versus Nothing* (Zurich: Haffmans Verlag, 1983), 108–09.

 | DOI 10.1163/9789004359062_009

What Way to Attract Attention

Many of the advertisements in the book display early on what may be considered typically Ulyssean features, the most striking being their affinity to motion (or wandering) and to transformation (or metamorphosis). An example at the opening of "Lestrygonians" can illustrate this:

> A sombre Y.M.C.A. young man, watchful among the warm sweet fumes of Graham Lemon's, placed a throwaway in a hand of Mr Bloom.
> Heart to heart talks.
> Bloo .... Me? No.
> Blood of the Lamb.
> His slow feet walked him riverward, reading. Are you saved? All are washed in the blood of the lamb.
>
> *U* 8.5–11

Motion is what makes this encounter possible, the advertisement passing from a roaming messenger to a wandering target-customer in the streets, and transformation is its promise. It represents one first attempt to attract attention and, although it does not appear to be very successful since it does not hold Bloom's interest for long, it still touches on themes that will be developed in the book, with regard to advertising in particular: It shows its similarities to religion and its promises of completion and of bliss, of salvation in the next life or of fulfilment in this one.[2] It further addresses the idea of circulation, clever placing and easy perception; the young man has his strategic approach (he is "watchful", he seems to know what he is looking for), he places the note directly into his target's hand, and Bloom finds himself holding the note almost before being aware of it. This is also reflected by the word order: "placed" precedes "a hand" and "Mr Bloom" himself, holding the note. It also touches on the advertiser's attempt to make what is essentially an impersonal message come across as personal, "heart-to-heart" communication. By coincidence, although for a different reason, Bloom is indeed fooled for a moment and reads the note personally ("Bloo ... Me? No"). After all, nothing seems easier to spot in a text than one's own name – a hint perhaps that we all read ourselves into a text. Senn points out that, when reading, "what we gather, select, recognize,

---

2 For a discussion of the idea of consumption amounting to an act of faith, with the consumer turning into believer, and of the "mythic aura of completeness" that advertising attaches to commodity, see Garry Leonard, *Advertising and Commodity Culture in Joyce* (Gainesville: University Press of Florida, 1998).

rearrange, construe ... we remake in our own likeness" and Bloom temporarily does so "when he hastily projects his own name into a word that for a few letters looks alike".[3]

Bloom soon loses interest, however, and moves on toward the river, where he is drawn by gulls and has his own go at trying to attract attention:

> Looking down he saw flapping strongly, wheeling between the gaunt quaywalls, gulls. Rough weather outside. If I threw myself down? Reuben J's son must have swallowed a good bellyful of that sewage. One and eightpence too much. Hhhhm. It's the droll way he comes out with the things. Knows how to tell a story too.
>
> They wheeled lower. Looking for grub. Wait.
>
> He threw down among them a crumpled paper ball. Elijah thirtytwo feet per sec is com. Not a bit. The ball bobbed unheeded on the wake of swells, floated under by the bridgepiers. Not such damn fools.
>
> *U* 8.51–59

Again not fooling anyone, the throwaway floats down the river and goes off on its own little Odyssey. It is interesting to note in passing how often the word *wheeling* appears in this passage (four times within relatively few lines [*U* 8.51–83]). *Wheeling* seems appropriate for a mind like Bloom's, who loves all things that swirl, and has numerous resonances in the book, as will be shown later.

Bloom soon chances on another wandering ad, the sandwich-board men advertising for Hely in their variation of an attempt to attract attention:

> A procession of whitesmocked sandwichmen marched slowly towards him along the gutter, scarlet sashes across their boards. Bargains. Like that priest they are this morning: we have sinned: we have suffered. He read the scarlet letters on their five tall white hats: H.E.L.Y.S. Wisdom Hely's. Y lagging behind drew a chunk of bread from under his foreboard, crammed it into his mouth and munched as he walked. Our staple food. Three bob a day, walking along the gutters, street after street. Just keep skin and bone together, bread and skilly.
>
> *U* 8.123–30

Advertising implicitly reflects the economic aspect of culture and, here, hunger is what drives the characters forward, appropriately for this chapter, where

3 Fritz Senn, *Inductive Scrutinies: Focus on Joyce* (Baltimore: Johns Hopkins University Press, 1995), 33.

food is a dominant topic. The scene observed by Bloom is interesting in itself for a web of connections it establishes with issues of the text at large, for example the idea of a sandwichman eating bread drawn from under his sandwich-board could carry cannibalistic overtones (Homer's Laestrygonians are a tribe of giant cannibals), or it may have echoes of the transubstantiation at Mass, a first link to the priest having already been made. However, Bloom's focus here is on the business. Seeing the men thus engaged sets him off to think about advertising as part of his experience. Since he is involved in the trade himself, he would be well aware of its techniques and practices. As a canvasser for ads, employed by the *Freeman's Journal*, he has only a limited role and rather little negotiating power, say, about the design or the placement of an advertisement. Semi-professionally, however, he would be aware of what might catch the eye.[4] Of Hely's sandwich-board ad he thinks it "doesn't bring in any business" (*U* 8.130–31) and remembers his own presumably more promising suggestion at the time about:

> a transparent showcart with two smart girls sitting inside writing letters, copybooks, envelopes, blottingpaper. I bet that would have caught on. Smart girls writing something catch the eye at once. Everyone dying to know what she's writing. Get twenty of them round you if you stare at nothing. Have a finger in the pie. Women too. Curiosity. Pillar of salt. Wouldn't have it of course because he didn't think of it himself first.[5]
>
> *U* 8.131–37

The showcart features again in "Ithaca", when Bloom mentions it to Stephen as an example of originality producing its own reward, though not necessarily leading to success. He thereby implicitly admits that his idea may not be the most triumphant as far as commercial ads go: "an illuminated showcart, drawn by a beast of burden, in which two smartly dressed girls were to be seated engaged in writing" (*U* 17.608–10). In 1904, Osteen tells us, travelling showcarts

4 See Matthew Hayward's nuanced discussion of Joyce's portrayal of Bloom as canvasser. He explains how Joyce uses advertising to characterize Bloom in his particular role, one he comes to describe as "progressive outsider"; Matthew Hayward, "Bloom's Job: The Role of the Advertisement Canvasser in Joyce's Dublin", *Modernism/modernity* 22, no. 4 (2015): 651–66.

5 For a discussion of the frequent use of the word "smart" in advertising and of its appeal and ambiguity in *Ulysses* see Matthew Hayward's essay "'But Who Was Gerty?': Intertextuality and the Advertising Language of 'Nausicaa'" and David Spurr's "Classified Advertising in Joyce" in this volume.

were “hackneyed promotional gimmicks”.[6] They would have looked like the picture in illustration 7.1:

ILLUSTRATION 7.1
Nineteenth century travelling showcart for Cherry Blossom.[7]

Or they might have looked like the picture in illustration 7.2:

ILLUSTRATION 7.2 *Nineteenth century advertising wagon.*[8]

The cart’s greatest strength is motion and, in Bloom’s case, it would be used to advertise, of all things, stationery, a play on words Osteen notices too: although

6 Mark Osteen, *The Economy of “Ulysses”: Making Both Ends Meet* (Syracuse: Syracuse University Press, 1995), 134.

7 “Collectibles: A Cherry Blossom Coach Card”, accessed 6 December 2016, http://www.webring.org/l/rd?ring=collectiblesunli;id=21;url=http%3A%2F%2Fgosnell%2Eorg%2Euk%2F.

8 “F.B. Keith’s Advertising Wagon ca. 1894”, artist unknown, accessed 6 December 2016, http://commons.wikimedia.org/wiki/File:BFKeiths_advertising_wagon_ca1894.png.

"it promotes stationery it would not be stationary" but would circulate in the city.[9] Thus, the words "stationery" and "stationary" acquire a mobile and unstable quality, too, with meaning bobbing between two terms.

It is true that Bloom's idea for an ad is rather fanciful, more than a little extravagant and probably questionable in terms of cost-effectiveness, but it is at least partially successful in that it certainly would attract attention and make passers-by stop and look. Indeed, it seems designed more like an excuse or a licence to observe than a serious attempt to sell (which, read against his habitual failure to get a substantial glimpse at a female body, may be comprehensible). His idea does, however, have its merits. Bloom, sensitive to the workings of curiosity, is aware of some features of the psychology of attention. Similarly, he knows about the power of connotation: the idea of the two attractive women is suggestive of the by now very familiar device of using sex-appeal to sell a product.

Bloom, then, can be said to have a silent understanding of the developing advertising techniques of his day. Matthew Hayward looks at this in more detail in his essay on Bloom and advertising, considering him as a canvasser who appears to have absorbed some of the knowledge of the new techniques in advertising emerging at the time.[10] Joyce took notes on Howard Bridgewater's *Advertising, Or the Art of Making Known* (c. 1910), which he listed under the heading "Advertising" in his "Notes on Business and Commerce".[11] These remarks used to be explained as part of Joyce's preparation for his employment at a private bank in Rome between 1906 and 1907, but the identification of their source (i.e. a series of advertising guides published in London in 1909–1910) allows us to analyse the precise suggestions.[12] Bridgewater offers a popularised version of the science of advertising based on the theories of the day, drawing on developing psychological concepts and techniques based largely on the works of the most influential theorists of the early twentieth century, like Harlow Gale and Walter Dill Scott. Some questions very much in the air at the time concerned the nature of human volition, the workings of voluntary and involuntary action or whether man was a predominantly rational

9 Osteen, *Economy of "Ulysses"*, 135.

10 Matthew Hayward, "The Bloom of Advertising: Joyce's 'Notes on Business and Commerce' and *Ulysses*", *Dublin James Joyce Journal* 5 (2012): 49–65.

11 Howard Bridgewater, *Advertising or the Art of Making Known* (London: Isaac Pitman & Sons, n.d., c. 1910); James Joyce, "Notes on Business and Commerce" (Cornell MS 38 and 63.1–13, reproduced in *JJA* 3:474–617).

12 Hayward, "Bloom of Advertising", 50.

or irrational being, all of which were reflected in the way advertising began to adapt its techniques. Indeed, Hayward describes the new approaches in advertising as marked by "a general change in the way in which human volition was conceived". While the early stages (roughly 1890–1910) tended to be characterised by a belief in the "dominant rationalistic image of man", assuming the key to human nature to be "rationality and rational understanding or self-interest", advertisements would tend to provide information about price, function, craftsmanship, durability, benefits, in short, all the reasons for which one should buy a certain product.[13] By the turn of the century, however, advertising "had gone well beyond merely announcing the price and availability of a product", as Leonard points out.[14] With a shift in views on the rationality of human action came a different approach to consumers, too. They began to be conceived as susceptible to the sway of emotive and unconscious appeals, as being liable to act even against reason and against their own self-interest, often enough buying for reasons unknown even to themselves. The impulse to buy came to be seen as directed by emotional and subconscious forces, the reasons for consumption as predominantly irrational. Around 1910–1930, the modern ad would, thus, strive to attract involuntary attention and be directed at largely unconscious desires.

Advertising Techniques Reflected through Bloom

Let us now turn to a few examples that show how the theoretical advances with which Joyce familiarised himself around 1910 surface in Bloom's reflections. Consider for example how Bloom re-designs the ad for a college sporting event, the Trinity College bicycle race, which he encounters on his walk:

> College sports today I see. He eyed the horseshoe poster over the gate of college park: cyclist doubled up like a cod in a pot. Damn bad ad. Now if they had made it round like a wheel. Then the spokes: sports, sports, sports: and the hub big: college. Something to catch the eye.
>
> *U* 5.550–54

What Bloom has in mind would look something like illustration 7.3 provided by Osteen:[15]

---

13 Hayward, "Bloom of Advertising", 52.

14 Leonard, *Advertising and Commodity*, 145.

15 Osteen, *Economy of "Ulysses"*, 138.

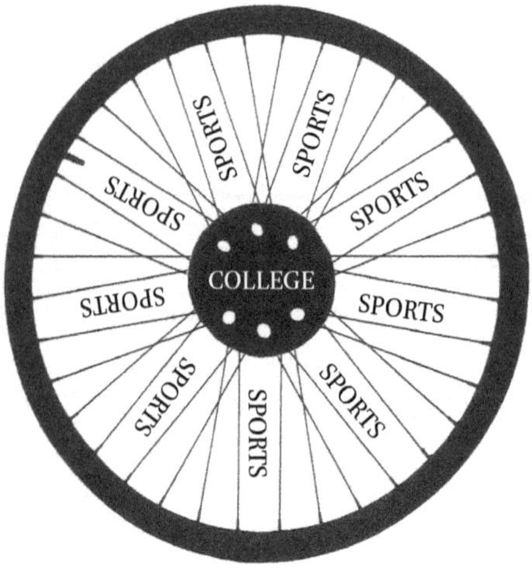

ILLUSTRATION 7.3
The re-designed college sports advertisement as imagined by Bloom.
COURTESY OF SYRACUSE UNIVERSITY PRESS.

His bicycle poster would capture the attention in a dual sense: not only by attracting the viewer's eye but by mirroring it, the hub-and-wheel design being reconstructed as an eye, magnifying and reflecting the visual organ that reads it.[16] Wheel and eye would merge, and the poster would stare back. (Incidentally, note that Bloom *eyes* the horseshoe poster in his mental redesigning of it, as though the text were underlining this fusion and transformation.) Further, the poster would also generate motion as one reads the spokes "sports, sports, sports" around and around the wheel, thus allowing the eye to move while staying in place. In this sense it is reminiscent of the effect of mobility-in-immobility in the example of the stationery stationary showcart.[17]

The theme of the mobile immobile is varied in another way in "Lestrygonians". Bloom has been marvelling at some animals' eating habits, wondering for example how birds can eat fishy flesh (only to conclude that there is "no accounting for tastes" [*U* 8.81]), or about what gives different types of meat their particular flavour (why it is for example that, when you feed a turkey on chestnuts it tastes of chestnut, but saltwater fish does not taste salty [*U* 8.85–86]). While wondering, his (wandering) eyes look for an answer, and it comes, sure enough, in the shape of an ad:

16 Osteen, *Economy of "Ulysses"*, 138.

17 This is, to mention in passing, also a variation on the theme of "eye" coinciding with "I", which turns up repeatedly throughout the book.

His eyes sought answer from the river and saw a rowboat rock at anchor on the treacly swells lazily its plastered board.

Kino's
11/-
Trousers

Good idea that.

U 8.88–93

The ad's power to arrest attention (to halt and anchor the roaming eye) paradoxically depends upon its wavelike motion. It "rocks at anchor", going up and down, back and forth, it is always moving but also fixed, to which it probably owes part of its allure. Note how the syntax does something to the same effect, as it too is in motion, or wobbling: at first reading we take "rock" to be intransitive (the boat rocks), but then it turns out to have an object: the boat rocks *its board*. The rowboat also introduces a fitting Odyssean element, suggestive of travel at sea, and succeeds in transporting its message into Bloom's field of vision. Thus, the text makes us aware of the paths on which the ads travel, but it is also an exploration of where the eye likes to go.

Joyce made notes relating to this, for example, on what is easy for the eye to take in and what might be harder to absorb. The eye, according to the "Notes", should be made to move neither too little nor too much. Illustration 7.4 shows an entry he heads "Optical Illusions" about the eye not liking to jump too much:

In my own transcription, with italic face added for emphasis:

Optical Illusions: Apperception <—>
>—<. Perspective: Garden 100 m long.
well done in ad. 6".4" *Easy Eye-Impressions. "Jumpy" ads avoided* Ex You
are
a
fair
dealing
man.

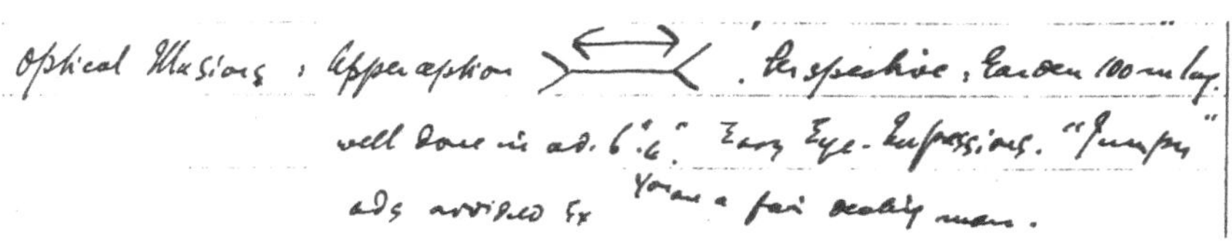

ILLUSTRATION 7.4 *Joyce's notes on optical illusions.*

Joyce copied this from Bridgewater's passage about optical illusions in *Advertising or the Art of Making Known*, as a scanned extract from the original shows in illustrations 7.5 and 7.6.[18]

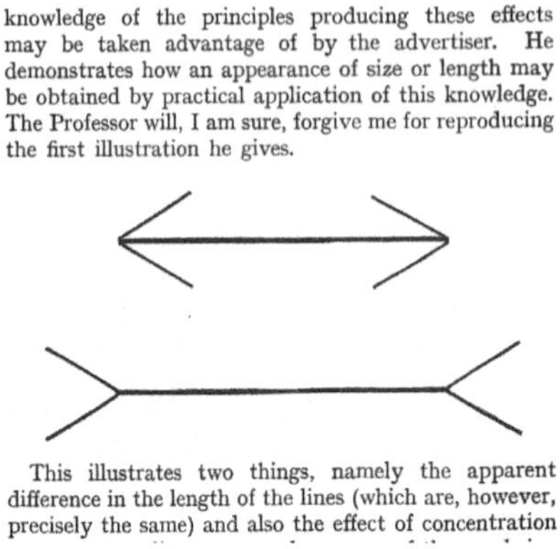

knowledge of the principles producing these effects may be taken advantage of by the advertiser. He demonstrates how an appearance of size or length may be obtained by practical application of this knowledge. The Professor will, I am sure, forgive me for reproducing the first illustration he gives.

This illustrates two things, namely the apparent difference in the length of the lines (which are, however, precisely the same) and also the effect of concentration

ILLUSTRATION 7.5
Bridgewater's original for Joyce's copy, page 29.

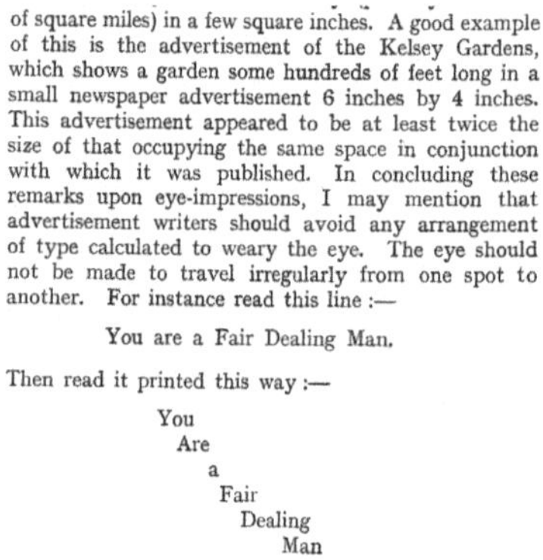

of square miles) in a few square inches. A good example of this is the advertisement of the Kelsey Gardens, which shows a garden some hundreds of feet long in a small newspaper advertisement 6 inches by 4 inches. This advertisement appeared to be at least twice the size of that occupying the same space in conjunction with which it was published. In concluding these remarks upon eye-impressions, I may mention that advertisement writers should avoid any arrangement of type calculated to weary the eye. The eye should not be made to travel irregularly from one spot to another. For instance read this line :—

You are a Fair Dealing Man.

Then read it printed this way :—

You
Are
a
Fair
Dealing
Man

ILLUSTRATION 7.6
Bridgewater's original for Joyce's copy, page 30.

Joyce also has an entry about posters, on the other hand, being too static (reproduced in illustration 7.7 and transcribed below, with italics added for emphasis):

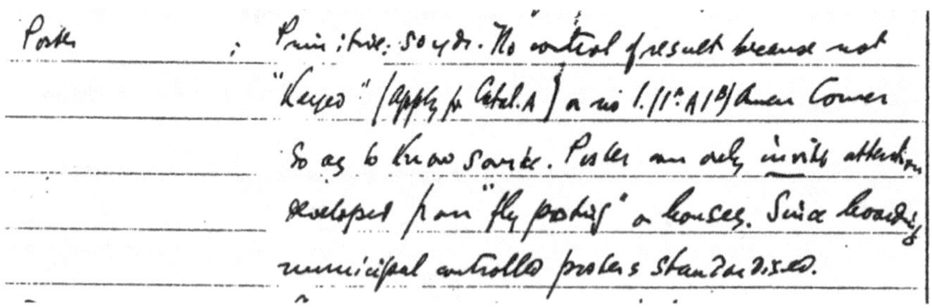

ILLUSTRATION 7.7 *Joyce's notes about posters.*

18 Bridgewater, *Advertising*, 29–30.

Transcription:

> Poster: Primitive: 50 yds. No control of result because not "keyed" (apply for Catal. A) or no I. II[A]. A I [B] 1 Amen Corner so as to know source. *Poster can only invite attention* developed from "fly posting" on houses. Since boarding municipal controlled posters standardised.

This entry goes back to Bridgewater pages 54–55, the aim being to find the means for print best suited to attract and hold the viewer's eye.

Similarly, Joyce's considerations about how best to present things in an interesting way become clear when read against the background of Bridgewater. Joyce notes under "Attention":

Transcription of handwritten text reproduced in illustration 7.8 (italics added for emphasis):

> Attention: Statistics show 4 visual limit. Headlines 4 limit. Absence of counter attractions. Ex. Motor "Ad" better in non-motor press. Intensity obtained by movement. Red(1, Green(2, Black(3. Contrast Black/white better than White/black. Variation of type consistent with harmony. *Still Life Taboo (Tailors' dummy) Ex. Smoking Cigarettes, Riding Bicycles.*

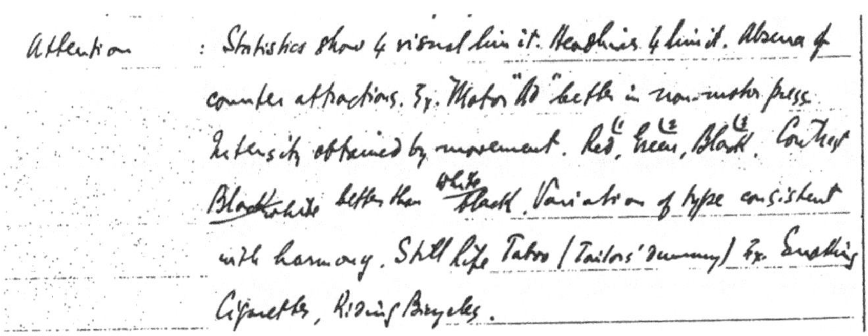
Attention : Statistics show 4 visual limit. Headlines 4 limit. Absence of counter attractions. Ex. Motor "Ad" better in non-motor press. Intensity obtained by movement. Red(1, Green(2, Black(3. Contrast Black/white better than white/Black. Variation of type consistent with harmony. Still Life Taboo (Tailors' dummy) Ex. Smoking Cigarettes, Riding Bicycles.

ILLUSTRATION 7.8 *Joyce's notes on attention.*

This note is out of a passage where Bridgewater suggests introducing what he calls "a human interest" into the ad, which is bound to attract more attention than the reproduction of a mere object would:

> Still-life illustrations are never interesting. If it is a house you want to interest one in, show someone entering or looking at it or out of it; if a

> bicycle, someone riding it (this is not so often done as it should be); if a cigarette, someone smoking it, or handling it in some way.[19]

Incidentally, Joyce's notes on cigarettes and bicycles are reminiscent of Reggy Wylie, the boy that Gerty admires for "the way he turned the bicycle at the lamp with his hands off the bars and also the nice perfume of those good cigarettes" (*U* 13.143–45). In this light, Reggy reads as if he had materialised out of Joyce's notes on good advertising. Gerty, of course, would love the ad-boy.[20]

Indeed, Gerty provides a good occasion to discuss the rewards of a good ad, being extremely responsive to the language of the novelette, of fashion magazines and of advertising, and describing herself in the following terms:

> Time was when those brows were not so silkily seductive. It was Madame Vera Verity, directress of the Woman Beautiful page of the Princess Novelette, who had first advised her to try eyebrowleine which gave that haunting expression to the eyes, so becoming in leaders of fashion, and she had never regretted it. Then there was blushing scientifically cured and how to be tall increase your height and you have a beautiful face but your nose?
>
> *U* 13.108–14

Harald Beck informs us that Joyce must have found a source for this in an advertisement for Eyebrowlin, which had been in circulation since 1916. He provides a reproduction of the original ad on his website (re-printed here with permission in illustration 7.9), which said "'EYEBROWLIN' produces that fascinating expression", the brand being modelled on "eyebrow line", a term frequently employed by artists and fashion writers. Beck notes further

---

19 Bridgewater, *Advertising*, 14.

20 As it happens, Bridgwater (spelled without "e") appears in *Ulysses* in the shape of a boat carrying Bath bricks, e.g. in: "Elijah, skiff, light crumpled throwaway, sailed eastward by flanks of ships and trawlers, amid an archipelago of corks, beyond new Wapping street past Benson's ferry, and by the threemasted schooner *Rosevean* from Bridgwater with bricks" (*U* 10.1096–99). Don Gifford notes: "The schooner *Rosevean*, announced in 'Shipping News,' *Freeman's Journal*, 16 June 1904, as 'from Bridgwater with bricks'"; *"Ulysses" Annotated: Notes for James Joyce's "Ulysses"*, 2nd ed. (Berkeley: University of California Press, 1988), 66. Whether Joyce's use of the name is coincidental or a deliberate allusion is worthy of consideration. I have not found any reference to this in scholarly work. The list of errata reproduced in *JJA* 12:180, however, shows that Joyce at least considered the spelling of the name important enough to request a correction from how it was printed in the first edition of *Ulysses*, "Bridgewater" (240), to e-less "Bridgwater".

that Joyce put down "eyebrowleine, produce that fascinating expression of eyes" and "used by leaders of fashion" in his notes for "Nausicaa" in 1919.[21]

Similarly, her "you have a beautiful face but your nose?" is fittingly reminiscent of advertisements of the time, such as the one in illustration 7.10, since "Nausicaa" is also a chapter about varieties of noses.

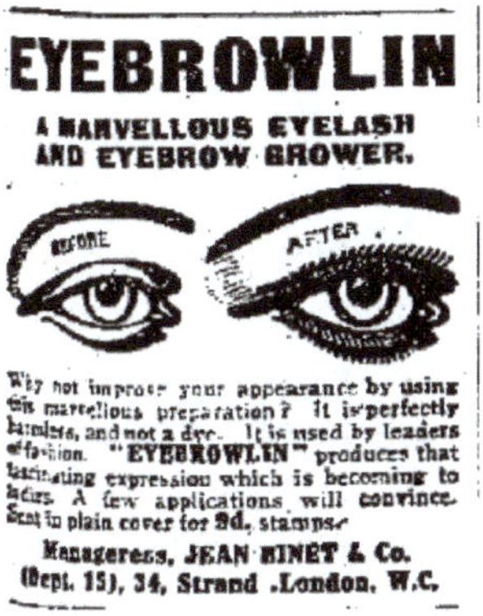

ILLUSTRATION 7.9
Advertisement for Eyebrowlin in Lloyd's Weekly News (*1916*).
COURTESY OF HARALD BECK.

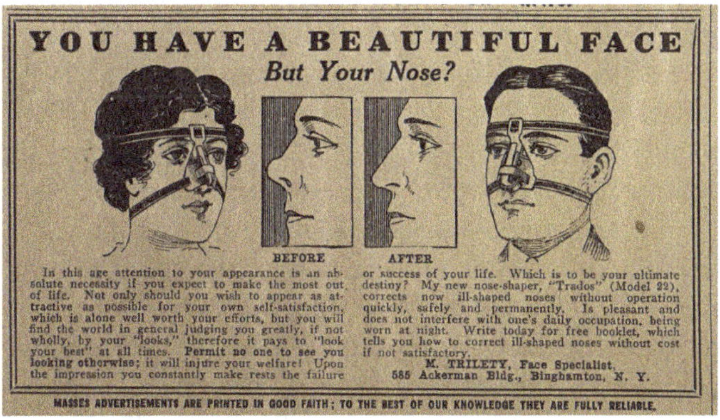

ILLUSTRATION 7.10 *Advertisement for nose shaper* (*1916*).[22]

Gerty is highly receptive to this sort of appeal. Bloom, at one point, also imagines a woman in terms of her responsiveness to a certain type of ad when he considers the widower O'Connor and the kind of woman that would be good for him:

21 Harald Beck, "Eyebrow Line", *James Joyce Online Notes*, accessed 6 December 2016, http://www.jjon.org/joyce-s-environs/eyebrow-line.

22 "You have a beautiful face but your nose", artist unknown, accessed 6 December 2016, https://commons.wikimedia.org/wiki/File:You_have_a_beautiful_face,_but_your_nose%C2%BF.jpg.

> Some good matronly woman in a porkpie hat to mother him. Take him in tow, platter face and a large apron. Ladies' grey flannelette bloomers, three shillings a pair, astonishing bargain. Plain and loved, loved for ever, they say.
>
> *U* 13.1233–36

The hint of the clothes she would wear and of the kind of ad to which she might respond makes for a very succinct rendering of her character. Indeed, responsiveness is a keyword, particularly for the figure of Gerty. She is a great believer in products' powers, or at least in the way they are advertised. In a sense, she can be read as a personification of the texts she enjoys or, more precisely, a personification of responsiveness to their language. In addition, she makes a mini-cycle of formation and transformation. Leonard realises this in pointing out the limitations of advertisements, which, he says, "cannot be anything more than what they persuade us to think we are doing".[23] I would take this a step further and argue that it is precisely this persuasive force that helps build the character of Gerty. She is aware of, and believes in, a particular linguistic universe, of which advertising is a part, and constructs herself out of it. She, thus, becomes a linguistic assemblage or, in Senn's terms, a "montage" of rhetorical figures, and reflects a world that is culturally and linguistically constructed.[24] Ultimately, she is text and generates or regenerates herself out of the texts she responds to.[25]

Gerty's responsiveness to advertised products, particularly those with transformative powers, points to an important feature Joyce exploits, with regard both to the ads in the book and to the art of advertising in general. It is perhaps no coincidence that (in real life as well as in the text) commodities are sometimes advertised as if they were things from another world, coming to us as the answer to all our questions, the solution we have been waiting for, a revelation even, promising to change our lives for good. As such, they may well act as the

---

23 Leonard, *Advertising and Commodity Culture in Joyce*, 41.

24 Fritz Senn, "Nausicaa", in *James Joyce's "Ulysses": Critical Essays*, ed. Clive Hart and David Hayman (Berkeley: University of California Press, 1974), 309.

25 See Matthew Hayward's essay "'But Who Was Gerty?'" in this volume for a language-focused reading of the figure of Gerty. It questions what he calls a "naturalistic" reading of her character, which interprets her as Joyce's depiction of a realistic figure through which he offers a critique of a certain type of female consumer and her culture. Instead, by studying specifically the language of the first part of "Nausicaa", Hayward is able to identify it as akin to and parodic of a particular kind of style, i.e. that of female-oriented advertising typical of the early decades of the twentieth century.

present-day variant of intercessory powers from above, a modern-day equivalent to intervening gods. There is some of this in the products Joyce employs. The pamphlet lying in Bloom's drawer, for example, is a:

> prospectus of The Wonderworker, the world's greatest remedy for rectal complaints, direct from Wonderworker, Coventry House, South Place, London E C, addressed (erroneously) to Mrs L. Bloom with brief accompanying note commencing (erroneously): Dear Madam.
>
> *U* 17.1819–23

Molly remembers it, too, in "some advertisement like that wonderworker they sent him addressed dear Madam" (*U* 18.715–16). It features again in "Ithaca":

> Quote the textual terms in which the prospectus claimed advantages for this thaumaturgic remedy.
>
> It heals and soothes while you sleep, in case of trouble in breaking wind, assists nature in the most formidable way, insuring instant relief in discharge of gases, keeping parts clean and free natural action, an initial outlay of 7/6 making a new man of you and life worth living.
>
> *U* 17.1824–29

As the name and the description of the article suggest, it is full of promises of miraculous transformation. The text of the pamphlet looks forward (it is a pro-spectus) to something like salvation ("remedy"), and it is salvation within reach, in *this* world ("instant" and making "life worth living"), which is bound to make the product all the more attractive. The magic has started to work, too, though it has also gone wrong: it has made Bloom a new man, but by giving him a new gender.[26]

Another brand with transforming powers which interests Bloom is self-advertising Sandow, with his tools and exercises. Bloom has had a go at his methods. One of his drawers contains:

> a chart of measurements of Leopold Bloom compiled before, during and after 2 months' consecutive use of Sandow-Whiteley's pulley exerciser (men's 15/-, athlete's 20/-) viz. chest 28 in and 29 1/2 in, biceps 9 in and 10 in, forearm 8 1/2 and 9 in, thigh 10 in and 12 in, calf 11 in and 12 in.
>
> *U* 17.1815–19

26 This is also noted by Osteen, *Economy of "Ulysses"*, 117. We should point out that saints too, by definition, have to be thaumaturgic: having performed miracles.

When Bloom has his narrow escape from the sandstrewer in "Circe", "Close shave that but cured the stitch. Must take up Sandow's exercises again. On the hands down. Insure against street accident too" (*U* 15.199–21), he is aware of the protective powers Sandow may presumably have. Bloom may or may not stick to his resolution (he does not seem as seriously dedicated to Sandow as Gerty is to her role models and their cures) but he is intrigued enough to try it out on himself. Bloom's interest in the product's effectiveness, however, may derive more from his susceptibility to the powers of science than faith or divinity. That this passage should occur in "Ithaca" is thus fitting in at least two ways: the episode's engagement with science (or pseudo science) and its exploration of latent potential. As Vike Plock explains, "'Ithaca' is Joyce's most engaging reflection on contemporary science", both embracing its empiricism and simultaneously satirizing its "widely accepted hegemonic stance".[27] The episode's "passion for dormant abilities and potential growth" aided by science would appeal to Bloom, who, in his embodiment of Flowerville, "is the product of self-improvement stretched to the utmost".[28] Although the significant development of muscular girth documented in Bloom's chart would be highly unlikely (reminiscent, e.g., of the unrealistic list of jobs for him imagined earlier [*U* 17.787–94]), it nevertheless encapsulates the episode's tendency to portray Bloom's fascination with science and self-potential. Advertised commodities, such as Sandow's pulley exerciser, often speak to the need to transform the self and to believe in the possibility of relief or alleviation, and it might indeed help at times to believe in the existence of a power one can call on.

The issues of motion and of transformation as discussed so far are dominant Ulyssean themes, acted out in numerous variations. Here is just one more example taken from Joyce's treatment of advertising, the well-known ad for Plumtree's potted meat. It is interesting for the way in which it varies the themes by refracting them through Bloom's perception. With regard to motion and direction, an advertisement usually carries a clear message: it puts one perspective on things and wants to guide the consumers in a certain direction and only in one, that of the product. It is meant to work like a signpost, needing to be placed well in order to be seen and able to direct its targets to a particular goal. Yet, Joyce plays precisely with the idea of directing and misdirecting, placement and misplacement as well as adverting and averting in Bloom's reaction to the Plumtree ad. In "Lestrygonians", he remembers the slogan, "What

27 Vike Martina Plock, "A Feat of Strength in 'Ithaca': Eugen Sandow and Physical Culture in Joyce's *Ulysses*", *Journal of Modern Literature* 30, no. 1 (Fall 2006): 129.

28 Plock, "A Feat of Strength in 'Ithaca'", 137, 130.

is home without Plumtree's Potted Meat? ...", and thinks, "His ideas for ads like Plumtree's potted under the obituaries, cold meat department" (*U* 8.138–39). Bloom thinks this ad particularly misplaced. Although, as Hayward tells us, no ad for potted meat was ever placed directly beneath the obituary in the *Freeman's Journal* or *Evening Telegraph* in 1904, this approach would have been in line with that of a nineteenth century advertiser, adhering to the key rational principle of the time that "a good position will draw attention".[29] Yet, it is blind to what Bloom is aware of, that is, the association of ideas prompted by its positioning, the ad now eliciting cadaverous associations. In this instance at least, it attracts attention but misdirects it, too.[30]

A little later on his walk, Bloom is reminded of the ad again. While trying to make a choice for his lunch from the selection at Davy Byrne's, he looks at the shelves, sees pots of Plumtree sitting there and has his thoughts diverted in all sorts of directions:

> Sardines on the shelves. Almost taste them by looking. Sandwich? Ham and his descendants musterred and bred there. Potted meats. What is home without Plumtree's potted meat? Incomplete. What a stupid ad! Under the obituary notices they stuck it. All up a plumtree. Dignam's potted meat. Cannibals would with lemon and rice. White missionary too salty. Like pickled pork. Expect the chief consumes the parts of honour. Ought to be tough from exercise. His wives in a row to watch the effect. *There was a right royal old nigger. Who ate or something the somethings of the reverend Mr MacTrigger*. With it an abode of bliss. Lord knows what concoction. Cauls mouldy tripes windpipes faked and minced up. Puzzle find the meat. Kosher. No meat and milk together. Hygiene that was what they call now. Yom Kippur fast spring cleaning of inside. Peace and war depend on some fellow's digestion. Religions. Christmas turkeys and geese. Slaughter of innocents. Eat drink and be merry. Then casual wards full after. Heads bandaged. Cheese digests all but itself. Mity cheese.
> – Have you a cheese sandwich?
>
> *U* 8.741–56

29 Hayward, "Bloom of Advertising", 59.

30 If the Plumtree ad is indeed made up it would be a good example of Joyce's own technique of montage: he would be inserting an invented note among those of a real newspaper, thus assembling fictitious and actual print, and highlighting the very technique of montage, which is part of newspaper practice in general, as was commented during the Zurich Workshop.

A few lines further down, he decides what to have: "A cheese sandwich, then. Gorgonzola, have you?" (*U* 8.764). To order a Gorgonzola sandwich in Dublin in 1904 might strike one as slightly odd but, then, we also know Bloom to be particular about his food. The play on mity–mighty seems to bring Bloom back to reality. The coincidence of the sound of "mighty" with that of "mity" is something he would be able to enjoy. Beck has an entry on "mity cheese", which explains that the play on mity–mighty "had been around in print for at least half a century before Bloom used it" in June 1904, for example in Russell Thacher Trall's cookbook, "Cheese is a mity elf, / Digesting all things but itself", and *mighty cheese* seems to have been "a not uncommon collocation" at the time, used for ads, too.[31]

It is through Bloom's reaction to and perception of advertisements that we gradually come to see what he thinks makes a good ad. He knows, for example, about the importance of repetition: "Because, you see ... for an advertisement you must have repetition. That's the whole secret" (*U* 12.1147–48); he is striving to obtain a three month renewal for Keyes (while Nannetti's eyes are fixed on repetition in financial terms, that is, a threefold payment for the ads). Bloom is also aware of the impact jingles have, which he compares to the litany in church: "Could hear them all at it. Pray for us. And pray for us. And pray for us. Good idea the repetition. Same thing with ads. Buy from us. And buy from us" (*U* 13.1122–24). The employment of repetition and the use of jingles were, however, nothing new at the time.[32] What was new were the developments in advertising theory that began to be felt around 1910, the year of Bridgewater's publication. The view was shifting to the new model, according to which the appeal of a well-made ad was considered to be essentially unconscious. There is a number of ads featuring in *Ulysses* that would hence have been considered old-fashioned, as Bloom is aware. One instance is provided by the sandwich-board men advertising Hely's. Although the walking characters may indicate that an ad needs to move and circulate to make a product known, Bloom does not think much of the technique. The clumsiness he sees in it is also reflected linguistically in the longwinded, awkwardly perambulating sentences that describe the men's walk:

---

31 Beck, "Mity Cheese", *James Joyce Online Notes*, accessed 6 December 2016, http://www.jjon.org/joyce-s-allusions/cheese.

32 See John Strachan's essay on the historical development of the advertising business in Dublin in the second half of the nineteenth and early twentieth centuries; Strachan, "*Ulysses* and the Dublin Advertising Business", in *James Joyce in the Nineteenth Century*, ed. John Nash (New York: Cambridge University Press, 2013), 100.

> A procession of whitesmocked sandwichmen marched slowly
>
> *U* 8.123

> H.E.L.Y'S filed before him, tallwhitehatted
>
> *U* 10.310

> Five tallwhitehatted sandwichmen between Monypeny's corner and the slab where Wolfe Tone's statue was not, eeled themselves turning H.E.L.Y'S and plodded back as they had come.
>
> *U* 10.377–79

The string seems always at risk of losing its tension, even of coming undone. Indeed Bloom sees "Y lagging behind" (*U* 8.126–27), then crosses Westmoreland street when "apostrophe S had plodded by" (*U* 8.155). These are further advertising ideas of Hely's that Bloom considers rather unfavourably:

> You can't lick 'em. What? Our envelopes.
>
> *U* 8.139–40

> Hello, Jones, where are you going? Can't stop, Robinson, I am hastening to purchase the only reliable inkeraser *Kansell*, sold by Hely's Ltd, 85 Dame street.
>
> *U* 8.140–42

The ads are reminiscent of the rather verbose and narrative-based advertisement, familiar at the time but becoming outdated, too.[33] The same holds for the following examples, which still rely on basically rational claims:

> Excellent for shade, fuel and construction
>
> *U* 4.193–94

> the world's greatest remedy
>
> *U* 17.1819–20

> The best obtainable
>
> *U* 6.462

33 Hayward, "Bloom of Advertising", 59.

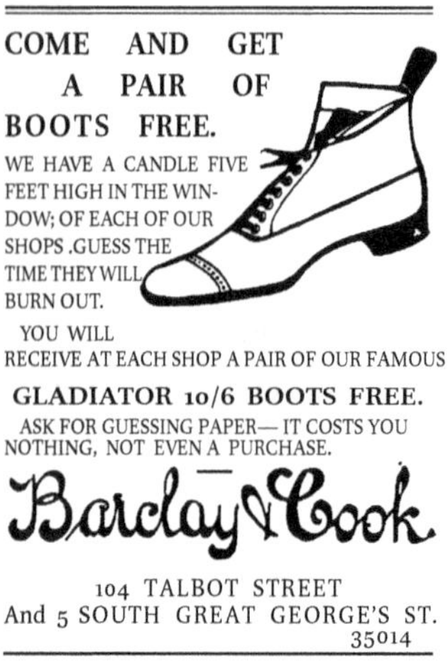

ILLUSTRATION 7.11
The Barclay & Cook shoe advertisement featuring in the reconstructed Dublin Evening Telegraph *of 16 June 1904, produced in 2004 to celebrate the centenary of Bloomsday.*[34]
COURTESY OF IAN GUNN.

Similar to this is the attention-grabbing nature of the shoe ad that Bloom finds rather uninspired (see illustration 7.11). It reads: "Look at this long candle. Calculate when it burns out and you receive gratis 1 pair of our special noncompo boots, guaranteed 1 candle power. Address: Barclay and Cook, 18 Talbot street" (*U* 17.589–91).

Bloom, who generally favours information, does not do so in advertising. He rejects the wordy ad and prefers the visual one that tells its story at a glance. His predilection is for the image (like his bicycle wheel and his showcart-girls) and for the modern style – even if, admittedly, with the showcart, he lapses back into an outdated mode.

The figure of the canvasser Bloom is interesting, however, precisely for this ambivalence, his Janus-faced nature. He moves backward and forward between a progressive and a retrogressive outlook, going back and forth between a fondness for Victorian gimmickry and the use of later psychological insight. Hayward makes this point by explaining that, while Joyce was composing *Ulysses* from 1914 to 1922, "advertisements were being designed on principles that modelled the consumer as essentially irrational and susceptible to unconscious influence", yet Joyce "set the novel in 1904, at a time when advertisers still largely adhered to the classical model of the rational consumer".[35] The novel, in other words, is set in a period of transition, when advertising

34 Ian Gunn, *Dublin Evening Telegraph 16 June 1904* (Edinburgh: Split Pea Press, 2004), 2, accessed 6 December 2016, http://www.harenet.co.uk/splitpea/.

35 Hayward, "Bloom of Advertising", 53.

techniques were starting to change. In 1904, new theoretical advances were beginning to emerge, which became widespread in the 1910s and 1920s. The ideas Joyce gives Bloom pull in both advertising directions of that period, as he looks forward "towards the future, even as his practice remains fixed in the past".[36] Bloom thus straddles the threshold between the older, flamboyant methods of advertising and the new, subtler approaches.

Straddling a period of transition and change also means being active during times when a process of renewal has set in and creative energy is at work. This "state of change" (to put it in somewhat contradictory terms), or of flux, is brought to a particular climax when we see Bloom's advertising fantasies flying at their highest. His ideas for designing a modern ad are presented most radiantly in "Ithaca", particularly in the following two passages. The first comes in answer to the question "What also stimulated him in his cogitations?" (*U* 17.576):

> the infinite possibilities hitherto unexploited of the modern art of advertisement if condensed in triliteral monoideal symbols, vertically of maximum visibility (divined), horizontally of maximum legibility (deciphered) and of magnetising efficacy to arrest involuntary attention, to interest, to convince, to decide.
>
> *U* 17.580–84

This description of the perfect ad, well visible, legible and of a certain magnetic power, is followed by the adman's ultimate dream. In answer to the question "What were habitually his final meditations?" (*U* 17.1769) we learn that they were:

> Of some one sole unique advertisement to cause passers to stop in wonder, a poster novelty, with all extraneous accretions excluded, reduced to its simplest and most efficient terms not exceeding the span of casual vision and congruous with the velocity of modern life.
>
> *U* 17.1770–73

The description of the ideal ad tells something about how it should be designed, the emphasis being on reduction and concentration (ironically, maybe, contrasting with the rather wordy, in places even tautological, language used

36 Hayward, "Bloom of Advertising", 53.

to describe it – three words, "one sole unique", to say 'one').[37] The description also says something about the ad's impact: it would first stand out like something magical, mesmerising, possibly even cause momentary confusion (reminiscent of what Bloom had thought about speaking Latin at mass, "Good idea the Latin. Stupefies them first." [*U* 5.350–51]) but it would still be absorbable at the pace of modern life and move the viewer to act on it. It is worth bearing in mind that Bloom thinks about his "poster novelty" just before going to sleep; these are "his final meditations". That is, he is drifting into a post-wake, pre-dream state, his ideas becoming fluid and metamorphic. The idea of a good ad is thus presented through a dreamlike, Bloomian focus on the art of advertising and of making known. Hard as it would be to miss the irony in the voice of the passage, it still speaks of a potentially inspired moment, a piece of successful rhetoric, the application of the imagination to the sale of goods by the medium of print. Incidentally, some of these qualities in ads are also pertinent to literature, *Ulysses* in particular, which managed to do just that when it was published: the literary world was certainly *adverted* to it.[38]

Closing Comments

The question that this essay set out to address, whether Joyce's use of advertising reflects Ulyssean features typical of the book as a whole, has led to a consideration of the nature of some of the more prominent ads that appear in the book, mainly filtered through the perception of the canvasser Bloom. We saw

---

37 This description of an ad and its design is also mentioned by David Spurr in his discussion of the artistic environment in which Joyce was working, characterized e.g. by such artistic movements as *De Stijl*. Spurr writes that this advertisement would be "very much in keeping with the design principle of *De Stijl* in its purity of form, its efficiency, and its congruity with the time and space of everyday life". He explains that "advertisements like the one Bloom imagines", appealing for its "synthesis of functionality with aesthetic value", were indeed "designed by *De Stijl* collaborators such as Bart van der Leck (for the Batavier steamship line from Rotterdam to London) and Vilmos Huszár (for Miss Blanche Virginia cigarettes)". For a more detailed discussion of the artistic ideals of the time and a positioning of Joyce within them see David Spurr, "The Machine Aesthetic in Joyce and *De Stijl*", in *A LONG THE KROMMERUN, Selected Papers from the Utrecht James Joyce Symposium*, eds. Onno Kosters, Tim Conley and Peter de Voogd, European Joyce Studies 24 (Leiden: Brill Rodopi, 2016), 7–19.

38 Joyce was not entirely uninvolved in creating the stir around his publication. See William S. Brockman's essay "'Clio's Clippings': From Newspaper to Press Cutting" in this volume

how Joyce, in his construction of this figure, makes Bloom move between old-fashioned and new techniques, bridging a period in which advertising methods were beginning to change and making visible a time of transition during the first decade of the twentieth century, when new ideas were emerging, reshaping and transforming the crafts. Joyce brings this course of transition to a particular climax when it intersects with a moment at which Bloom's consciousness is itself in a state of pre-dream flux, where ideas are not fixed but in the process of taking shape. This concentration on the dreamlike meditations about an art that is for its part in the midst of being transformed brings into focus the Odyssean nature of Joyce's use of advertising: it is akin to a book that seems in perpetual motion and which has a predilection for showing things in a state of becoming.[39] The advertisement comes to enact the commercial equivalent of the Ulyssean themes in Joyce's book of metamorphoses and its protean nature.

---

for a discussion of how he compiled and distributed his own "Extracts from Press Notices", assembled between 1907 and 1922 for the purpose of self-promotion, and was thus able to turn the press's interest in him to his advantage.

39 Senn has discussed in various places Joyce's pervasive concern with the stage at which things are in the process of taking shape, e.g. on how Joyce strives repeatedly to "catch thoughts *in statu nascendi*, before articulation"; Fritz Senn, "Syntactic Glides", in *James Joyce and the Difference of Language*, ed. Laurent Milesi (Cambridge: Cambridge University Press, 2003), 30.

CHAPTER 8

"Aeolus" – A Sightseeing Tour

Harald Beck

Abstract

"Aeolus", the newspaper-office episode in *Ulysses*, is one of the least understood when it comes to indoor topography. And yet, although the book says relatively little about Bloom's passing through the offices, it is possible to see how the descriptions in *Ulysses* tally with what is known about them by drawing on contemporary resources. Various materials – such as a 1910 plan showing the *Freeman's Journal* public office where Bloom talks with Murray about Keyes's ad, an 1893 fire insurance map, reports about events in the building in 1916, extracts from *Thom's Directory* of 1910 or a photograph of the interior of the *Freeman's* printers' room – are valuable documents to partly reconstruct the premises and to trace Bloom's route through the *Freeman's* building: from ground floor, to caseroom, through gallery, to upper floor, down the staircase to the editor's office on the ground floor, and out of *Freeman* on to the streets toward Williams's Row. "Aeolus", the windy memorial palace of the press, turns out to be a near-documentary fictional resurrection of a reality James Joyce knew had been irreversibly destroyed in the Easter Rising of 1916.

Keywords

"Aeolus" – *Ulysses* – *Freeman's Journal* – *Evening Telegraph* – documentary material – *Freeman's Journal* printers' room – Bloom's path

The map in illustration 8.1 shows – in outline – Bloom's route in "Aeolus" from the cab stand through the *Freeman*'s offices and on to Dillon's in Bachelor's Walk. Particularly the portion of the route within the *Freeman*'s offices has until now remained something of a mystery. While it is not possible to plot Bloom's path through the offices precisely, a close reading of the text of "Aeolus", along with an examination of contemporary documents, shows that the description in *Ulysses* tallies in its essentials with what is known about the interior layout at the *Freeman's Journal*.

In spite of the fact that the episode swarms with detailed descriptions like "he lifted the counterflap, as he passed in through a sidedoor and along the warm

 | DOI 10.1163/9789004359062_010

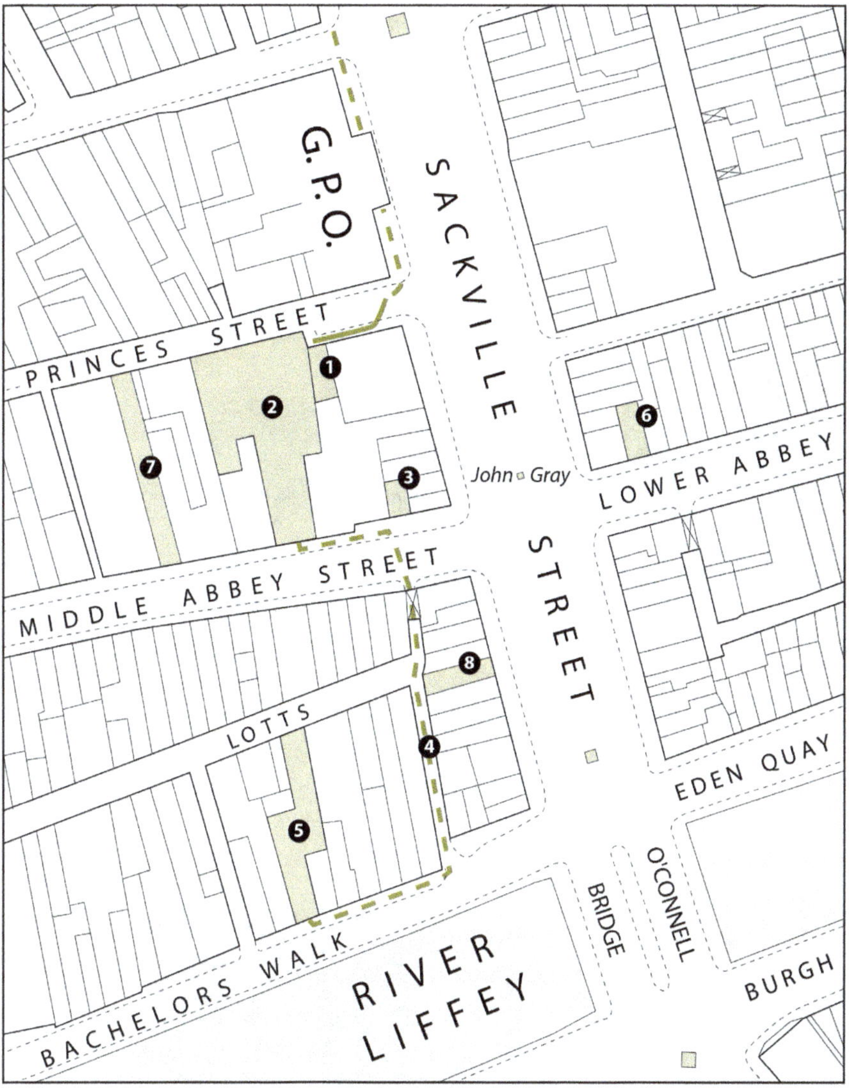

ILLUSTRATION 8.1 *Map showing Bloom's route in "Aeolus" from the cab stand through the* Freeman's *offices and on to Dillon's in Bachelor's Walk. (1) The Prince's Stores, (2) The* Freeman *offices and printing works, (3) The Oval, (4) Williams's Row, (5) Dillon's auction rooms, (6) Mooney's, (7) The Irish Catholic, (8) Graham Lemon, confectioner.*
COURTESY OF IAN GUNN.

dark stairs and passage" (*U* 7.69–70), "Aeolus" is one of the least understood episodes in *Ulysses* when it comes to its primarily indoor topography. Even readers' perceptions of its outdoor locations are faulty at times. Bracketed by two episodes, "Hades" and "Lestrygonians", in which we can almost trace every single step Bloom takes, our understanding of his exact whereabouts in "Aeolus" is strangely blurred. History is – no doubt – to blame: to be more precise, the British incendiary bombs which were dropped on the area surrounding the GPO during the Easter week of 1916. The destruction was dramatic, as the shaded areas in illustration 8.2 (indicating destroyed structures) and the remains of the *Freeman* building show:

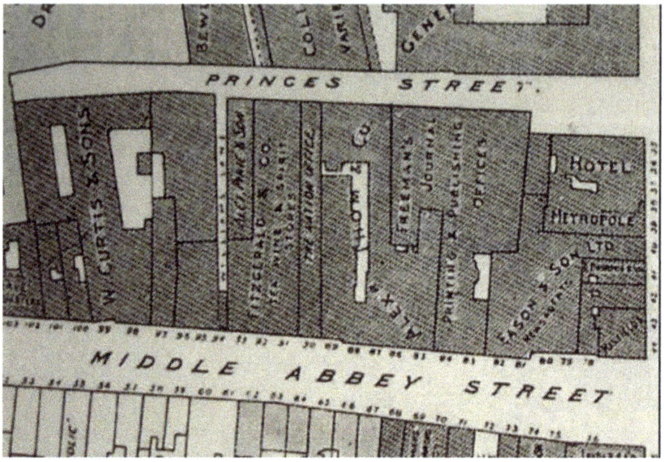

ILLUSTRATION 8.2 *Map indicating destroyed structures (shaded areas) and remains of the* Freeman *building.*
COURTESY OF THE NATIONAL LIBRARY OF IRELAND.

ILLUSTRATION 8.3 *Irish Rebellion, May 1916, ruined* Prince's Stores and *Freeman's Journal.*
COURTESY OF AIDA YARED.

When the "Aeolus" episode was first published in the *Little Review* it began like all the other episodes before (and most after) *in medias res*:

> Grossbooted draymen rolled barrels dullthudding out of Prince's stores and bumped them up on the brewery float. Grossbooted draymen rolled barrels dullthudding out of Prince's stores and bumped them up on the brewery float.
> — There it is, John Murray said. Alexander Keyes.
> — Just cut it out, will you? Mr Bloom said, and I'll take it round to the *Telegraph* office.[1]

The final text of *Ulysses* precedes this scene with a whole new paragraph that introduces the reader to "The Heart of the Hibernian Metropolis".

It starts at Nelson's Pillar on Sackville Street, a likely place for the funeral cabs to drop off their passengers, more specifically, Simon Dedalus, Ned Lambert and Hynes,[2] who seem to have gone straight to the *Evening Telegraph* office, and Bloom, who enters the building at the Prince's Street end. The additional section (*U* 7.1–19) follows the path of a person who, like Bloom for

ILLUSTRATION 8.4
Nelson's Pillar on Sackville Street.[3]

1 *Little Review* 5, no. 6 (October 1918): 26. The second sentence is not yet inverted as in the 1922 first edition.

2 When Bloom meets Hynes and tells him that the cashier is just going to lunch he is obviously coming from the Middle Abbey Street end of the building because we are told: "He hurried on eagerly towards the *Freeman's Journal* office." (*U* 7.118).

3 "Nelson's Pillar Dublin", accessed 6 December 2016, https://commons.wikimedia.org/wiki/File:XXI_OCTOBER_MDCCCV_(8636135413).jpg.

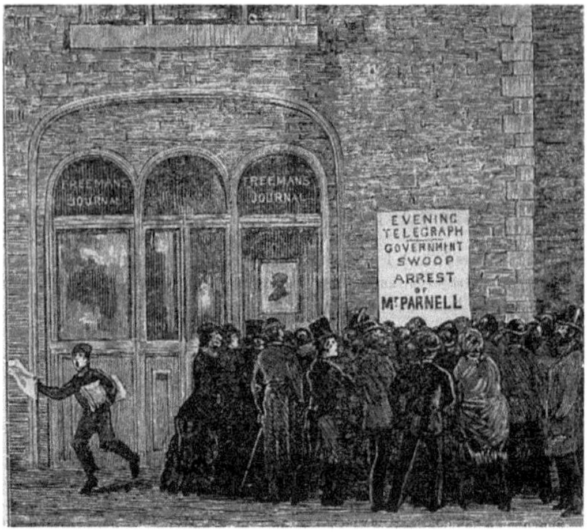

ILLUSTRATION 8.5
Main entrance to the Freeman's *public office, facing Sackville Street.*
ILLUSTRATION (1881) COURTESY OF AIDA YARED.

ILLUSTRATION 8.6
This enlargement from a picture of the Hotel Metropole shows the Prince's Stores and the entrance to the Freeman *office familiar from the drawing above.*
COURTESY OF THE NATIONAL LIBRARY OF IRELAND.

all we know, walks from Nelson's Pillar to the *Freeman* offices. We pass the United Tramway's famous time-keeper, Richard Delany (right behind the tram in the picture above), the General Post Office and turn right into the cul-de-sac of North Prince's Street where the mail cars are parked opposite the *Freeman*'s public office and enter the building through its main entrance facing Sackville Street, not the GPO (see illustration 8.5).

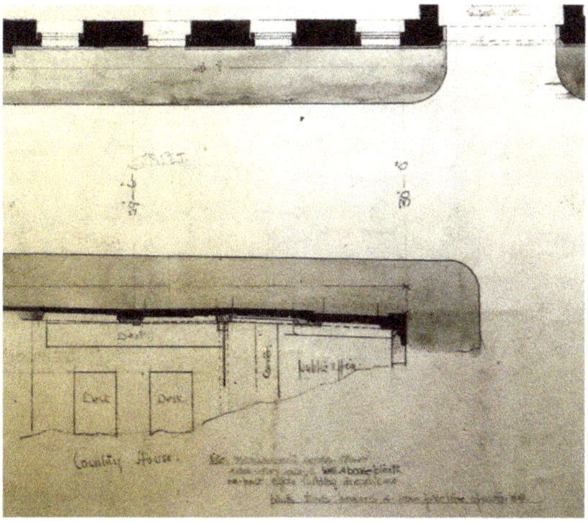

ILLUSTRATION 8.7
A 1910 plan showing the location of the Freeman's *public office where Bloom and Murray discuss Keyes's ad.*
IMAGE COURTESY OF EAMONN FINN.

Before that he passes a then well-known public house, immediately adjacent to the Hotel Metropole and the *Freeman*'s Office, called the Prince's Stores (see illustration 8.6). When it is mentioned in *Ulysses* (*U* 7.21–22), Bloom is obviously looking through the door visible in the picture above at the goings-on in the street in front.

It deserves to be mentioned that Bloom obviously goes straight to the cashier's, Rutledge's, office when he enters the building, so before he talks to Red Murray.[4] A 1910 plan, unearthed by Eamonn Finn, shows the location of the *Freeman's* public office (see illustration 8.7), where Bloom and Murray discuss Keyes's ad, and which Bloom leaves through a counter flap and a sidedoor in accordance with his announcement, "I'll go through the printingworks" (*U* 7.33).

Before he does so the paper's editor William Brayden "enter[s] the dingy archway, and passe[s] on into the dark and dirty interior"[5] behind Bloom, who has to turn round to see him, and walks up a staircase to his first-floor office (*U* 7.42–46).[6]

Thanks to John Smurthwaite an 1893 fire insurance map has come to light that allows us to at least partly reconstruct the destroyed premises and Bloom's progress from the Prince's Street entrance to the Middle Abbey Street end, a

---

4 Bloom's visit is not only to be deduced from his hint to Hynes at *U* 7.111–18, but is confirmed by the entry in Bloom's budget at *U* 17.1459: "Commission recd. *Freeman's Journal*".

5 This description of the building is to be found in Francis P. Jones, *History of the Sinn Fein Movement and the Irish Rebellion of 1916* (New York: P.J. Kenedy, 1917), 322.

6 Compare also with the following description: "Mr. MacSweeny of the *Weekly Freeman* … was a bearded man of polite manners, and he led me up the ramshackle stairs, through printing rooms, to his own private office."; L. MacManus, *White Light and Flame: Memories of the Irish Literary Revival and the Anglo-Irish War* (Dublin: Talbot Press, 1929), 18.

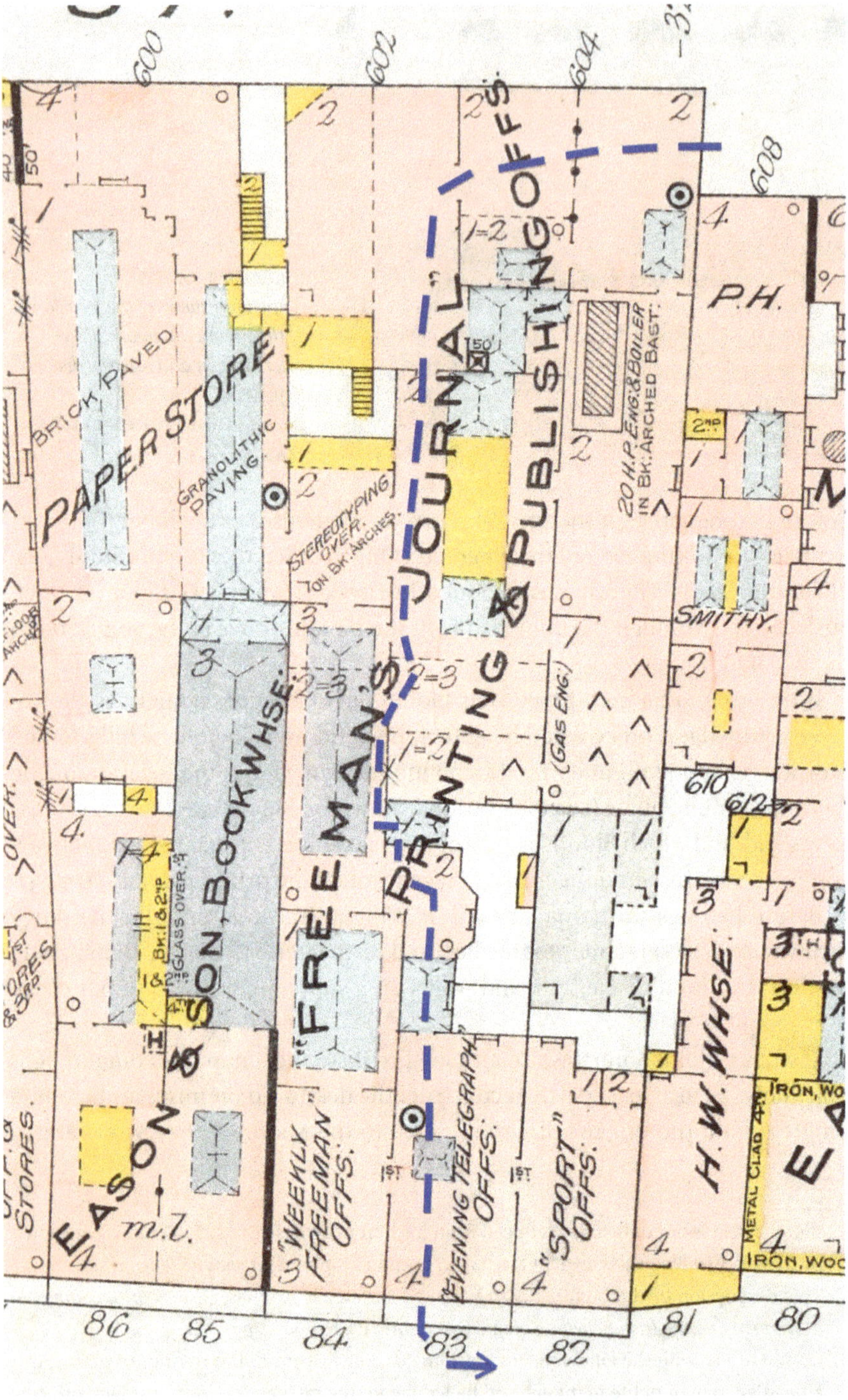

ILLUSTRATION 8.8 *Bloom's possible route (blue arrow) through the buildings from North Prince's Street to Middle Abbey Street (not more than a suggestion).* Insurance Plan of the City of Dublin *(London: Charles E. Goad, 1893), vol. 1, sheet 7.*

MAP COURTESY OF THE BRITISH LIBRARY.

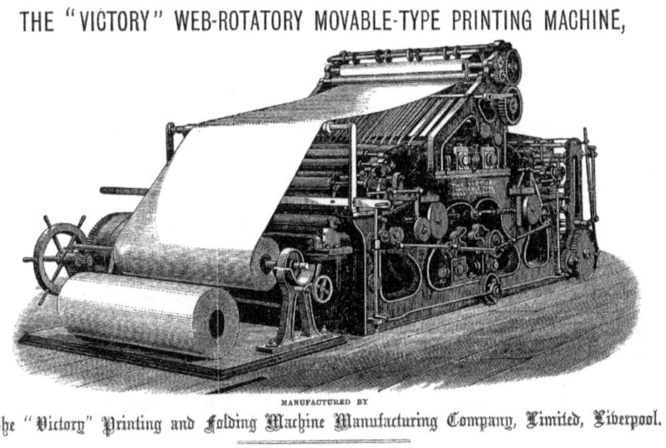

ILLUSTRATION 8.9 *Printing Press "Victory" web newspaper machine, with folding apparatus.*[7]

distance of around 65 metres in a group of buildings bought (and occasionally sold) by the Gray family over the course of decades.

It has to be pointed out here that Joyce's memories of the newspaper offices stem from August and September 1909. But although the Goad map dates from 1893 very little seems to have changed in the newspaper offices and printing works, as reports about the events of 1916 in the building suggest (see footnote 4).

A key to the fire insurance maps can be found here: http://www.bl.uk/onlinegallery/onlineex/firemaps/england/northwest/goadlegendmanchester.html

Walking towards the printing works, Bloom can feel the floorboards vibrating from the printing machines driven by the engines in the area nearby (*U* 7.69–72). The *Freeman's Journal* used the Liverpool-built "Victory" web newspaper machine, with folding apparatus.

His destination is the reading closet of Nannetti, the foreman printer, at the head of the composing-room, as this rare photograph of the interior of the *Freeman's Journal* works discovered by David Pierce suggests (illustration 8.10):[8]

---

7 James Moran, *Printing Presses: History and Development from the Fifteenth Century to Modern Times* (London: Faber, 1973), 200.

8 Pierce is wrong when he suggests that the person seemingly in charge might be Nannetti; *Reading Joyce* (Harlow: Pearson Longman, 2008): 258. Photographs of Nannetti in the National Portrait Gallery show that this is not the case. See: "The National Portrait Gallery", accessed 6 December 2016, http://www.npg.org.uk/collections/search/portraitLarge/mw213482/William-Coffey-Joseph-Patrick-Nannetti. It might, however, be Patrick Mead, the real-life equivalent of Myles Crawford in *Ulysses*.

ILLUSTRATION 8.10 *A view of the composing room at the* Freeman's Journal, *taken between the mid-1890s and 1904.*
COURTESY OF DAVID PIERCE.

This view from above hints at the existence of the gallery mentioned later when Bloom leaves the printing works for the *Evening Telegraph* office (*U* 7.217–18). Sadly a few years later the printing works looked like this:

ILLUSTRATION 8.11 *A view showing the complete destruction of the linotypes.*[9]

Bloom basically stays on the ground floor of the building as the heavy printing and linotype machines and the engines they required were all in that area. Matthias McDonnell Bodkin, who worked for the *Freeman* in the early 1870s, describes in his novel *White Magic* the atmosphere on the upper floors where the editor and the journalists worked:

9 *The Linotype Bulletin* 13 (1916–17): 106.

> They went down a long, narrow, ramshackle passage, with little numbered doors on either side like a shabby hotel. "Leader writers' room", "Special wire", "Editor", were under the numbers .... He stopped at the end of the passage at a door with a battered zinc plate and on it in half-obliterated black letters, "Reporters' room". St. John turned the handle, without knocking, and walked right in.
>
> It looked a particularly dilapidated school-room, given over to the tender mercies of particularly mischievous school-boys. The long desk was knife-scarred and ink-stained, and strewn with pens, pencils, reporting "slips", and newspapers, especially newspapers ... The walls were adorned with what may be called combination cuts. Half-a-dozen illustrations combined to produce a single effect ...[10]

With Nannetti's instructions Bloom proceeds through the caseroom and finally out of the "clanking noises through the gallery on to the landing" (*U* 7.217–18). He must have moved up to that gallery that would have given easy access to the compositors from the reporters' rooms on the first floor as he goes down the house staircase at the Middle Abbey Street end of the building (*U* 7.222) to reach the *Evening Telegraph* editor's office on the ground floor, which is above street level by about three feet. The editor himself resides in an inner office with a telephone, which Bloom wants to use to reach Alexander Keyes. When Bloom is told that he is in town at Dillon's on Bachelor's Walk he leaves the office and crosses the street towards Williams's Row pursued by a "file of capering newsboys"[11] and ridiculed by Lenehan and McHugh on watch from a window looking out on Middle Abbey Street (*U* 7.439–46).

When at Stephen Dedalus's instigation the pressmen eventually leave the *Evening Telegraph* office for a drink at Mooney's across Sackville Street (*U* 7.959–64), Bloom comes back puffing (like Ulysses to the island of "Aeolus") near the *Irish Catholic* and *Dublin Penny Journal* at 90 Middle Abbey Street (see excerpt below from *Thom's Directory* of 1910) by a seemingly roundabout route. The most plausible explanation is a shortcut through the so-called Lotts and a passageway onto Middle Abbey Street, a common manoeuvre in Dublin and one that Bloom has performed earlier, in "Lotus Eaters", when entering St Andrew's Church at the back and leaving it at the front.

---

10 Matthias McDonnell Bodkin, *White Magic: A Novel* (London: Chapman & Hall, 1897), 132.

11 The timing for the newsboys running out into the street at the end of the episode corresponds perfectly with reality as the first edition of the *Evening Telegraph* was published at 1 o'clock p.m.

ILLUSTRATION 8.12 *Bloom's destination is on the quays at J. Dillon, auctioneer, 25 Bachelor's Walk, the seventh house from the right.*
COURTESY OF THE NATIONAL LIBRARY OF IRELAND.

ILLUSTRATION 8.13 *83 Middle Abbey Street from Sackville Street.*
COURTESY OF THE NATIONAL LIBRARY OF IRELAND. THE NUMBERS HAVE BEEN ADDED FOR THIS ESSAY AND REFER TO ADDRESSES CORRESPONDING TO THE MAP OF MIDDLE ABBEY STREET REPRODUCED AT THE OPENING OF THIS ESSAY.

Stephen Dedalus, Professor McHugh, Lenehan and the other gentlemen of the press cross Sackville Street at John Gray's[12] pavement island (*U* 7.1067) and

12 John Gray (1815–1875) was a one-time owner of *The Freeman's Journal.* As Joyce chose the newspaper office as the equivalent of the palace of "Aeolus", the word "island" has the true ring of Homeric rightness.

..*here Sackville-street, Lower, intersects*.
78 Egan, John J., wine and spirit merchant, *The Oval*, also at 81 and 82 Talbot-street, 70*l*.
79 & 80 Eason & Son (limited), wholesale newsagents, &c. head office —managing director, Charles Eason, M.A., J.P.—res. Harvieston, Cunningham-road, Dalkey, 170*l*.
81 & 82 Eason & Son (limited), wholesale booksellers, stationers, and newsagents, 320*l*.
83 *Evening Telegraph, Freeman's Journal* art department, 63*l*.
84 *Sporting News*, 36*l*.
" *Weekly Freeman and Irish Agriculturist*—editor's office (first floor); *Fireside Club* (first floor); *Sport* office (ground floor); Art Department (ground floor), 36*l*.
" *Freeman's Journal* (limited), and at 211, Strand, London, and 95, Rathmines-road

ILLUSTRATION 8.14 *Excerpt from* Thom's Dublin Directory (*1910*)*: 1461, third column.*

move on to Mooney's public house just at the corner at 1 Lower Abbey Street (see illustration 8.15). Bloom, who has been left slightly flabbergasted by the rude Crawford (*U* 7.993–94), eventually turns into Sackville Street after them, as we find him in front of Graham Lemon, confectioners, at 49 Sackville Street when the next episode opens (*U* 8.6).

What seems to be a location seen "like all through a mist", to use Molly Bloom's words (*U* 18.636–37), at a first reading turns out to be a near-documentary fictional resurrection of a reality Joyce knew was irretrievably destroyed.

ILLUSTRATION 8.15 *Statue of John Gray in the middle of Sackville Street. Mooney's is on Lower Abbey Street to the right.* COURTESY OF THE NATIONAL LIBRARY OF IRELAND.

Bloom, Mr Dedalus and Stephen have made their entrances into and exits from this windy memorial palace of the press, but real and mythological father and son are only "almosting" a meeting. Only at the end of the day will Stephen and Bloom finally sit down together in the Maternity Hospital, the cabman's shelter and 7 Eccles Street.

Acknowledgements

I am grateful to Eamonn Finn (Dublin), Ian Gunn (Edinburgh), John Simpson (Cheltenham) and John Smurthwaite (Leeds) for their help with this attempt at literary archaeology.

CHAPTER 9

"Aeolus", Interrupted: Heady Headlines and Joycean Negotiations of Closure

Tamara Radak

Abstract

The continuous narrative in "Aeolus", presented in a linear fashion, is soon discontinued and constantly interrupted by the very means that purports to shape it, that is, the form of the newspaper. In this episode, interruptions and disturbances abound both in terms of form and of content. With its experimental layout and its thematising of two opposing drives, unstoppable forward movement and haphazard interruptions, I argue that "Aeolus" can be seen as a synecdoche for the tension between teleological and anti-teleological (or closural and anti-closural) processes and strategies present in *Ulysses* as a whole. On the one hand, the text introduces formal elements that give it structure and drive it forward, while at the same time enabling it to draw attention to itself as artefact, thus giving it a self-reflexive quality that makes the readers pause in their suspension of disbelief, implicitly exposing the artificial nature of structural ordering principles of narrative, such as beginnings, middles and ends. On the other hand, however, it is precisely the repetitive and circular aspect of this self-reflexivity which serves an opposing end in providing instances of the text intruding upon itself and disturbing its own linear progress. Joyce's texts constantly negotiate form, essentially rejecting closure and propagating openness. In "Aeolus", as in *Ulysses* as a whole, attempts at superimposing a definite and ultimately reductive form onto the exuberance of life fail.

Keywords

"Aeolus" – *Ulysses* – narrative – narrative closure – structure – teleology – linearity – interruption – self-reflexivity – technology

In this essay, I will investigate the interconnection between the idea of interruption, which occurs both in terms of form and of content in "Aeolus", and the complex negotiation and questioning of closure that *Ulysses* as a whole

 | DOI 10.1163/9789004359062_011

undertakes. In many ways, "Aeolus" serves as a node between earlier, linearly told chapters with relatively straightforward narratives and the radical experimentalism of later chapters, which it prefigures.[1] Taking my cue from Barbara Herrnstein Smith, who acknowledges the protean and process-like quality of closure by suggesting that "closure is a relative matter"[2] and that "allusions to closure may appear at points in a poem"[3] other than their final lines, I argue that "Aeolus" serves as a synecdoche for the anti-closural strategies and processes displayed in *Ulysses* as a whole.[4] The inclusion of often only distantly related headlines at seemingly random points in the continuous narrative could furthermore be seen as an allusion to the Homeric origin of the episode, in which Odysseus's shipmates let loose the sack of winds given to them by Aeolus, which blows them off track. Indeed, the headlines in "Aeolus" mimic scattered parts of a once potentially coherent newspaper that may well have been blown to pieces. In this, they metaphorically embody a typically modernist "tension between unity and fragmentation".[5] In the present context of interruption and closure, it is particularly noteworthy that the crew is headed for but fails to reach Ithaca, the place of Odysseus's eventual return, finding themselves continuously side-tracked on their way home. As Joyce famously proclaimed, in his own refashioning of the *Odyssey* "Ithaca" is "in reality the

1 Karen R. Lawrence notes that "Aeolus" "offers a departure from the 'novel' of the first six chapters and an adumbration of the experimentation in the subsequent chapters. It seems that Joyce *deliberately* altered the chapter [from the linear narrative which appeared in the *Little Review*] to make it predict the antics of the later chapters and to give the reader early notice that the form of the novel was becoming obsolete" ("'Aeolus': Interruption and Inventory", *James Joyce Quarterly* 17, no. 4 (1980): 390, emphasis mine). While the seemingly random and arbitrary headlines and headings have been commented upon by Lawrence, her approach only touches on the issue of closure, focussing on structuralist and post-structuralist theories of continuity and narrative rather than engaging with studies of narrative closure, such as Barbara Herrnstein Smith's *Poetic Closure* (1968), on which my own essay will draw.

2 Barbara Herrnstein Smith, *Poetic Closure: A Study of How Poems End* (Chicago: University of Chicago Press, 1968), 211.

3 Smith, *Poetic Closure*, 178.

4 In my forthcoming monograph, *No(n)Sense of an Ending? Modernist Aporias of Closure*, I investigate the complex relationship between modernist fiction and its "anti-closural" (Smith, *Poetic Closure*, 6) textual strategies in greater detail, arguing that questions of closure are not only negotiated in the final sections of these texts but form a recurring motif on different narrative levels.

5 Sean Latham and Gayle Rogers, *Modernism: Evolution of an Idea*, New Modernisms (London: Bloomsbury, 2015), 5.

end" (*Letters I* 172). "Aeolus" is thus connected to the text's questioning of closure on a conceptual level as well.

The study of narrative closure, spearheaded by scholars such as Frank Kermode, Barbara Herrnstein Smith, Marianna Torgovnick and Rachel Blau DuPlessis,[6] is an arena of occasionally conflicting sets of definitions and terminologies.[7] The most immediately relevant approach for the present context is Smith's *Poetic Closure*. This seminal contribution to the field, although it investigates closure in poems, proves valuable for a discussion of narrative prose, too. Smith defines closure as follows:

> Closure occurs when the concluding portion of a poem creates in the reader a sense of appropriate cessation. It announces and justifies the absence of further development; it reinforces the feeling of finality, completion, and composure which we value in all works of art; and it gives ultimate unity and coherence to the reader's experience of the poem by providing a point from which all the preceding elements may be viewed comprehensively and their relations grasped as part of a significant design.[8]

Smith's approach builds on Aristotle's contention that "well-constructed plots must neither begin nor end in a haphazard way, but must conform to the pattern [he has] been describing", i.e. create a "whole [...], which has a beginning, a middle, and an end".[9] The idea of "ultimate unity and coherence" in the reader's experience is challenged throughout *Ulysses*, but "Aeolus" is the first chapter in which disturbances to the coherence of "well-constructed plots" manifest themselves *visually*. In "Aeolus" (as in *Ulysses* as a whole), "haphazard" interruptions abound, parodying the notion of "finality, completion, and composure" and foregrounding the chaos and contingency of human life, or

6 See Frank Kermode, *The Sense of an Ending: Studies in the Theory of Fiction* (Oxford: Oxford University Press, 1967; reprint 2000); Smith, *Poetic Closure*; Marianna Torgovnick, *Closure in the Novel* (Princeton: Princeton University Press, 1981) and Rachel Blau DuPlessis, *Writing Beyond the Ending: Narrative Strategies of Twentieth-Century Women Writers* (Bloomington: Indiana University Press, 1985).

7 In the first chapter of *Ending in Progress: Final Sections in James Joyce's Prose Fictions* (Utrecht: Universiteit Utrecht, 1999), 2–14, Onno Kosters comments on some of the problematic aspects and imprecisions inherent in previous approaches to the topic of closure in literature.

8 Smith, *Poetic Closure*, 36.

9 Aristotle, "On the Art of Poetry", *Aristotle/Horace/Longinus: Classical Literary Criticism*, ed. T.S. Dorsch (Harmondsworth: Penguin Books, 1965), 41.

"messy reality".[10] In its challenging of conventional novelistic forms, the "Aeolus" chapter of *Ulysses* not only metaphorically exemplifies but truly embodies the larger modernist quest for new modes of expressing human experience, for which clear-cut, uncontested, inflexible ideas such as those of beginnings, middles and ends proved unsatisfactory.

From a formal point of view, the introduction of headlines[11] in "Aeolus" marks the beginning of a break with linear narrative, which becomes even more pronounced in later episodes.[12] The provocation to traditional novelistic style put forth in "Aeolus" goes further than the odd experimental stylistic outbreak in previous episodes in that "the disturbance created by the headings is stylistic and tonal, *as well as visual*".[13] While previous episodes (notably "Proteus") make – occasionally extensive – use of interior monologue or include other unusual stylistic elements (such as the onomatopoetic rendering of "Mrkgnao" [*U* 4.25]), "Aeolus" introduces graphic markers which divide the text into separate units of discourse.[14] This "overt intrusion and conspicuous

10 Fritz Senn, "Transmedial Stereotypes in the 'Aeolus' Chapter of Joyce's *Ulysses*", in *Word and Image Interactions: A Selection of Papers Given at the Second International Conference on Word and Image, Universität Zürich, August 27–31, 1990*, ed. Martin Heusser (Basel: Wiese Verlag), 67.

11 As Terence Killeen noted at the Zurich James Joyce Foundation Workshop in August 2013, the choice of vocabulary for this type of graphic intrusion is difficult, as the entries would technically be called "subheads" in journalistic terms. This would, however, imply the preexistence of clearly marked headlines, which would precede the subheads in question spatially (and thus hierarchically). To avoid confusion, I will refer to these graphic markers by the broader and more inclusive term "headlines" henceforth. See also Cheryl Herr's comment that "some readers have questioned whether Joyce's capitalized lines are actually headlines. Whether these phrases are viewed as headlines, subheads, or captions is not necessarily important to understanding 'Aeolus'"; "Irish Censorship and 'The Pleasure of the Text': The 'Aeolus' Episode of Joyce's *Ulysses*", *Irish Renaissance Annual* 3 (1982): 160.

12 See e.g. David Mikics's claim that "Joyce's use of newspaper headlines before each brief section marks it as *Ulysses*' first radical departure from realist convention"; "History and the Rhetoric of the Artist in 'Aeolus'", *James Joyce Quarterly* 27, no. 3 (1990): 535; and also Archie K. Loss's statement that the subheads "interrupt an otherwise sequential account ... of a particular period of time"; "Joyce's Use Of Collage In 'Aeolus'", *Journal of Modern Literature* 9, no. 2 (1982): 175. Or note Eric Smith's suggestion that the "bold typographic variation disrupt[s] the continuity of the normal reading process"; "How a Great Daily Organ Is Turned Out: 'Aeolus,' *Techne*, and the Recording of *Ulysses*", *James Joyce Quarterly* 41, no. 3 (2004): 460.

13 Lawrence, "'Aeolus': Interruption and Inventory", 392 (emphasis mine).

14 Fritz Senn also highlights the importance of the subheads as a graphic element, suggesting that they present a contrast to "the relative paucity of graphic material" usually found in newspapers of that time; Senn, "Transmedial Stereotypes", 62. For a genetic exploration

labelling"[15] clearly sets the headlines apart from the continuous text underneath, challenging readers' assumptions about genre and calling into question their expectations of "well-constructed plots".

The continuous narrative placed under the headlines in "Aeolus" is, however, of an essentially sequential and linear nature. Far from the disparate and disjointed snapshots of Dublin life in "Wandering Rocks", this chapter seemingly attempts to convey an ordered, straightforward story. Such an undertaking is, however, made to fail through the intrusive nature of the headlines. Although the headlines formally act as an ordering principle, they in fact interrupt the text's continuity and its narrative development at seemingly random intervals and do not appear to obey a logical pattern. Not only do these interruptions become more intrusive in the course of the episode; the continuous narrative is also punctuated by multiple disturbances in the form of interrupted conversations, "*Missed Understandings*" (FW 175.27) caused by the "hell of a racket" (*U* 7.128) produced by the printing machinery[16] and newspaper boys storming into offices.[17] As the intrusions within the continuous text gain a momentum of their own, the headlines also become more intrusive and more obscure as the episode progresses, until they take up almost the same amount of space as the continuous text.[18] In this regard, it is particularly noteworthy that Joyce not only added headlines and rhetorical devices during the revision phase,[19] but also introduced additional interferences and signs of difficulties

of this topic, see Eli Z. Lassman, "'Scribbled Words': The Usage of the *Ulysses* Notebooks in 'Proteus' and 'Aeolus'", *James Joyce Quarterly* 45, no. 2 (2008): 301–22.

15 Senn, "Transmedial Stereotypes", 62.

16 The noise subsides considerably once the characters reach the editorial office. However, communication is then impeded as a result of other events.

17 Concrete examples of unsuccessful, or interrupted, quests include Bloom's (putative) failure to place an ad, Lenehan's attempt to tell a riddle, and Stephen's (in)famous "*Parable of The Plums*" (*U* 7.1057–58). Stephen's telling of the latter almost mimics a publication in instalments, with the headlines dividing the story into individual segments and other characters (i.e. the audience) intruding upon his storytelling and even urging him to invent a pompous title for an essentially mundane story.

18 See in particular the last few sections (*U* 7.1006–1075).

19 See *JJA* 23:3–84. See also Hsin-Yu Hung's claim that the 1922 "Aeolus" "became radically 'visual' and 'spatial', immediately recognizable by its showy journalistic headlines" as a result of being subjected to "considerable modification"; Hsin-Yu Hung, "Avant-Garde Metamorphoses: Newspaper Typography and Joyce's Rewriting of 'Aeolus'", in *James Joyce, Metamorphosis and Re-Writing*, ed. Franca Ruggieri, Joyce Studies in Italy 11 (Rome: Bulzoni, 2010), 78.

in communication (e.g. "He doesn't hear it", *U* 7.128) into the continuous text during the revision process.[20]

The most persistent cause of these interruptions is the printing machinery, which in turn forms part of a motif in *Ulysses* as a whole that relates to technology as a potential source of disturbance both in a concrete and in a metaphorical sense. From the very first pages, it becomes clear that "machines dominate the scene with their incessant noise"[21] in "Aeolus". The opening passage of the chapter gives a vivid account of the fast-paced "HEART OF THE HIBERNIAN METROPOLIS" (*U* 7.1–2):

> Before Nelson's pillar trams slowed, shunted, changed trolley started for Blackrock, Kingstown and Dalkey, Clonskea, Rathgar and Terenure, Palmerston Park and upper Rathmines, Sandymount Green, Rathmines, Ringsend and Sandymount Tower, Harold's Cross. The hoarse Dublin United Tramway Company's timekeeper bawled them off:
> — Rathgar and Terenure!
> — Come on, Sandymount Green!
> Right and left parallel clanging ringing a doubledecker and a singledeck moved from their railheads, swerved to the down line, glided parallel.
> *U* 7.3–12

The "shocks of everyday industrial modernity"[22] and the mercilessly fast rhythm of modernised Dublin life are compellingly illustrated by the quick succession of verbs ("shunted", "changed", "started", "swerved") and place names. These acts of "dynamic verbalism"[23] in combination with accumulative references to public transportation ("trams", "trolley", "doubledecker", "singledeck", etc.) and the onomatopoetic description of the trams' movement as "clanging" and

20 One particularly interesting example of a later addition that introduces a sense of ambiguity with regard to the "saviour's" identity as well as an additional disturbance is the scene in which the telephone rings. In the *Little Review* instalment, the text read: " – His grace phoned down twice this morning, Red Murray said gravely … Mr Bloom said slowly: – Well, he is one of our saviours also" (*Little Review* 5, no. 6 [October 1918], 27). Then an addition was made and the text now reads: "– His grace phoned down twice this morning, Red Murray said gravely … A telegram boy stepped in nimbly, threw an envelope on the counter and stepped off posthaste with a word: – *Freeman!* Mr Bloom said slowly: – Well, he is one of our saviours also" (*U* 7.62–68).

21 Herr, "Irish Censorship", 165.

22 Nicholas Daly, *Literature, Technology, and Modernity, 1860–2000* (Cambridge: Cambridge University Press, 2004), 15.

23 Hung, "Metamorphoses", 82.

"ringing"[24] further contribute to a crowded, busy and noisy atmosphere. The scene seems to be buzzing with technological progress and evokes the image of "SPEEDPILLS VELOCITOUS" (*U* 7.1022).[25]

The unstoppable onward drive of the printing press and the threat of technology overpowering its creator are topics frequently employed in this episode and they provide a fertile ground for Bloom's musings:

> The machines clanked in threefour time. Thump, thump, thump. Now if he got paralysed there and no-one knew how to stop them they'd clank on and on the same, print it over and over and up and back. Monkeydoodle the whole thing.
>
> *U* 7.101–04

In Bloom's mind, the rhythm of the printing press imitates a musical piece, or *danse macabre,* "in threefour time".[26] Evoking the image of a waltz, this reference introduces a positive, light-hearted circular movement and stands in contrast to the negative evaluation of mechanical movement in the rest of the episode. However, Bloom reverts to the aspect of oppressive, Sisyphean circularity in the very same train of thoughts, as he considers the possibility of the printer's becoming "paralysed". The impossibility of the machinery coming to a standstill ("they'd clank on and on the same, print it over and over and up and back") is juxtaposed with the imagined paralysis of the human printer in Bloom's mind. The printer is not only overwhelmed and "paralysed" by the force of the machines; he is equally unable to master them once they start "clanking on" and stop their repetitive and aimless movement ("on and on the same"). Although the printing press was built to serve a pre-defined purpose

24 The lack of punctuation (notably between "clanging" and "ringing"), which would provide a stronger sense of internal structure to the paragraph, creates the effect of disordered, quickly succeeding impressions enumerated in a random order rather than a linearly progressing narrative, evoking the form of an impressionist or futurist poem.

25 See also David Spurr's observation that "Joyce arranges the names of the destinations according to poetic metre, beginning with a series of trimeter trochees, … followed by a series of choriambs" as a way of "herald[ing] the new monumentality of the urban system" and "celebrat[ing] [a] new form of heroism" ("The Machine Aesthetic in Joyce and *De Stijl*", in *A LONG THE KROMMERUN, Selected Papers from the Utrecht James Joyce Symposium*, eds. Onno Kosters, Tim Conley and Peter de Voogd, European Joyce Studies 24 (Leiden: Brill Rodopi, 2016), 13.).

26 Spurr also acknowledges the musical implications of "threefour time", considering the machines' movement as an anticipation of Fernand Léger's *Ballet mécanique* (1923–24) ("Joyce and *De Stijl*", 14).

and its movement is directed towards a goal, or *telos* (the actual release of the next issue), in assuming a life of its own, the machinery becomes unproductive (by economic standards) as a result of its compulsively repetitive movement. In Bloom's imagination, the machinery indeed "speaks in its own way" (*U* 7.177): the formerly "obedient" machines manage to break free from human control and develop a language of their own. As this kind of language is, however, not intelligible to humans, they are essentially faced with the same failure to communicate as the characters in this episode. Paradoxically, then, technological progress deteriorates into paralysis, since the printing press does not produce any meaningful discourse (by standard measures), but a large amount of randomly generated "Monkeydoodle"[27] of questionable content and textual affiliation. From Bloom's (always somewhat practical) point of view, this essentially failed end product acts as a testimonial to the destructive power of unsupervised technology.

The human fear relating to the possibility of machines getting "out of hand" (*U* 7.82), reminiscent of horror visions from Goethe's "Der Zauberlehrling" (1797)[28] or Mary Shelley's *Frankenstein* (1818), constitutes a central image in "Aeolus":

> Machines. Smash a man to atoms if they got him caught. Rule the world today. [Dignam's] machineries are pegging away too. Like these, got *out of hand*: fermenting. Working away, tearing away. And that old grey rat tearing to get in.
>
> *U* 7.80–83, emphasis mine

Bloom's imaginary parallelisation of machines with the human body explores the topic of the inescapable teleological drive of life and death as its ultimate *telos*. It is debatable to which extent the dominance of machines in this chapter is "*countered* by Bloom's tendency to humanize the mechanical processes he witnesses",[29] or in which respect "Aeolus" displays a "utopian view

27 The term "Monkeydoodle" itself is remarkable as it can be regarded as a nonsense word and thus, in this case, "does, in appearance, what it is about" (Senn, "Transmedial Stereotypes", 61), but also evokes the idea of "aping" human discourse, which is, in a sense, one of the functions of newspapers. As Fritz Senn also pointed out (private conversation, August 2013), doodling is the opposite of goal-oriented writing.

28 Spurr similarly reads "the immense power of the machine" and "its potentially uncontrollable operation in time" as "a modern version of the enchanted brooms" in Goethe's text ("Joyce and *De Stijl*", 14).

29 Herr, "Irish Censorship", 165 (emphasis mine).

of technology", as both Herr and Kiberd suggest.[30] Rather, Bloom's "tendency to humanize the mechanical process" and, vice versa, to ascribe mechanical features to the human body,[31] serves as a typical example of Joyce's tactic of reducing complex abstract concepts and issues to tangible and thus more easily accessible subject matters by mediating them through the mind of Bloom as the archetypal Everyman (as opposed to Stephen's highly complex abstract musings on time and art).[32]

Bloom's ambivalent attitude towards machines in "Aeolus" is embedded within a complex web of allusions in the intricate intratextual fabric of *Ulysses*, testifying to the fact that machines function as forces of disruption throughout the text: in "Lotus Eaters", "a heavy tramcar honking its gong" (*U* 5.131) prevents Bloom from taking a closer look at a "proud: rich" woman across the street in "silk stockings" (*U* 5.122). This missed opportunity, an inverted "Pisgah Sight" (*U* 7.1057) and interrupted act of voyeurism, is taken as a personal insult by Bloom:

> Lost it. Curse your noisy pugnose. Feels locked out of it. Paradise and the peri. Always happening like that. The very moment. .... The tram passed. They drove off towards the Loop Line bridge, her rich gloved hand on the steel grip. Flicker, flicker: the laceflare of her hat in the sun: flicker, flick.
> *U* 5.132–40

The "heavy tram" is juxtaposed with the elegant and light, but also mocking "flicker" of the woman's hat lace. This short section is quite revealing in that it incorporates a number of motifs which are taken up at several points in *Ulysses* (e.g. missed opportunities, voyeurism and the power of contingency). One such recurring motif is that of Bloom's bodily desires and drives, which he is seldom

30 Kiberd, *Irish Classics*, 468.

31 See in particular his parallelisation of Dignam's body as (faulty) "machiner[y]" in this chapter (*U* 7.82) and the heart as an "old, rusty pump" in "Hades" (*U* 6.676): "Broken heart. A pump after all, pumping thousands of gallons of blood every day. One fine day it gets bunged up: and there you are" (*U* 6.673–75). It is moreover noteworthy that Joyce himself, by assigning particular organs to episodes, also in a way ascribes bodily attributes to his text, thus figuratively making the word flesh.

32 Poignant examples of this phenomenon are malfunctioning watches: "Gerty could see him taking out his watch, listening to it and looking up and clearing his throat and he said he was very sorry his watch was stopped" (*U* 13.545–47), "I never know the time even that watch he gave me never seems to go properly" (*U* 18.344–45). These mundane everyday objects reflect the novel's highly complex layering of time and its eventual transgression in "Penelope" on a mundane level.

able to satisfy. The tram obstructing Bloom's view and the woman's vehicle (which eventually drives away) function as embodiments of modernity, which he dismisses as "noisy pugnose" at this point.[33] While in this case, Bloom's reaction is based on personal resentment and the feeling of being "locked out of ... Paradise", his considerations in "Aeolus" revolve around broader issues of the increasing technologisation of everyday life and the consequences of the inexorable drive of modernity. Both passages, however, share the idea that technology, even when originally designed to serve human (inter)action, is often also directly responsible for interrupting it.

In "Aeolus", the printing press as an ever-moving, unstoppable force serves as a source of disruption on various levels. Apart from obstructing human communication, as indicated in the aforementioned examples, this particular machine is also responsible for disruptions on a different level that relates to the reading process of the text. The passages dealing with the physical creation of the newspaper make this most evident. References relating to the physical production of the paper occur on several occasions, for example when the "obedient reels feeding in huge webs of paper" are mentioned and the characteristic sound of clanking is heard: "Clank it. Clank it" (*U* 7.136), and thereby introduce a self-referential element into the text. Similarly, the telling headline "ORTHOGRAPHICAL" (*U* 7.164) features an account of the act of typesetting, highlighting the editor's "proof fever" and his fear of typographical errors, as seen through Bloom's eyes:

> Want to be sure of his spelling. Proof fever ... It is amusing to view the unpar one ar alleled embarra two ars is it? double ess ment of a harassed pedlar while gauging au the symmetry with a y of a peeled pear under a cemetery wall.
>
> *U* 7.165–69

Bloom's thoughts, although they are not printed in the newspaper text by the machines, are part of the novel's text and cause a noteworthy disturbance in the reading process. Onomatopoetic interjections, too, become more intrusive in the course of the episode as the machines begin to "call attention"[34] to themselves and cause grammatical misconstructions in the reading:

33 It does not become clear to whom or what Bloom addresses this insult. Considering that instances of synaesthesia are probably not an altogether uncommon phenomenon in free-flowing thought, the insult can most likely be read as a combination of an aural and a visual stimulus (noisy tram/pug-nosed driver).

34 This quotation is taken up at a later point in Bloom's conversation with Myles Crawford: "But he wants a par to call attention in the *Telegraph* too, the Saturday pink" (*U* 7.973–74).

> Sllt. The nethermost deck of the first machine jogged forward its flyboard with sllt the first batch of quirefolded papers. Sllt. Almost human the way it sllt to call attention. Doing its level best to speak. That door too sllt creaking, asking to be shut. Everything speaks in its own way. Sllt.
>
> *U* 7.174–77

By disrupting the linear, teleologically oriented progression of the text, the accumulation of intrusions and deliberately caused misreadings in this passage undermine the basic function of a newspaper: presenting information in a straightforward, objective and unambiguous way.[35] The disturbance in the reading process gives the readers pause, jolting them out of their willing suspension of disbelief and indeed making them see the "machinery" behind the material text they are reading. Such self-reflexive interruptions in the textual flow question the very concept of "ultimate unity and coherence" which Smith considers central "to the reader's experience"[36] of closure. By inviting the reader to look behind the scenes, the self-reflexive passages in "Aeolus" expose any ordering principle of narrative, such as the idea of clear-cut beginnings, middles and ends, as artificial constructs.

The inexorable onward drive of the printing press, which refuses to come to a standstill, and the structural markers of the headlines, which purportedly impose an order onto the narrative, can be seen as exemplifications of the struggle between "messy reality" and literary form. Joyce demonstrates how such structural scaffoldings fail at keeping the exuberance of life in check; he demonstrates the inadequacy of traditional novelistic principles of order by, for example, undermining them through the insertion of headlines, thus holding them up to ridicule. In the case of "Aeolus", these ordering principles in fact interrupt the text, thus taking away from a sense of coherence and order rather than contributing to it. The attempts at breaking free from the confines of the printed page and the fixed nature of the written word undertaken in "Aeolus" form part of a larger project within the text as a whole. The text's resistance to linear, univocal narrative and its attempts at escaping the necessity of a fixed form can be traced from the opening chapters (most notably "Proteus") throughout *Ulysses*. Although the final triumph of (carefully planned) chaos over order is only achieved in Molly's overflowing discourse in "Penelope", the text does "get out of hand" on several other occasions.

---

35 Ironically, the faulty typeset occasionally breaking through in "Aeolus" seems to anticipate the cumbersome printing process of *Ulysses* itself, which necessitated Sylvia Beach to produce a preamble to the first edition, asking "the reader's indulgence for typographical errors unavoidable in the exceptional circumstances".

36 Smith, *Poetic Closure*, 36.

Both "Aeolus" and *Ulysses* as a whole question the very concept of closure by constantly renegotiating and subverting seemingly fixed boundaries of the novel by means of experimental techniques and a narrative which not only "seems to have lost the ability to know where to stop", as Lawrence suggests, but also, in the case of the machines in "Aeolus", compulsively reiterates "the same again" and deliberately refuses to stop. By refusing to "cut it out" (*U* 7.26),[37] i.e. to stop intruding and disrupting the teleology of its own narrative, "Aeolus" not only demonstrates but in fact embodies the dialogism and essential "unfinalizability"[38] of Joycean texts. Its many interruptions on the surface as well as the metaphorical level draw attention to the haphazard nature of disturbances in everyday life, but also self-reflexively comment on the problems of "reduc[ing] reality into a linguistic equivalent"[39] or, in Georg Simmel's words, of imposing form on life, which is "always in latent opposition to the form".[40] "Aeolus" foregrounds intrusions, "missed understandings" and "Pisgah sights", interrupting the flow of the narrative on a number of levels. It features attempts to impose form which, eventually, become counter productive, as the technique used threatens to get out of hand itself, paradoxically both impeding progress and deferring closure. Later episodes, such as "Cyclops" or "Ithaca", dwell on the limits of representation, questioning the very concept of ultimate closure in literary texts. Finally, the complex web of references in *Ulysses* contributes to the idea that the reading process of this text must always remain a provisional, circular, unfinished, "unfinalizable" and never-ending work in progress, since the multivalence of its allusions alone precludes the very idea of a singular, or indeed "final", meaning.

37 Ironically, this ambivalent imperative containing the idea of stopping an ongoing action is the very first utterance by Bloom in "Aeolus" and thus stands at the beginning of the chapter.

38 Although Bakhtin applies this concept in connection with the impossibility of accurately representing the human psyche in a linear, monologic fashion in novels, he eventually extends "the rigorous unfinalizability and dialogic openness" of discourse to the whole of "Dostoevsky's artistic world"; *Problems of Dostoevsky's Poetics*, trans. Caryl Emerson (Manchester: Manchester University Press, 1984), 272. The term seems particularly fitting in the present context, since Joyce's text leaves so many Iserian gaps, some of which can only be understood retrospectively (or not at all), and constantly negotiates the boundaries of closure and openness, whole and fragment, that any attempt at making sense of this multifaceted narrative always appears provisional. The text, thus, while "finished" in the formal sense, always remains "unfinalizable" in terms of meaning-making.

39 Lawrence, "Interruption and Inventory", 401.

40 Georg Simmel, "The Conflict in Modern Culture", repr. in *The Conflict in Modern Culture and Other Essays*, trans. K. Peter Etzkorn (New York: Teachers College Press, 1968), 12.

Acknowledgements

Ideas for this paper were presented at the Zurich James Joyce Foundation Workshop in 2013. Further research for this paper was facilitated by a visiting research scholarship granted by the Friends of the Zurich James Joyce Foundation. I am very grateful to the Foundation's staff, and notably to Fritz Senn, for their unwavering support and their willingness to provide me with access to any material I needed. Some of the ideas in this paper resulted from discussions and conversations with Senn, as well as other Joyceans and members of the reading groups at the Foundation.

CHAPTER 10

The Self-Reflexive Text of "Aeolus"

Sangam MacDuff

Abstract

"Aeolus" brings an intense, self-reflexive scrutiny to processes of textual production, reproduction, circulation, and recirculation. Thematically, this is foregrounded through the setting, printing, distribution and recycling of newspapers; metatextually, Joyce's focus on the materiality of print, notably through orthography and onomatopoeia, emphasizes the processes of linguistic production and dissemination under investigation. From the outset of the episode, this cycle is linked to public transportation and the postal system, reflecting on the structures which put citizens and their missives into circulation. Added to the *Little Review* version of October 1918, these opening sections bring circulation to the fore, and Joyce's other revisions also reflect upon the text through highly wrought rhetoric and the insertion of cross-headings. Both changes revel in revealing and concealing the intricate tapestry of the text, bringing language centre-stage. In retrospect, it has always, and necessarily, occupied this position, but it takes the strikingly self-reflexive text of "Aeolus" to make the self-evident evident. I argue that this self-reflexivity is the real focus of the episode, underscored by Joyce's ironic return to the biblical origins of speech and writing.

Keywords

"Aeolus" – *Ulysses* – circulation – self-reflexivity – onomatopoeia – boustrophedon

Set in the world of publishing, "Aeolus" reflects on processes of print production, including the production of its own text. The majority of the episode takes place in the offices of the *Freeman's Journal* and the *Evening Telegraph*, whose early evening edition is literally coming off the press even as the "late pink" (*U* 17.325) is being set.[1] The episode is populated with "GENTLEMEN

1 I am grateful for information provided by Terence Killeen, who confirms that what is being printed must be "the very earliest edition of the *Telegraph*", there being "at least two printings of the *Evening Telegraph*, as of all Dublin evening papers, in the course of the day" at the time.

 | DOI 10.1163/9789004359062_012

OF THE PRESS" (*U* 7.20), from William Brayden and Myles Crawford, respective editors of the papers, to Ruttledge, the business manager, Nannetti, the printing foreman, Monks, a union representative, and an unnamed typesetter who is busily at work on Paddy Dignam's funeral notice. Twelve hours later "L. Boom" is nettled by his own misnomer when he reads this account in the cabman's shelter, alongside Deasy's letter on foot and mouth disease, delivered by Stephen, and an account of the Ascot Gold Cup run earlier in the day. Thus, texts produced in "Aeolus" are reproduced in the newspaper Bloom reads in "Eumaeus", where they appear alongside real news items Joyce culled from the *Evening Telegraph* late pink edition of 16 June 1904. In this way, the text of *Ulysses* literally reflects back on itself, offering a tangible example of the self-reflexivity that dominates "Aeolus".

At the same time, this metafiction invites comparisons between the printed form of Joyce's text and the newspapers he partially reproduces. Marshall McLuhan has suggested that "*Ulysses* is, newspaperwise, an abridgement of all space in a brief segment of time",[2] but beyond its ambitions to include everything in a single day, the *ad hoc* arrangement of subject matter in *Ulysses*, whether through the free association of interior monologue or the vagaries of the "Arranger",[3] is not unlike the random assortment of news items, pictures and advertisements in early twentieth century newspapers.[4] Likewise, the

He further explains that the paper which is being printed in "Aeolus" cannot be the same that Bloom later reads in the cabman's shelter. The latter contains an account of the Ascot Gold Cup race (*U* 16.1276–89), which has not yet happened when Bloom is in the newspaper office; and "Eumaeus" refers to "the pink edition extra sporting" (*U* 16.1232) of the paper, the description clearly indicating that this is the latest edition, with all the sporting news. Private correspondence, August 2016.

2 Marshall McLuhan, "Joyce, Mallarmé, and the Press", *Sewanee Review* 62, no. 1 (January-March 1954): 50.

3 David Hayman, *"Ulysses": The Mechanics of Meaning* (Englewood Cliffs: Prentice Hall, 1970), 70.

4 For instance, the first page of the late pink is almost entirely devoted to advertisements, save for brief notices of births, marriages and deaths, and a column of trivia "Gleaned From All Sources"; page two intersperses advertisements, weather, tide times, theatre listings and court proceedings with the sinking of the General Slocum on 15 June (advertised by billboard in "Wandering Rocks" [*U* 10.89–92; cf. *U* 8.1146–47, *U* 10.725–30]), two articles on the upcoming Gordon-Bennett motor race, updates on the Russo-Japanese War, and the "Essence of Everyday's News"; likewise, on page three, the sinking of two Japanese transport ships is followed by the Berlin child murders, the renewal of a lease for the Dublin and Kingstown train line, a farmer attempting to pass counterfeit coins, Parliament news, Gaelic League and love affairs, the day's cricket scores and a report on the Ascot Gold Cup, alongside "The Very Latest" briefings (including the shooting of the Governor of Finland at 11 a.m. Helsinki

hotchpotch of contemporary periodicals is accurately represented in Bloom's list of "Nature notes. Cartoons. Phil Blake's weekly Pat and Bull story. Uncle Toby's page for tiny tots. Country bumpkin's queries. Dear Mr Editor" (*U* 7.94–95), etc., which can also be read self-reflexively, particularly following Bloom's reflection that "it's the ads and side features sell a weekly, not the stale news in the official gazette" (*U* 7.89–90). His point here is borne out by the fact that the front pages of contemporary newspapers like the *Freeman's Journal* and the *Evening Telegraph* were almost entirely given over to advertisements, and it may be significant that the *Little Review* version of "Aeolus" (October 1918) begins with Bloom seeking a renewal for Keyes's advertisement (illustrations 10.1–10.2).[5] Spacehound, or rather "spacetimehound"[6] that he is, Bloom sells advertising space for a set period of time (quantifying reprints), which offers a paradigm for all commercial print production.[7] Thus in the first edition, Joyce foregrounds a self-reflexive focus on the economics of publishing; the revisions he made to the episode extend the self-reflexivity to circulation in general.

Although the revisions Joyce made to the "Aeolus" episode have been well documented,[8] their significance has never been fully explained. First, the headlines, or more accurately, crossheads, which punctuate the 1922 text draw attention to the form of the episode, which is not only set in a newspaper office, but also set in the style of a newspaper.[9] Secondly, two new sections at the beginning of the episode suggest that newspaper production is linked to

---

time, alluded to by J.J. O'Molloy in "Aeolus" [*U* 7.601–02]), further classifieds, and a touching memorial; cf. *U* 16.1232–89. Ian Gunn and Alistair McCleery, eds., *Evening Telegraph: Dublin, Thursday, June 16, 1904* (Edinburgh: Split Pea Press, 1990).

5 "Ulysses", *Little Review* 5, no. 6 (October 1918): 26–51.

6 Frank Budgen, *James Joyce and the Making of "Ulysses", and other Writings* (Oxford: Oxford University Press, 1972), 95.

7 Joyce became adept at selling his own work in similar terms, calculating the value of *Ulysses* according to length: "It is an extremely cheap … edition of the equivalent of 8 English novels of standard size … at the normal selling price today or less …" (*Letters I* 196; cf. also *Letters I* 221); or to time, estimating that it cost him twenty thousand hours of work (*JJII* 510). See Mark Osteen, *The Economy of "Ulysses": Making Both Ends Meet* (Syracuse: Syracuse University Press, 1995), 26–29.

8 See Michael Groden, *"Ulysses" in Progress* (Princeton: Princeton University Press, 1977), 64–114. Sebastian Knowles gives a detailed account of the genesis of the episode, particularly the "Orthographical" section in *The Dublin Helix: The Life of Language in Joyce's "Ulysses"* (Gainesville: University Press of Florida, 2001), 31–37.

9 The most extensive discussion of crossheads is Stephen Donovan's "'SHORT BUT TO THE POINT': Newspaper Typography in 'Aeolus'", *James Joyce Quarterly* 40, no. 3 (Spring 2003): 519–41. On the newspaper form of *Ulysses*, see McLuhan, "Joyce, Mallarmé". Declan Kiberd makes a similar argument in *"Ulysses" and Us: The Art of Everyday Living* (London: Faber and

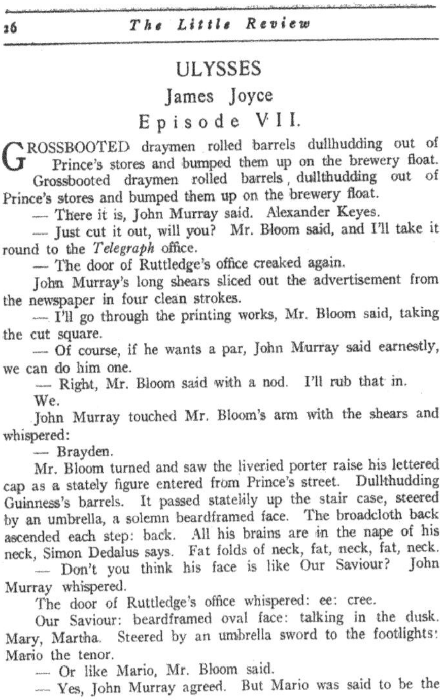

26 *The Little Review*

ULYSSES

James Joyce

Episode VII.

GROSSBOOTED draymen rolled barrels dullhudding out of Prince's stores and bumped them up on the brewery float.

Grossbooted draymen rolled barrels, dullthudding out of Prince's stores and bumped them up on the brewery float.

— There it is, John Murray said. Alexander Keyes.

— Just cut it out, will you? Mr. Bloom said, and I'll take it round to the *Telegraph* office.

— The door of Ruttledge's office creaked again.

John Murray's long shears sliced out the advertisement from the newspaper in four clean strokes.

— I'll go through the printing works, Mr. Bloom said, taking the cut square.

— Of course, if he wants a par, John Murray said earnestly, we can do him one.

— Right, Mr. Bloom said with a nod. I'll rub that in.

We.

John Murray touched Mr. Bloom's arm with the shears and whispered:

— Brayden.

Mr. Bloom turned and saw the liveried porter raise his lettered cap as a stately figure entered from Prince's street. Dullthudding Guinness's barrels. It passed statelily up the stair case, steered by an umbrella, a solemn beardframed face. The broadcloth back ascended each step: back. All his brains are in the nape of his neck, Simon Dedalus says. Fat folds of neck, fat, neck, fat, neck.

— Don't you think his face is like Our Saviour? John Murray whispered.

The door of Ruttledge's office whispered: ee: cree.

Our Saviour: beardframed oval face: talking in the dusk. Mary, Martha. Steered by an umbrella sword to the footlights: Mario the tenor.

— Or like Mario, Mr. Bloom said.

— Yes, John Murray agreed. But Mario was said to be the

ILLUSTRATION 10.1
Opening of "Aeolus" printed in the Little Review *of October 1918.*
COURTESY OF THE MODERNIST JOURNALS PROJECT.

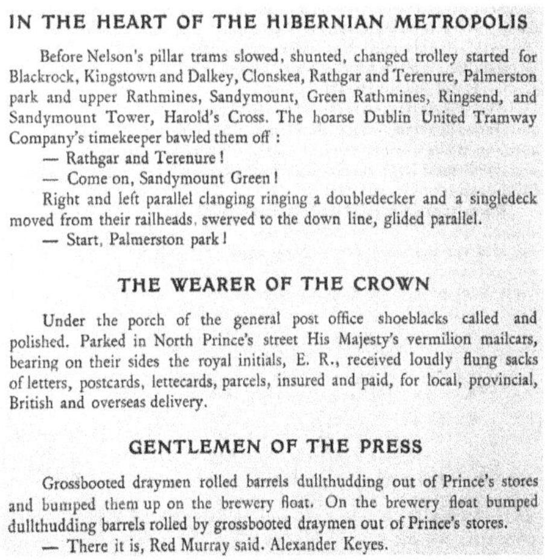

IN THE HEART OF THE HIBERNIAN METROPOLIS

Before Nelson's pillar trams slowed, shunted, changed trolley started for Blackrock, Kingstown and Dalkey, Clonskea, Rathgar and Terenure, Palmerston park and upper Rathmines, Sandymount, Green Rathmines, Ringsend, and Sandymount Tower, Harold's Cross. The hoarse Dublin United Tramway Company's timekeeper bawled them off :

— Rathgar and Terenure !

— Come on, Sandymount Green !

Right and left parallel clanging ringing a doubledecker and a singledeck moved from their railheads, swerved to the down line, glided parallel.

— Start, Palmerston park !

THE WEARER OF THE CROWN

Under the porch of the general post office shoeblacks called and polished. Parked in North Prince's street His Majesty's vermilion mailcars, bearing on their sides the royal initials, E. R., received loudly flung sacks of letters, postcards, lettecards, parcels, insured and paid, for local, provincial, British and overseas delivery.

GENTLEMEN OF THE PRESS

Grossbooted draymen rolled barrels dullthudding out of Prince's stores and bumped them up on the brewery float. On the brewery float bumped dullthudding barrels rolled by grossbooted draymen out of Prince's stores.

— There it is, Red Murray said. Alexander Keyes.

ILLUSTRATION 10.2
Opening of "Aeolus" printed in the 1922 edition.

public transportation and the postal system, implying an analogy between the circulation of humans through the city, of mail through the post and of

Faber, 2009), 113–23, as does Terence Killeen in *"Ulysses" Unbound: a Reader's Companion to James Joyce's "Ulysses"* (Bray: Wordwell, 2005), 72–73.

newsprint. Thirdly, the misprint of the first sentence (printed twice) in the *Little Review* is reappropriated through a chiastic reversal in the 1922 text ("On the brewery float bumped dullthudding ...", *U* 7.22–23), along with a hundred or so other rhetorical figures, most of which Joyce added in the galleys. Just as the crossheads foreground the form of the episode, Joyce's rhetorical figures draw attention to linguistic form, even at the expense of clarity. Indeed, their opacity often enforces a heightened awareness of the materiality of the text, setting in motion cycles of self-reflexivity, both within the text and for the reader. Again, the crossheads are exemplary here, because their late addition imposes "a kind of retrospective arrangement" (*U* 10.783) on the chapter, and one which makes increasingly elliptical demands of the reader to close the circle between passages and their headings. In fact, I believe it is this circular form of self-reflection that links Joyce's revisions, for in the circuitous route to publication, each change suggests that the circulation of people, writing and newspapers is connected to the circulation of language. Thus, I argue that the processes of setting, printing, distributing and recycling newspapers described in "Aeolus" bring an intense, self-reflexive scrutiny to broader processes of textual production, reproduction, circulation, and recirculation. I will try to show this through the materiality of print, its circulation, and the self-reflexive relationship between them.

Print Matters

In both the Gilbert and Linati schemata, the art attributed to "Aeolus" is rhetoric, the organ lungs.[10] Accordingly, a good deal of the talk in the chapter focuses on great orators of the past, from Demosthenes to John F. Taylor, and the episode itself is interlarded with almost as many rhetorical figures as in Quintilian.[11] But even "Doughy" Dawson's (*U* 7.336, 340) speech on the eve of Bloomsday is dated (and lambasted) when it goes to press, showing how close the relationship is between public oratory and those modern organs of persuasion, newspapers. Aeolia, the "Floating Island" of the "Press" (Gilbert), could be associated with the "Mutability" of the latter (Linati) or with the circulation and recycling of print, but it is important to note that the first symbol of the Linati schema is "Machines", and the scene given by Gilbert is "Newspapers"

10 These two schemata are compared in Richard Ellmann, *Ulysses on the Liffey* (London: Faber, 1974), 187.

11 See Don Gifford, "Rhetorical Figures in 'Aeolus'", in *"Ulysses" Annotated: Notes for James Joyce's "Ulysses"*, 2nd ed. (Berkeley: University of California Press, 1988), 635–43.

(not their offices, but the periodicals themselves). Thus, all the hot air and windy bombast of rhetoric is grounded in the mechanical production of printed paper, which is itself presented as a kind of respiratory cycle. There is perhaps an analogy here with Aeolus trapping adverse winds in a bag for Odysseus, only for his men to release them, blowing their ship back to Aeolia:[12] Joyce too seems to capture the gusts of rhetoric in the materiality of print, notably through orthography and onomatopoeia, only to scatter those letters and phonemes to the winds once more, where they circulate freely in the breath of vocalised air and the inky currents of dissemination. In both cases there is a return: the winds return to the sky, the mutability of print is restored; but there is a difference between the beginning and end of the cycle: Odysseus's men now know what the bag contains, and the text manifests a new, self-reflexive awareness of its material form.

Perhaps the clearest example of this is the "Orthographical" section:

> ORTHOGRAPHICAL
>
> Want to be sure of his spelling. Proof fever. Martin Cunningham forgot to give us his spellingbee conundrum this morning. It is amusing to view the unpar one ar alleled embarra two ars is it? double ess ment of a harassed pedlar while gauging au the symmetry with a y of a peeled pear under a cemetery wall. Silly, isn't it? Cemetery put in of course on account of the symmetry.
>
> I should have said when he clapped on his topper. Thank you. I ought to have said something about an old hat or something. No. I could have said. Looks as good as new now. See his phiz then.
>
> Sllt. The nethermost deck of the first machine jogged forward its flyboard with sllt the first batch of quirefolded papers. Sllt. Almost human the way it sllt to call attention. Doing its level best to speak. That door too sllt creaking, asking to be shut. Everything speaks in its own way. Sllt.
>
> *U* 7.164–77

To put the passage in context, Nannetti has been given a galley page to proofread, and it is worth noting that this proof-sheet is produced by "silent typesetters" before being checked "silently" by the foreman (*U* 7.162–63, 109), in contrast to the noise of the printing machines "thumping" away (*U* 7.72–101). Bloom himself notes the way Nannetti slips "his words deftly into the pauses of the clanking" (*U* 7.139), as though the machines have monopolised the talk; but they have not yet silenced it. Despite the noise of printing – that is, of

12 Homer, *Odyssey*, bk. 10.

reproduction – silent typesetters go on filling their chases to produce new formes.[13] Likewise, in the absence of speech at the start of this section, Bloom's thoughts slip deftly into the text: "Proof fever" leads him to the "spellingbee conundrum" (which, as Harald Beck has shown, goes back to at least the 1860s).[14] It is indeed amusing to see the way words get broken down into letters (correctly spelled, as words: "ar", "ess", "y") as spelling is interrogated, and this self-reflexive quality of Bloom's thoughts is evident again in the comment "Silly, isn't it?" which seems to belong as much to the editor or arranger of the text as to Bloom. This quality is even more marked in the last sentence of the paragraph, where "cemetery" has ostensibly been put in on account of its aural similarity to, and orthographical difference from, "symmetry": in fact, only the first stressed vowel differs, and it is perhaps this consonance which, according to the *Waterloo Daily Courier* (Iowa) of 13 December 1897, led one student to write "gaze on the cemetery of a pealed hair".[15]

It is doubtful whether Joyce had this particular source in mind; more likely "cemetery" was put in on account of the symmetry with "Hades". Indeed, in the next paragraph Bloom recalls John Henry Menton's dinged hat at the end of the previous episode, still thinking what he should or could have said to conciliate his antagonist, as he dwells on Menton's curt "Thank you" (*U* 6.1015–33). Some twelve hours later, Bloom is still niggled by the incident, comparing Menton's "Thank you" unfavourably to Parnell's (*U* 16.1336), whose headgear he also claims to have "set to rights", "history repeating itself with a difference" (*U* 16.1523–26). Trivial as it is in itself, this textual recycling is significant insofar as it represents one transaction in the symbolic economy of *Ulysses*, which, as we shall see, is facilitated by the circulation of language.

Before broaching wider questions of linguistic circulation in the novel, I want to attend to its constituent elements in speech and writing, that is, phonemes and graphemes, via the onomatopoeic and orthographical conventions

13 The actual offices of the *Freeman's Journal* contained both monotype and linotype machines. The typesetter "neatly distributing type" (*U* 7.204) must be setting by hand, since linotype printers would resort type automatically, but the line of bitched type in "Eumaeus" is the result of a botched linotype slug.

14 The *Belfast News-letter* of 26 August 1862 offered the following sentence as an orthographical challenge: "It is agreeable to see the unparalleled embarrassment of a harassed pedlar gauging the symmetry of a peeled pear". The test was repeated (with amusing variations) in the *Huddersfield Chronicle* of 25 September 1876, The *Daily Gazette* of Fort Wayne, Indiana of 5 February 1869, and even the *Freeman's Journal* of 12 March 1869; Harald Beck, "Spellingbee Conundrum", *James Joyce Online Notes*, accessed 6 December 2016, http://www.jjon.org/joyce-s-allusions/spellingbee-conundrum.

15 Quoted in Beck, "Spellingbee Conundrum".

which constrain them. Etymologically, "orthography" means correct writing (Skeat) or spelling (OED).[16] The focus on correct spelling in "Orthographical" has already been remarked upon; but "orthography" also means a "system of spelling or notation", or more generally "the branch of knowledge which deals with letters and their combination to represent sounds and words", and *Ulysses* explores the conventions of writing and spelling like few books before or since. Some of the more memorable examples include Martha Clifford's typographical error, "I do not like that other world" (U 5.245), the "Greek ees" Henry Flower replies with (U 11.860, 889), the theosophico-orthographical joke, "tālāfānā, ālāvātār, hātākāldā, wātāklāsāt" (U 12.354), Molly's misspelt words, "symph̸athy I always make that mistake and new̸phew with 2 double yous" (U 18.730–31), and Milly's

> infantile epistle, dated, small em monday, reading: capital pee Papli comma capital aitch How are you note of interrogation capital eye I am very well full stop new paragraph signature with flourishes.
>
> U 17.1791–94

The same unlocked drawer in "Ithaca" also contains Bloom's cache of not-so-secret letters from Martha, which, presumably at his behest, have "the transliterated name and address of the addresser of the 3 letters in reversed alphabetic boustrophedonic punctated quadrilinear cryptogram (vowels suppressed) N. IGS./WI. UU. OX/W. OKS. MH/Y. IM" (U 17.1798–1801). Amusing or puerile as Bloom's code may be, there is, I think, a serious side to the wordplay.

Boustrophedonic (βουστρόφος, ox-turning) writing, used in ancient Greek inscriptions, runs "alternately from right to left and from left to right, like the course of the plough".[17] This snaky movement shows up the arbitrary nature of our own writing conventions, a theme which echoes back to "Aeolus". When Bloom watches a typesetter "neatly distributing type" (U 7.204), initially it appears that he is composing the paragraph for Hynes: "Reads it backwards first .... mangiD kcirtaP" (U 7.205–06).[18] This leads Bloom to think of "poor papa ... reading backwards" (U 7.206–07), just as he imagines doing in "Circe" when he "*unrolls a paper and reads solemnly* Aleph Beth Ghimel Daleth" (U 15.1622–23),

16 Walter W. Skeat, *An Etymological Dictionary of the English Language*, new ed. (Oxford: Clarendon Press, 1910), 416; OED *Online*, accessed 6 December 2016, http://oed.com.

17 "Boustrophedon", OED *Online*, accessed 6 December 2016, http://oed.com.

18 In fact, he is "distributing" the individual letters from the chase back into their respective boxes (which explains how he "Seems to see with his fingers" [U 7.215–16]). Strictly speaking, the words themselves should be set in mirror image: mɒngiᗡ ʞɔiɿtɒꟼ.

although he can get no further in the alphabet,[19] and the rest of his text is gibberish, while Rudy *"reads from right to left inaudibly, smiling, kissing the page"* (*U* 15.4959–60). This circular relationship between Semitic and Roman scripts is a recurrent concern (cf. *U* 15.4708–16); in "Aeolus", where the relationship between Hebrew and Greek is compared to that between Gaelic and English, ancient Greek can be seen to mediate between them, because all typesetters in any of these languages are fluent boustrophedonic scribes.

Nevertheless, they are also apt to make mistakes, as the par Bloom reads in the Last Pink makes clear:

> *The mourners included: Patk. Dignam (son), Bernard Corrigan (brother-in-law), Jno. Henry Menton, solr, Martin Cunningham, John Power,.)eatondph 1/8 ador dorador douradora* (must be where he called Monks the dayfather about Keyes's ad) *Thomas Kernan, Simon Dedalus, Stephen Dedalus B.A., Edw. J. Lambert, Cornelius T. Kelleher, Joseph M'C Hynes, L. Boom, CP M'Coy, – M'lntosh and several others.*
>
> *U* 16.1255–61

Of the twelve named, three were absent, "L. Boom" is nettled by his misnomer, and amongst "the usual crop of nonsensical howlers of misprints" (*U* 16.1267) we find the line of "bitched type" (*U* 16.1263) "*.)eatondph 1/8 ador dorador douradora*".[20] Aside from the comedy of errors, these misprints suggest both the unreliability of information in the media, and the impermanence of type. Again, this is a recurrent concern in *Ulysses*. When first we encounter "Plasto's high grade ha" (*U* 4.69–70), unless we are reading carefully, we might think it a misprint, but when the "sweated legend" is repeated (at *U* 5.24), we realise the last letter has faded. "POST NO BILLS. POST 110 PILLS" (*U* 8.101) provides another famous example, but perhaps the most telling incubism of dissolute and

---

19 Cf. the "glyphic comparison of the phonic symbols" of ancient Irish and Hebrew in "Ithaca", where Stephen writes "the Irish characters for gee, eh, dee, em, simple and modified, and Bloom in turn wrote the Hebrew characters ghimel, aleph, daleth and (in the absence of mem) a substituted qoph" (*U* 17.731–39).

20 As John Simpson explains, "when a compositor made an error" on a linotype machine, "he would often cancel the line by running his fingers down one or more columns of keys to generate enough garbled metal print characters to complete the line – which would then be extracted and replaced by the correct line ... Needless to say, it wasn't long before readers started to find evidence of *etaoin shrdlu*, as compositors forgot to remove slugs of garbled type before the page was set" (e.g., *Freeman's Journal*, 17 April 1899). See John Simpson, "Eatondph and Douradora", *James Joyce Online Notes*, accessed 6 December 2016, http://www.jjon.org/joyce-s-words/eatondhp.

degenerative letters occurs in "Hades". Amongst the "saddened angels, crosses, broken pillars" (*U* 6.928–29) of Glasnevin cemetery, the (faded?) epigraph on the gravestone of Robert Emery (mis)leads Bloom to Robert Emmett (*U* 6.977–78), whose immortal words reappear in "Sirens"; yet these ghostly characters on and beneath the gravestones are but ancient legends in comparison to the "inked characters fast fading on the frayed breaking paper" (*U* 6.160) of the morning *Freeman*.

As letters fade and words break up, they become loosed to reform in new combinations; hence the significance of the sandwich-board men parading round the city for H.E.L.Y'S (*U* 8.126–54, *U* 10.310, 377–79, 1237–38, etc.). Life-sized and embodied, these letters literally circulate through the city, but as Y lags behind and "apostrophe S" plods after (*U* 8.126–27, 155), the signs themselves begin to decompose, like the letters of "mangiD kcirtaP", which were not after all being composed, but disassembled and distributed back into their separate cases. In typesetting, this process releases letters from set forms, liberating them to form new words, and a similar process takes place in *Ulysses* as individual letters spawn new words, new text, like Bloom's lilted alphabet, "Ahbeesee defeegee kelomen opeecue rustyouvee doubleyou" (*U* 4.137–38), or the books Stephen was "going to write with letters for titles" (*U* 3.139–40).

This process of letter recycling and word formation creates the poetics of *Finnegans Wake,* but in *Ulysses* it is most clearly seen through onomatopoeia. Derived from the Greek *ὀνοματοποιία*, the word literally means word-making. The sole example of onomatopoeia Gifford cites in "Aeolus" is "sllt", an interesting choice not only because the word has evidently been formed in imitation of the sound of the printing machines,[21] but also because of the words it suggests. According to Richard Ellmann, "sllt" is "the repeated sound of slitting",[22] but just as the source is uncertain, the sound could also elide slat, slet, slot, slut, salt, selt, silt, or even "Silly, isn't it?" (*U* 7.169). The word is repeated five times in the paragraph, as though to multiply its possible forms, and indeed, while the single-sentence intrusions seem to be nouns, the third occurrence is a verb ("sllt to call attention") and the fourth is either an adverb or an unhyphenated compound verb: "sllt creaking" (*U* 7.177). This transformation is effected through prosopopeia: "Almost human the way it sllt to call attention. Doing its level best to speak", causing Bloom to reflect that "Everything speaks

21 Although the precise sound imitated is open to question (is it caused by the exhalation of quirefolded papers on the flyboard, or is it rather the sound produced by the suction caps which would lift the papers off?) this ambiguity itself suggests the respiratory cycle of the pulmonary machines, in keeping with the organ, the lungs.

22 Ellmann, *Ulysses on the Liffey*, 72.

in its own way" (*U* 7.175–77). This maxim could be regarded as the generative principle of onomatopoeia, where the figure is understood according to its usual definition as word-formation in imitation of sound, and Joyce revels in attempting just this: to take only a few of the most celebrated examples, think of the "fourworded wavespeech: seesoo, hrss, rsseeiss, ooos" (*U* 3.456–57), Davy Byrne's smile-yawn-nod, "Iiiiichaaaaaaach!" (*U* 8.970), or the sound of vessels being filled, "Diddleiddle addleaddle ooddleooddle" (*U* 11.984). However, in the last case, it is not clear whether Bloom really hears glasses being filled or only imagines it during a complicated train of associations that stems from a metatextual pun on "Chamber Music", as both the title of Joyce's first published poems and the variable pitch of the chamber pot during the act of micturition, a homely thought which returns Bloom (rather anxiously) to Molly (*U* 11.979–85).

This ambiguity, amusing in itself, provides a neat illustration of Derek Attridge's claim that onomatopoeia "necessarily displaces that to which it refers".[23] Going back to "sllt creaking", even if the "sllt" here is read as an interruption – the sound of the press irrupting into the sentence – it has still displaced the creaking door. In fact, the door does speak in its own way: early in the episode, Ruttledge's door memorably whispers "ee: cree" (*U* 7.50), a whisper that circulates back into the text of "Sirens": "Sea, wind, leaves, thunder, waters, cows lowing, the cattlemarket, cocks, hens don't crow, snakes hissss. There's music everywhere. Ruttledge's door: ee creaking. No, that's noise" (*U* 11.963–65). The curious thing about this noise, though, is that, like a Chinese whisper, it passes into the phonic representation of Bloom's "wee little wind pip[ing] eeee" (*U* 11.1203) just before he lets wind under cover of the tram, an act which is echoed and extended by the "pianissimo eeeee" Molly emits between the "sweeeee … tsong" of a distant train (*U* 18.908), as though Joyce wanted to tease us by finally uniting husband and wife in the bodily expression of love's old sweet song. Here again the free circulation of wind is associated with the circulation and recirculation of letters, first forming new words (ὀνοματοποιία), like "sllt" or "ee" and then multiplying their associations through recirculation (that is, repetition). In doing so, Joyce's onomatopoeia not only "displaces that to which it refers", it also displaces the signifiers which do the referring, thereby providing a stereoscopic perspective on Attridge's observation that "onomatopoeia can be seen as a paradigm for all language".[24]

23 Derek Attridge, "Language as Imitation: Jakobson, Joyce, and the Art of Onomatopoeia", *MLN* 99, no. 5 (1984): 1136.

24 Attridge, "Language as Imitation", 1136.

The circulation of individual letters and phonemes is obviously part of a much larger cycle in *Ulysses*. We have already seen how "Orthographical" recycles text printed earlier in "Aeolus" and "Hades", as well as recycling a well-known "spellingbee". Going through numerous reprints from c. 1860 to 1904, this conundrum belongs to the public domain, but as it is circulated via Martin Cunningham's discourse into the private domain of Bloom's interior monologue it becomes increasingly personalised. As I have shown, "cemetery" is probably Bloom's addition, although initially the connection to "Hades" appears almost unconscious; in "Circe" the line passes (subconsciously?) into Bloom *"feeling his occiput dubiously with the unparalleled embarrassment of a harassed pedlar gauging the symmetry of her* [Zoe's] *peeled pears"* (*U* 15.1993–94); and in "Eumaeus" Bloom seems to ghost-write his own free indirect borrowing as he "look[s] away thoughtfully with the intention of not further increasing the other's [Stephen's] possible embarrassment while gauging her [Molly's] symmetry of heaving *embonpoint*" (*U* 16.1466–68). On reflection, though, this can also be seen as a return from private, verbalised thought to the public domain of the story Bloom imagines writing, while the entire circuit is obviously and necessarily mediated through the text, enhancing its self-reflexive quality. A similar cycle is retraced in the difference between the machine "Doing its level best to speak" in "ORTHOGRAPHICAL" (*U* 7.176), Ben Dollard "Doing his level best to say it" (*U* 11.1011) and baby Boardman, who "did his level best to say it" (*U* 13.388). Bloom's thoughts are proverbial, drawn from a common idiom, but on the one hand they become personalised (in the first sentence only Bloom knows what part of the machine "sllt"s, while the second contains imponderable depths) while, on the other hand, there is a shift from Bloom's interior monologue to the "namby-pamby jammy marmalady drawersy" (as Joyce wrote to Frank Budgen in 1920) style of "Nausicaa's" "circumlocutions" (*Letters I* 135), which seem to belong as much to Gerty as to Bloom. Again, though, the "it" is instructive: mimicking her own speech in infantile form, Cissy tells baby to "Say pa pa pa pa pa pa pa" and is presumably interrupted during the fourth repetition by the baby's attempt to do so: "Haja ja ja haja" (*U* 13.387–92). The interesting point about this is that it returns speech to the repetition of phonemes, whose simple alternation leads to endless variation ("A jink a jink a jawbo" [*U* 13.28]), showing again how language is produced, reproduced, and constantly recirculated. Indeed, the great cycle of life and death Bloom imagines in "Lestrygonians" always commences with the same repeated vagitus: "maaaaaa" (*U* 8.483), extending the first vowel indefinitely from its voiced bilabial origins into the newborn's first word, calling back the mother.

Circulation, Circularity, Self-Reflexivity

Circulation is not only a recurrent motif, but a governing principle in *Ulysses*. Like the texts Joyce returns to – the *Odyssey*, *Hamlet*, the *Commedia* – *Ulysses* involves a return; but Bloom's homecoming does not simply close the circle: Stephen's departure promises a new cycle, while Molly's monologue recirculates the text. The infinite time of "Penelope" (Linati) indicates the "endlessnessnessness" (*U* 11.750) of this textual cycle, as well as all the cycles in the text. For instance, in the "maaaaaa" passage quoted above, Bloom's thoughts turn from the circulation of trams ("ingoing, outgoing, clanging") to "Useless words", as though still blown by the prevailing winds of "Aeolus" (*U* 8.476–77); this train of thought then takes him to the endless cycles of time ("Things go on same, day after day"), life and death ("One born every second somewhere. Other dying every second"), and space, as not only the citizens, but the city itself, passes, "worn away age after age", only to spring up again in "mushroom houses built of breeze" (*U* 8.477–92), showing again how "Aeolus" blows through the narrative, constructing an imaginary city from rhetorical breezeblocks. As the passage indicates, there is a certain circularity between "Hades", "Aeolus" and "Lestrygonians": in death, "the circulation stops" (*U* 6.434), just as the trams are short-circuited at the end of "Aeolus" (*U* 7.1043–49), while in "Lestrygonians", their recirculation is linked to the life cycle, but only so long as the digestive cycle continues ("have to feed it like stoking an engine" [*U* 8.930]). These mechanics of the body are in play again when Bloom thinks of a swallowed pin coursing through the "pipes" of the digestive tract (*U* 8.1046–48), and since his thoughts are "turned back" by the sight of a plumber's window, Bloom's intestinal cycle can be linked to the watercourse in "Ithaca" (*U* 17.163–82), as well as the various aqueous cycles he admires (*U* 17.216–28). Amongst these, Bloom remarks on the ubiquity of water "as constituting 90% of the human body" (*U* 17.226–27), which is something of an overestimate, although plasma does in fact contain about 90% water.[25] As the organ of "Wandering Rocks", blood circulates through the city, just as in "Aeolus" "'THE GREAT DAILY ORGAN' at 'THE HEART OF THE HIBERNIAN METROPOLIS' pump[s] misinformation into the heart of the collective bloodstream", and "the transportation system circulates the characters, like corpuscles on odysseys around the city's

25 The quantity of water in the average adult is approximately 60%, although it varies according to age, gender and body type. Arthur C. Guyton and John E. Hall, *Textbook of Medical Physiology*, 12th edition (Jackson: Saunders, 2010), 293.

arteries".[26] Bloom's physical wanderings around the city, as well as the course of his interior monologue, can be read in just this way. For instance, when contemplating roaring seashells in "Sirens", he thinks: "The blood it is. Souse in the ear sometimes. Well, it's a sea. Corpuscle islands" (*U* 11.945–46). Exploring this internal sea more deeply, in "Ithaca" Bloom meditates on "the universe of human serum constellated with red and white bodies, themselves universes of void space" (*U* 17.1063–64), a thought which might return us via the composition of plasma to those "aquacities of thought and language" Stephen distrusts (*U* 17.240) – a curiously self-reflexive moment when one considers that these aquacities constitute his entire fictional life, as well as 100% of *Ulysses*.[27]

As with Bloom's throwaway remark to Bantam Lyons in "Lotus Eaters", which circulates on the waters of civic discourse, or the "throwaway" Bloom tosses into the Liffey (*U* 8.57), from whence it circulates through the urban space of the text (resurfacing, amongst other places, in the life cycles Bloom imagines "washed in the blood of the lamb" [*U* 8.480–83]), *Ulysses* constantly recycles itself: "Buzz. Buzz", "Queen Anne is dead" (*U* 9.207, *U* 7.90) – this is very much old news, "published by authority in the year one thousand and" (*U* 7.90–91); but it has not yet, I think, gone stale. Perhaps the best study to date is Maud Ellmann's 2008 essay, "*Ulysses:* The Epic of the Human Body", in which she shows how "the city in *Ulysses* takes the form of a gigantic body circulating language, commodities, and money, together with the Dubliners whirled round in these economies",[28] yet her remarks on the self-reflexive quality of this epic body are limited to a stylistic break from realism, which she regards as a kind of onanistic indulgence.[29] Similarly, in *The Economy of "Ulysses"* Mark Osteen provides

26 Maud Ellmann, "*Ulysses:* The Epic of the Human Body", in *A Companion to James Joyce*, ed. Richard Brown (Malden: Blackwell Publishing, 2008), 55.

27 Stephen's *volte-face* is particularly surprising in view of the watery words he composes in *Portrait:* "like waters circumfluent in space the liquid letters of speech, symbols of the element of mystery, flowed forth over his brain" (*P* V.1746–48).

28 Ellmann, "The Epic of the Human Body", 55.

29 "If exile can represent a form of homecoming", Ellmann argues, "return can also represent a form of exile. This principle applies to the style of *Ulysses,* which tugs in two directions, towards the realist tradition in the novel and away from it at once. … Ultimately *Ulysses* remains faithful to the novel in much the same way that Bloom remains faithful to Molly – by indulging in a bit on the side. To pursue this analogy a little further, Bloom's masturbation corresponds to the self-reflexiveness of Joyce's language, which offers a relief, as opposed to a divorce, from the constraints of realism"; Ellmann, "The Epic of the Human Body", 65.

a compelling analysis of monetary circulation and the linguistic or intertextual economies of *Ulysses*. His thesis that Joyce sought to reconcile spendthrift habits with bourgeois thrift through an aesthetic economy of the gift, where loss is gain, offers an interesting reading of the relationship between Stephen and Bloom, but it is only in "Penelope", he argues, that those tendencies are synthesised "into a single infinitely circulating system".[30] By contrast, I would argue that this circularity (*Making Both Ends Meet,* as Osteen's subtitle puts it), is present from the beginning of the text, and its doubling back is precisely self-reflection.

All texts can be said to be in circulation; indeed, language only exists in circulation; but print journalism is the form that depends upon it. Early in "Aeolus", Bloom wonders whether William Brayden, editor of the *Freeman's Journal,* will "save the circulation" (*U* 7.71), for his own livelihood as ads canvasser depends on a healthy readership. This economic bottom line is linked to the physical circulation of the printed word, but just as Homer's Aeolia is the floating island, circulation in "Aeolus" takes more aerial and afflated forms. Like Odysseus's bag, visible to all (though its contents are known only to himself and the wind-god), the winds of "Aeolus" first appear in Bloom-Ulysses's ellipsis: "The door of Ruttlege's office whispered: ee: cree. They always build one door opposite another for the wind to" (*U* 7.50–51). Readers, like Odysseus's mariners, might wonder what this elliptical bag contains: "pass through" is possible, as is "blow", but "circulate" fits best. Thus, at the beginning of the episode, the winds of "Aeolus" hardly seem to circulate at all: enclosed in the text, rhetorical figures like ecphonesis ("Start, Palmerston Park!"), metonymy ("WEARER OF THE CROWN") and diasyrm ("his brains are in the nape of his neck") (*U* 7.13, 14, 47)[31] are barely noticeable;[32] whereas by the end of the chapter, the winds of rhetoric are released, as in the speeches of Seymour Bushe and John F. Taylor. By contrast, from the start of the episode, the headlines stand out, like a visible form of the bag over the text. As with the rhetorical figures, or the wind motif which blows though the episode,[33] initially these headlines are relatively

30 Osteen, *Economy of "Ulysses"*, 34.

31 Gifford, "Rhetorical Figures", 636.

32 The obvious exception is the chiasmus Joyce added to the 1922 edition ("Grossbooted draymen ..." [*U* 7.21–24]), whose circular form is of special interest, as we shall see.

33 E.g., in the space of 50 lines we encounter: "High falutin stuff. Bladderbags ... gale days. Windfall ... what's in the wind ... Reaping the whirlwind ... Funny the way those newspaper men veer about when they get wind of a new opening. Weathercocks. Hot and cold in the same breath" (*U* 7.260–310). M.J.C. Hodgart, "Aeolus", in *James Joyce's "Ulysses": Critical Essays*, eds. Clive Hart and David Hayman (London: University of California Press, 1974), 117, provides a more extensive list.

unobtrusive (although the relevance of "THE CROZIER AND THE PEN" to "his grace", the archbishop – or is it the editor? – takes some working out, and "DISSOLUTION" is a curious synonym for death); as the chapter progresses, though, the relationship between crossheads and the text they frame becomes increasingly obscure, until the virtually unutterable headline "???" lets the wind out of the bag. As usual, the men are talking at cross-purposes, so that the three question marks can be attributed to three questions in the text: "What opera resembles a railwayline?", "Who?" and "Who tore it?" (*U* 7.514–21). The second question is answered immediately: "Mr Garrett Deasy, Stephen said"; the third can be answered by an attentive reader, recalling that Stephen tore "the blank end off" "Old Deasy's letter" in "Proteus" (*U* 3.404–5); but for Lenehan's riddle we must do as he commands: "Reflect, ponder, excogitate, reply" (*U* 7.514–15).

The form of the riddle demands reflection on the part of the reader, as well as Lenehan's listeners, and by printing three question marks as a headline, Joyce's text seems to reflect on itself. This doubling back from questions in the text to a title which puts the text into question sets up a reflexive loop which is not only typical of "Aeolus", but paradigmatic of *Ulysses* as a whole. Moreover, as Lenehan's answer makes clear, this loop exists not only between text and title, or heterogeneous passages, but within each part of the text itself: "*The Rose of Castile.* See the wheeze? Rows of cast steel" (*U* 7.591). One does indeed have to *see* the wheeze, for only in the difference between sound and spelling does the joke become apparent, at which point one might double back from the gag to the windy breath of the wheeze made visible. This circular form of paranomasia, based on phonetic and orthographical similarities (and differences) between near-homonyms, is typical of Joyce's wordplay. Its self-reflexive form indicates that its function is twofold: first, it leads out into pure play, a kind of linguistic frivolity, through the free association of sound, form and meaning; then by reflecting back on the nature of the associative rules which govern that play, the text goes into analysis.

I don't have space to analyse these games in detail, but a brief survey of the crossheads of "Aeolus" will provide numerous examples, as Joyce takes the wordplay of real newspaper headlines to farcical extremes: "DAMES DONATE DUBLIN'S CITS / SPEEDPILLS VELOCITOUS AEROLITHS, BELIEF" (*U* 7.1021–22). In this example, the dames are Anne Kearns and Florence MacCabe, the Dublin vestals in Stephen's parable; "CITS" abbreviates the citizens on whom they rain speedpills (a short-lived baseball term),[34] or velocitous aeroliths (meteorites) – that is, plumstones, from the heights of Horatio Nelson's

34 Harald Beck, "The Benefit of Speedpills", *James Joyce Online Notes*, accessed 6 December 2016, http://www.jjon.org/joyce-s-words/speedpill.

tower ("HORATIO IS CYNOSURE THIS FAIR JUNE DAY" [*U* 7.1063]). Yet the point of Joyce's riddles is not to find the solution, as though there were such a thing (after all, what does Stephen's "vision" [*U* 7.917] signify?), but rather the process of reflection itself, because this leads the reader to question both the significance of the text and its form. Indeed, by foregrounding form through rhetorical figures, Joyce brings a self-reflexive awareness to the text. In Burgess's terms, he is a pre-eminently "class 2" writer: making the "surface" of the text opaque, he simultaneously enhances its material reality, as ink on the page, and its semantic uncertainty; breaking the illusion of a transparent relationship between language and that to which it refers (one typically sustained by "class 1" writing), rhetorical winds are released and language is free to disseminate.[35] Yet the circulation of language is never entirely free; it is always constrained by the (mutable) sounds and shapes of its media, and however widely the "wind of wild air of seeds" (*U* 3.266–67) disseminates, it always comes back to the seminal structure of linguistic form.

Thus, circulation is recirculation in *Ulysses,* and as the text circles back to itself, it becomes self-reflexive. Lenehan's circumlocutions are symptomatic of this condition as his gentle ribbing doubles over to laugh in all seriousness at its own wordplay, "O, my rib risible!" (*U* 7.448) is raised to a floating rib, suggesting the creation of that first mother, Eve; "as we read in the first chapter of Guinness's" takes us back to "Our old ancient ancestors" (*U* 7.496–97); and so it is no surprise to find him recycling a joke as old as the hills, proclaiming the first speech of mankind in the cyclical form of a palindrome: "Madam, I'm Adam" (*U* 7.683). Clearly, Joyce is having fun here, but not only: in a similar vein, it is striking that the one passage in *Ulysses* Joyce chose to record phonographically is the recycled speech of John F. Taylor. According to Ellmann, Joyce heard Taylor's speech in defence of Gaelic at the Law Students' Debating Society on 24 October 1901, but he also appears to have relied on the report in the *Freeman's Journal* ("The Irish Revival", 25 October 1901), as well as an anonymous pamphlet entitled "The Language of the Outlaw" (c.1903; see *JJII* 91, 756). Yeats also recalled the speech, even quoting from it in his autobiography, although the speech itself was never recorded.[36] Hence, Joyce's version in "Aeolus" recirculates a text whose origins can never be established. This quasi-legendary status leaves room for rhetorical embellishment, and Professor MacHugh's memorial reconstruction of "the finest display of oratory I ever

35 Anthony Burgess, *Joysprick: An Introduction to the Language of James Joyce* (New York: Harcourt Brace Jovanovich, 1975), 15–16. See also Jennifer Schiffer Levine, "Originality and Repetition in *Finnegans Wake* and *Ulysses*", *PMLA* 94, no.1 (1979): 106–07.

36 Gifford, *"Ulysses" Annotated,* 148.

heard" (*U* 7.792–93) borders on grandiloquence. Sylvia Beach noted that Joyce chose the passage for its "declamatory" quality, but also believed it "expressed something he wanted said and preserved in his own voice",[37] a view many have shared,[38] for the speech itself records the epiphanic origins of writing in the Judeo-Christian tradition, as Moses comes down from Mount Sinai "*with the light of inspiration shining in his countenance and bearing in his arms the tables of the law, graven in the language of the outlaw*" (*U* 7.867–69).[39]

However ironic these passages may be, it is evident that Joyce is investigating the origins of language. Why he chose to do so in an episode concerned with newspapers is an interesting question. One possibility is that *Ulysses* itself can be compared to the ideal newspaper for 16 June 1904,[40] in which case the form of the book is reflected in the form of the chapter, so that newspaper production reflects on the textual production of the novel. Another possibility is that print journalism, as a medium that by definition depends on circulation, comes closest to Joyce's conception of *Ulysses* as circulating text. As I have shown, the newspaper cycle described in "Aeolus" – typesetting, printing, distribution, recycling – corresponds, in a general way, to wider cycles of linguistic production, reproduction, circulation and recirculation. On closer inspection, though, "Aeolus" seems to suggest that language is always in (re)circulation, for as soon as speech or writing is produced, it is already reproduced, in the deictic form of the sign, which both points away from, and doubles back on, itself.

37 Sylvia Beach, *Shakespeare and Company* (New York: Harcourt Brace, 1956), 171. An unpublished letter to Harriet Weaver suggests the choice was more pragmatic: "the gramophone people wanted the record made at once. Interior monologue would not go nor the growl of the cyclops nor the sirens so I read the late J.F. Taylor's speech from *Eolus*. That's done", but the two accounts are not necessarily incompatible; James Joyce to Harriet Shaw Weaver, 28 November 1924, Harriet Shaw Weaver Papers, Add MS 57347, British Library, London.

38 E.g., Hodgart regards the passage as "a truly inspired statement of Joyce's artistic credo"; Hodgart, "Aeolus", 121.

39 In fact, there are two editions of Moses's tables: after destroying the first tablets (Ex. 32:19), Moses hews a new pair on which God rewrites the Ten Commandments (Ex. 34:1–4). In Derridean terms, this suggests that there is no point of origin, for the first biblical writing supplements a lost original. I am indebted to Fritz Senn for pointing this out to me, as well as for suggesting some of the ways in which "Aeolus" investigates the origins of language (*Ulysses* seminar, 2013).

40 McLuhan approaches "the structure of *Ulysses* as a newspaper landscape"; McLuhan, "Joyce, Mallarmé, and the Press", 50. Kiberd suggests that Joyce creates a "two-way paper" or "counter-newspaper" "in which writers and readers [enjoy] a more interactive relationship" by providing "a dense set of background to the day's most trivial happenings"; Kiberd, *"Ulysses" and Us*, 118.

Hence, the circular form of Lenehan's speech is not peculiar to palindromes; it *is* the *doubling back* of self-reflexivity, suggesting that the origins of language are to be found in self-reflection. This explains why the investigation of origins in "Aeolus" is conducted through an exploration of print production and the materiality of the text; indeed, the two are inseparable. As Kenner puts it, Joyce is "post-Victorian enough to believe that all in a novel has the reality of text and no other reality"; but since "reality is immediate experience, and in a book is the immediate experience of language, streaming through what *Finnegans Wake* will call 'the eye of a noodle'",[41] textual reality is self-reflexive. Hence, it is no surprise that language takes centre-stage in "Aeolus". In retrospect, it has always, and necessarily, occupied this position, and after "Aeolus" we rarely lose sight of the fact again, because as the text becomes self-reflexive, we learn to reflect more closely on the text.

41 Hugh Kenner, *Ulysses* (London: George Allen & Unwin, 1980), 119, 32; *FW* 143.9.

CHAPTER 11

"Clio's Clippings": From Newspaper to Press Cutting

William S. Brockman

Abstract

Newspapers, pamphlets, handbills and other printed ephemera pervade Joyce's letters as well as his works of fiction. He subscribed to Irish newspapers and to newspaper clipping services. As Joyce's works were published, he became increasingly attuned to press coverage, either keeping stories clipped from the newspapers or sending them as enclosures in his letters. One of his main means of communication with supporters was via clippings. Of interest here is Joyce's use of the newspaper after it had served its function as carrier of the latest information. Examples of clippings sent to Ezra Pound and to Harriet Weaver document his fascination with the treatment he was receiving in the press and his ability to turn the press's interest in him to his advantage. In his works, a newspaper clipping forms part of the opening scene of "A Painful Case", three clippings are enumerated in the "Ithaca" episode of *Ulysses* and remnants of press notices appear in *Finnegans Wake*. Clippings form part of the multitude of cultural references that permeate Joyce's works. Extracting them from their original sources, Joyce puts them to a variety of uses and offers them to be viewed from multiple perspectives.

Keywords

newspaper clippings – letters – "Extracts from Press Notices" – "A Painful Case" – *Ulysses* – "Ithaca" – *Finnegans Wake*

On 10 November 1922 Joyce wrote to his Aunt Josephine, "Send me any news you like, programmes, pawntickets, press cuttings, handbills. I like reading them" (*SL* 294). Bits and pieces of printed ephemera pack his works of fiction, grounding them in the mundane and enlivening them with connections to commerce and culture.[1] While such things as newspapers and handbills were

1 This essay draws upon the author's "Press Cuttings: From 'Noise about Joyce' to 'Tress Clippings'", *Genetic Joyce Studies* 16 (Spring 2016), accessed 6 December 2016, http://www.geneticjoycestudies.org/articles/GJS16/GJS16_Brockman.

 | DOI 10.1163/9789004359062_013

intended initially to serve the moment as simple transmitters of announcement and trade, removing pieces of them from their original context and collecting them transformed their designs and messages from their original intent to a meaning determined by the beholder, by the new context and by the collection of which they are a part.

Joyce lived and wrote at a time of transformation of the newspapers from being carriers of the latest information and the most timely advertising to more – a resource for historical information, a basis for archival research. Libraries had begun to collect newspapers in earnest in the later nineteenth century, and the news clipping services, having originated in the 1880s, were booming. Newspapers were being retained and put to new uses. The adage "Today's news is tomorrow's fish-and-chip paper" was no longer valid for the twentieth century. Newspapers were part of the urban landscape in *Dubliners* and featured heavily throughout *Ulysses* and *Finnegans Wake*. This essay will examine Joyce's use of newspapers after they served their function as carriers of the latest information and as they were fragmented and then transformed by readers for their own ends. Joyce used the terms cutting and clipping interchangeably (though favouring the latter), and this essay will do the same.

Newspaper clipping services originated in the late nineteenth century and by the twentieth century were well established. The first well-known agency was Argus de la Presse, founded in Paris in 1879.[2] The industry's most

ILLUSTRATION 11.1 *Romeike Press Clipping Bureau readers' room, from* American Magazine *93 (February 1922): 15.*

2 Anke te Heesen, *The Newspaper Clipping: A Modern Paper Object* (Manchester: Manchester University Press, 2014), 57.

prominent name was that of Henry Romeike, who opened an agency in Paris in the early 1880s and then moved to London where he established a press cutting agency with Edward Curtice, Sr. He moved to the United States in 1887 where his firm became a great success, a model for a number of similar enterprises.[3] The clipping agencies fed the vanity of artists and politicians seeking to track public opinion through sightings of their names in the papers;[4] later the agencies became more affiliated with the corporate world. In all cases, the procedure was to identify a name or topic, to search through issues of many newspaper titles for any mention, and then to supply the articles to paying customers. The output of these agencies was impressive. In 1922 the Romeike Press-Clipping Bureau of New York (at this point led by Henry Romeike's son, Georges) covered some one thousand five hundred newspapers every day, employing between thirty and fifty readers (see illustration 11.1).[5] These readers – primarily women – had to memorize several thousand names and subjects of interest to subscribers. They would mark relevant articles which were then cut out by other employees wielding shears. Articles were identified as to date and source, attached to a slip bearing the name of the cutting agency, and mailed to the subscribers on a frequent, sometimes even daily basis (see illustration 11.2). Subscribers would be charged by the quantity of clippings. The corporate slogan from Robert Burns's "To a Louse" printed on the slips provided by Romeike's firm, "O wad some power the giftie gi'e us | To see oursel's as ithers see us" has an unintended echo that Joyce must have appreciated in Bloom's "see ourselves as others see us". (*U* 8.662)

Evidence of Joyce's collecting of newspaper clippings can be found in several of the library collections devoted to his life and works. The collection of Joyce's clippings preserved in the National Library of Ireland, though undoubtedly selective, shows the diversity of his interests.[6] The 108 extant items, almost all from the 1930s, include reviews of his works and of books about him, items reporting on his precarious eyesight, reports of the jail sentence of his

3 J.O. Baylen, "Romeike, Henry", *American National Biography Online*, accessed 6 December 2016, http://www.anb.org/articles/16/16-01406.html.

4 Of course, not only the famous want to see their names in print; Master Dignam thinks of his father's death notice and that other schoolboys will "all see it in the paper and read my name printed and pa's name" (*U* 10.1160).

5 Georges D. Romeike, "Who Is Mentioned Oftenest in the Newspapers?", *American Magazine* 93 (February 1922): 15.

6 "Newsclippings Arranged in Chronological Order", *The James Joyce – Paul Léon Papers in the National Library of Ireland: A Catalogue*, ed. Catherine Fahy (Dublin: National Library of Ireland, 1992), 232.

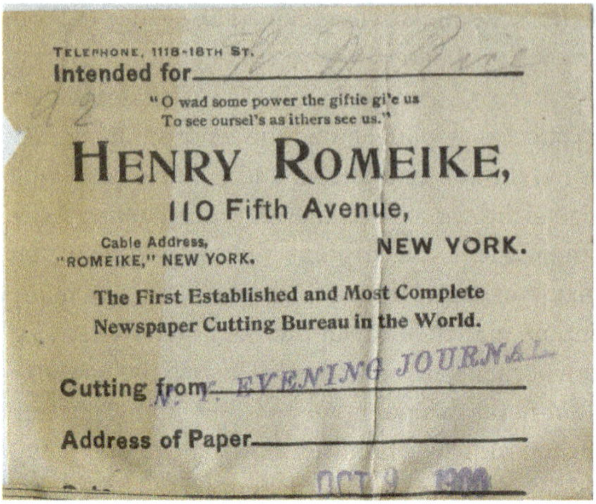

ILLUSTRATION 11.2 *Romeike Press Clipping Bureau slip.*
COURTESY OF RICE UNIVERSITY HISTORY CORNER.

literary agent Eric Pinker for theft, and, maybe most intriguingly, an 1877 article from *The World* about John Henry Newman. Where did this last item come from, and how long did Joyce have it with him? The most extensive evidence of Joyce's fascination with clippings is in the University at Buffalo James Joyce collection, so far undescribed except for a locally held catalogue but reportedly including thousands of items collected by Joyce from 1922.[7]

An unidentified clipping held in the Cornell University James Joyce collection raises similar questions. Entitled "Remarkable Romance", it recounts the story of a Galway woman who "had gone to a situation in Dublin and there made the acquaintance of a young man of good family and high educational attainments". They moved to Venice, but the husband "is just now on a visit to Galway and he has with him one of the handsomest little boys one could wish to see". Such sappy journalistic language echoes in "Nausicaa": Gerty is "as fair a specimen of winsome Irish girlhood as one could wish to see" (*U* 13.80–81), though a direct influence of this clipping on *Ulysses* is unlikely. Probably a local interest filler written by a local journalist, it is nevertheless (with some veiled

7 Luca Crispi, "ReCollecting Joyce at Buffalo: Revising and Completing the Catalog", in *Genitricksling Joyce,* eds. Sam Slote and Wim Van Mierlo, European Joyce Studies 9 (Amsterdam: Rodopi, 1999), 15–16. Dirk Van Hulle makes extensive use of the Buffalo collection to "give an impression of the immediate reception of 'Work in Progress' in the press"; *James Joyce's "Work in Progress": Pre-Book Publications of "Finnegans Wake" Fragments* (London: Routledge, 2016): 9.

facts, such as substituting "Venice" for "Trieste") a story about James and Nora Joyce. The clipping might have been acquired by Joyce during his visit with Giorgio to Galway in 1909; in some way it came into his possession but most importantly was saved, either as an account or as a "remarkable" coincidence.[8]

Joyce's attentiveness to news of himself is even more apparent in his fascination with a clipping sent to Harriet Weaver on 26 August 1919 that he identified as "from a Trieste paper which a friend of mine has sent me" (*Letters II* 449–50; see illustrations 11.3 and 11.4).[9] Written in Italian by Oscar Schwarz, an English language student of Joyce's (though published anonymously), the substantial article hyperbolically praises Joyce the artist who, it claims, has written novels and dramas celebrated throughout Europe. Actually, at this point he had published but one novel, *A Portrait of the Artist as a Young Man,* and a play, *Exiles,* which had recently been performed in Munich but was barely noticed and closed after the first performance. As a portrait of Joyce, however, the article is remarkably vivid and was, Joyce's comments to Weaver show, of great interest to him. He points out with amusement that the writer cited an article that Joyce had written from the Isle of Wight – actually a piece on the Aran Isles.[10] Schwarz writes appreciatively of Joyce's humour, his style of teaching, memorization of poetry, command of Italian, sharing of new poems and notes (apparently for *Ulysses*). He evokes the image of Joyce speaking in the evening, eyes behind strong glittering lenses, working his magic on those present. He portrays the two Joyce brothers James and Stanislaus as familiar figures in the city but distinct from each other in stature and pace. A reader of the article – perhaps Joyce, though the handwriting is difficult to identify – underlined "nel passo" with a reference to a handwritten note in Italian describing Stanislaus's distinctive walk as being well known; as Joyce wrote to Weaver, "nicknamed in Trieste 'omo salta' (the man on springs) on account of his walk".[11] Schwarz

8 David Rando, "A Remarkable Romance", in *Modernist Fiction and News: Representing Experience in the Early Twentieth Century* (New York: Palgrave Macmillan, 2011), 49–53.

9 Oscar Schwarz, "Di un poeta irlandese a Trieste", *L'era nuova* (14 August 1919), 2. Add MS 57345, Harriet Shaw Weaver Papers, British Library.

10 "Il miraggio del pescatore di Aran: La valvola dell'Inghilterra in caso di guerra", *Il piccolo della sera* (5 September 1912): 2.

11 Although *Letters II* gives "salta", the word to which Joyce refers looks more like "susta", which is also what he wrote in his letter to Weaver. A transcription error must have occurred at some point, perhaps on Weaver's or on Ellmann's part. "Susta" means "spring" in Triestine dialect, making "omo susta" into "spring man", "a man on springs".

notes Joyce's exile in Zurich as an asylum to all the souls not called by the governments to celebrate the war. Joyce, avoiding British conscription, underlined these last words and wrote "bene!" next to them.[12] Clearly this article impressed him and, despite the inaccuracies, stimulated his pride.

Di un poeta irlandese a Trieste

Sul prof. James Joyce, che durante la guerra ha scritto romanzi e drammi, celebrati da tutta la critica europea, così ci scrive un suo ammiratore:

Giovedì scorso fu rappresentato allo «Schauspielhaus» di Monaco un nuovo lavoro, gli «Exiles», scritto a Trieste, da un giovane scrittore irlandese, che fu qualche anno fa una delle figure più note e popolari a Trieste: il prof. James Joyce. Abitavano tra noi i due fratelli Joyce, diversi nel fisico, nell'indole, nel passo, due maestri di inglese ambi due, cioè il professore della Scuola Revoltella e l'«habitué» del Caffè agli specchi. Da alcun tempo la stampa inglese, francese, americana, spagnola, olandese, greca, cinese, pubblica critiche lusinghiere dei lavori del James maggiore, ne parlò anche il Benco nell'«Umana».

ILLUSTRATION 11.3 *Beginning of article; Oscar Schwarz, "Di un poeta irlandese a Trieste",* L'era nuova *(14 August 1919), 2.*[13]

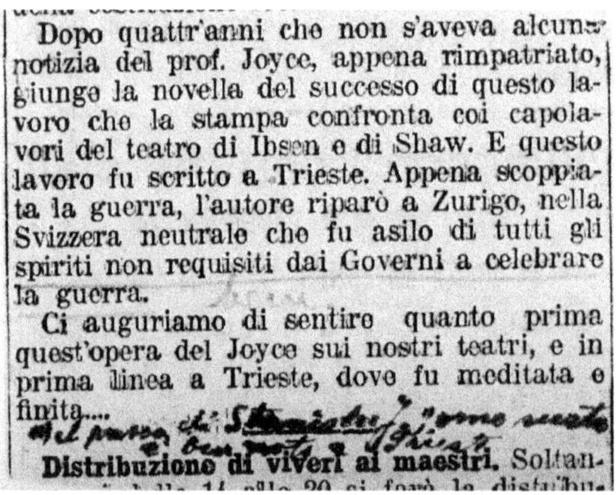

Dopo quattr'anni che non s'aveva alcuna notizia del prof. Joyce, appena rimpatriato, giunge la novella del successo di questo lavoro che la stampa confronta coi capolavori del teatro di Ibsen e di Shaw. E questo lavoro fu scritto a Trieste. Appena scoppiata la guerra, l'autore riparò a Zurigo, nella Svizzera neutrale che fu asilo di tutti gli spiriti non requisiti dai Governi a celebrare la guerra.

Ci auguriamo di sentire quanto prima quest'opera del Joyce sui nostri teatri, e in prima linea a Trieste, dove fu meditata e finita....

Distribuzione di viveri ai maestri. Soltan-

ILLUSTRATION 11.4 *End of article; Schwarz, "Di un poeta irlandese", 2.*

12 "spiriti non requisiti dai Governi a celebrare la guerra".

13 I am grateful to Erik Schneider for his assistance in identifying the author and determining bibliographic details.

Joyce's letters make dozens of references to newspaper cuttings. His fascination with newspapers is well documented.[14] He maintained subscriptions to Irish newspapers throughout much of his time on the continent. Stories clipped or torn from the newspapers were a means of communication for Joyce, which could be as urgent, expressive, and direct as telegrams or telephone calls. Clippings were, of course, news, but also advertisement, self-promotion, and proof or disproval of rumour. A letter of 15 March 1905 (*Letters II* 84) to Stanislaus, still living in Dublin at the time, enclosed a clipping from a Trieste newspaper about the publication of Ibsen's letters by his son. On 19 August 1906, homesick for Trieste, Joyce asked Stanislaus from Rome, "If there is anything interesting (Ferrero etc) in the *Piccolo della Sera*, you might send it" (*Letters II* 152). He lived with and among clippings and, from a relatively early age, used them as documentation of his own life and concerns.

As Joyce's works were published, he became increasingly attuned to press coverage. One of his main means of communication with supporters was via clippings. Joyce was relatively isolated in Zurich during the war years from 1915 to 1919 and depended upon communications from Harriet Weaver and Ezra Pound in London to obtain information about the publication and reception of his works. A letter from Harriet Weaver in 2 March 1917 states:

> You will see from the enclosed cutting that The Times Literary Supplement has given a special review in the body of the paper, not in the ordinary novel review column. This should be a great help to the sales. Mr. Pound had written to Mr. Clutton Brock, who writes their leading articles, and got him to ask the editor to let him have the book to review.[15]

This prompted Joyce to write directly to Arthur Clutton-Brock to thank him, which in turn prompted Clutton-Brock's question of whether "the sad scepticism of [*Portrait*] is merely recollection for you or whether it is your own state of mind".[16] Clippings could verify superstitions. Confirmation of his words to Harriet Weaver in a letter from 20 July 1919 that "as soon as I mention or include any person in [*Ulysses*] I hear of his or her death or departure or misfortune" (*SL* 241) came shortly afterward when, in his next letter from 6 August (*SL* 242),

14 For example, R. Brandon Kershner, *The Culture of Joyce's "Ulysses"* (New York: Palgrave Macmillan, 2010).

15 John Firth, "Harriet Weaver's Letters to James Joyce 1915–1920", *Studies in Bibliography* 20 (1967): 169.

16 As quoted in Firth, "Harriet Weaver's Letters", 169.

he enclosed a clipping of the obituary of solicitor J.G. Lidwell, who as a character in "Sirens" flirts with the barmaids.[17]

One of Joyce's first actions on arriving in Paris in July 1920 was to subscribe to a press cutting agency. In fact, he wrote Harriet Weaver on 16 August 1920 that he was surprised not to have received anything from the agency for a long time (*Letters III* 15). Although he did this at a time when his name was still obscure (there would have been few reports or reviews to collect) and his finances were a ruin, he had some prescient sense of the service's value. In October of that year a complaint was lodged in New York by the New York Society for the Prevention of Vice against Margaret Anderson and Jane Heap for sending through the mails the issue of the *Little Review* containing the opening section of the "Nausicaa" episode in *Ulysses*. Joyce's lawyer and supporter John Quinn had managed to delay the trial, but it went to court in February 1921. Though Joyce's main venue for publication at the time was the United States (with *Dubliners*, *Exiles* and *A Portrait of the Artist as a Young Man* published by Huebsch in New York), his contact with publishers and others in the country was sporadic. In April 1921 he sent Harriet Weaver a note written on a calling card accompanying a clipping from the *New York Times* and followed up that "I should know nothing whatever about it but for the fact that I was given one day in a bookshop here [presumably Shakespeare and Company] a cutting which the owner had received by chance from New York" (*Letters I* 160). The paper reported Quinn's statement that though *Ulysses* was "cast in a curious style … it was in similar [sic] vein to the work of an [unspecified] American author with which no fault was found, and he thought it was principally a matter of punctuation marks".[18] Both outraged and amused, Joyce wrote Weaver that "The offense is less grotesque than the defence!"[19] Later that year he wrote to Weaver of his pleasure at receiving a cutting of "a very friendly article" which lambasted the legal action as "an absurd act of puritanic spleen" and praised the *Little Review*'s *Ulysses* as "one of the most interesting literary symptoms in the whole literary world", asserting that "such sincerity, such energy, such fearlessness as Mr. Joyce's are rare in any epoch, and most of all in our own".[20] As

17 "Ulysses", *Little Review* 6, no. 4 (August 1919): 41–64 and 6, no. 5 (September 1919): 46–55.

18 "Improper Novel Costs Woman $50", *New York Times* (22 February 1921): 6.

19 James Joyce to Harriet Shaw Weaver, 11 March 1921, Harriet Shaw Weaver Papers, Add MS 57346, British Library, London.

20 James Joyce to Harriet Shaw Weaver, 5 May 1921, Harriet Shaw Weaver Papers, Add MS 57346, British Library, London; R.H.C., "Readers and Writers", *New Age* 28, no. 26 (28 April 1921): 306.

late as 1940 Joyce was still fascinated by the press's treatment of him. A clipping from a Rotterdam newspaper sent to him by a friend, Daniel Brody, prompted a letter of thanks from Joyce on 7 March 1940. Joyce found that the article, "even though unfavourable, is ably and intelligently hostile – when it is hostile".[21] It could not have been too critical, however, as the writer apparently referred to Joyce as "goochelaar", or magician.

Joyce was able to turn the press's interest in him to his advantage through the several *Extracts from Press Notices* that he had a hand in compiling between 1907 and 1922 (*Letters II* xlv; see illustration 11.5–11.6). These leaflets gathered excerpts from reviews of *Chamber Music, Exiles, A Portrait of the Artist as a Young Man* and *Ulysses* to serve as advertisement for these and succeeding

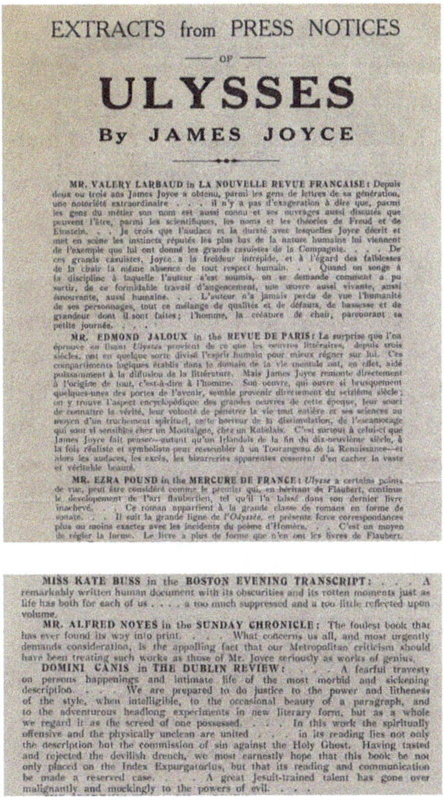

EXTRACTS from PRESS NOTICES

— OF —

ULYSSES

By JAMES JOYCE

MR. VALERY LARBAUD in **LA NOUVELLE REVUE FRANCAISE:** Depuis deux ou trois ans James Joyce a obtenu, parmi les gens de lettres de sa génération, une notoriété extraordinaire . . . il n'y a pas d'exagération à dire que, parmi les gens du métier son nom est aussi connu et ses ouvrages aussi discutés que peuvent l'être, parmi les scientifiques, les noms et les théories de Freud et de Einstein. . . Je crois que l'audace et la dureté avec lesquelles Joyce décrit et met en scène les instincts réputés les plus bas de la nature humaine lui viennent de l'exemple que lui ont donné les grands casuistes de la Compagnie. . . . De ces grands casuistes, Joyce a la froideur intrépide, et à l'égard des faiblesses de la chair la même absence de tout respect humain. . . Quand on songe à la discipline à laquelle l'auteur s'est soumis, on se demande comment a pu sortir, de ce formidable travail d'angencement, une œuvre aussi vivante, aussi émouvante, aussi humaine. . . L'auteur n'a jamais perdu de vue l'humanité de ses personnages, tout ce mélange de qualités et de défauts, de bassesse et de grandeur dont il sont faites; l'homme, la créature de chair, parcourant sa petite journée. . . .

MR. EDMOND JALOUX in the **REVUE DE PARIS:** La surprise que l'on éprouve en lisant *Ulysses* provient de ce que les oeuvres littéraires, depuis trois siècles, ont en quelque sorte divisé l'esprit humain pour mieux régner sur lui. Ces compartiments logiques établis dans le domain de la vie mentale ont, en effet, aidé puissamment à la diffusion de la littérature. Mais James Joyce remonte directement à l'origine de tout, c'est-à-dire à l'homme. Son oeuvre, qui ouvre si brusquement quelques-unes des portes de l'avenir, semble provenir directement du seizième siècle; on y trouve l'aspect encyclopédique des grandes oeuvres de cette époque, leur souci de connaître la vérité, leur volonté de pénétrer la vie tout entière et ses sciences au moyen d'un truchement spirituel, cette horreur de la dissimulation, de l'escamotage qui sont si sensibles chez un Montaigne, chez un Rabelais. C'est surtout à celui-ci que James Joyce fait penser—autant qu'un Irlandais de la fin du dix-neuvième siècle, à la fois réaliste et symboliste peut ressembler à un Tourangeau de la Renaissance—et alors les audaces, les excès, les bizarreries apparentes cesseront d'en cacher la vaste et véritable beauté.

MR. EZRA POUND in the **MERCURE DE FRANCE:** *Ulysse* a certains points de vue, peut être considéré comme le premier qui, en héritant de Flaubert, continue le développement de l'art flaubertien, tel qu'il l'a laissé dans son dernier livre inachevé. . . Ce roman appartient à la grande classe de romans en forme de sonate. . . Il suit la grande ligne de *l'Odyssée*, et présente force correspondances plus ou moins exactes avec les incidents du poème d'Homère. . . C'est un moyen de régler la forme. Le livre a plus de forme que n'en ont les livres de Flaubert.

MISS KATE BUSS in the **BOSTON EVENING TRANSCRIPT:** . . . A remarkably written human document with its obscurities and its rotten moments just as life has both for each of us . . . . a too much suppressed and a too little reflected upon volume.

MR. ALFRED NOYES in the **SUNDAY CHRONICLE:** The foulest book that has ever found its way into print. . . . What concerns us all, and most urgently demands consideration, is the appalling fact that our Metropolitan criticism should have been treating such works as those of Mr. Joyce seriously as works of genius.

DOMINI CANIS in **THE DUBLIN REVIEW:** . . . A fearful travesty on persons happenings and intimate life of the most morbid and sickening description. . . . We are prepared to do justice to the power and litheness of the style, when intelligible, to the occasional beauty of a paragraph, and to the adventurous headlong experiments in new literary form, but as a whole we regard it as the screed of one possessed. . . . In this work the spiritually offensive and the physically unclean are united . . . . in its reading lies not only the description but the commission of sin against the Holy Ghost. Having tasted and rejected the devilish drench, we most earnestly hope that this book be not only placed on the Index Expurgatorius, but that its reading and communication be made a reserved case. . . . A great Jesuit-trained talent has gone over malignantly and mockingly to the powers of evil. . . .

ILLUSTRATION 11.5–6
From Extracts from Press Notices of "Ulysses" by James Joyce. *See footnote 21.*

21 James Joyce to Daniel Brody, 7 March 1940, James Joyce Collection, box 2 folder 1, Harry Ransom Center, Austin.

works.[22] In these he could be seen as fulfilling the role of "scissors and paste man" (*Letters I* 297), as he referred to himself when negotiating with George Antheil for an opera based on Byron's *Cain* – Joyce willing not to rewrite Byron but to excise and rearrange. The leaflets were intended primarily to be inserted in later publications sent to reviewers to validate Joyce's reputation, as for instance his request to Grant Richards of 8 May 1914 to insert a leaflet of reviews from *Chamber Music* (published in 1907) into the newly-published *Dubliners* (*Letters II* 332), but also for shameless self-promotion, such as to Harriet Monroe, editor of *Poetry* magazine, on 12 August 1917 (*Letters II* 403). Correspondence shows him to have been highly attuned to the reception of his works. On 19 and 22 April 1915 he wrote Grant Richards querying him about reviews of *Dubliners* in the *Freeman's Journal* and *Sinn Féin*, suggesting that Richards's press clipping agency was failing to do its job (*Letters II* 339, 340). Though Joyce wanted to bathe in the press's praise of his work, he was aware that any notice is better than none. Reacting to the *Dublin Review*'s scathing criticism of *Ulysses* by Shane Leslie under the pen name of "Domini Canis" ("A fearful travesty on persons happenings and intimate life of the most morbid and sickening description") he wrote to Harriet Shaw Weaver in November 1922,

> I leave you to make your choice from his article which is having the effect I foresaw. It is the best thing he could have done for the book to give it prestige in England. The fact that it is adverse, in my opinion will not count .... I have also received the press-cuttings which might be called 'Noise about Joyce'. I do not think that Mr Noyes has read the book but you can take a few sentences from his article in the *Sunday Chronicle* ["the foulest book that has ever found its way into print"] to add to the press extracts.[23]
>
> *Letters I* 192

A newspaper clipping forms part of the opening scene of "A Painful Case" in the description of the contents of James Duffy's desk. In the desk is "a little sheaf of papers held together by a brass pin. In these sheets a sentence was inscribed from time to time and, in an ironical moment, the headline of an

22 *Extracts from Press Notices and Reviews of "Dubliners"* (London: Grant Richards, 1914); *Extracts from Some Press Notices of "A Portrait of the Artist as a Young Man" by James Joyce* (London: Egoist Press, 1916); *Extracts from Press Notices of "Ulysses" by James Joyce* (Harlesden: Leveridge, 1922).

23 *Extracts from Press Notices of "Ulysses"*, 4.

advertisement for bile beans had been pasted on to the first sheet" (*D* 11.23–27). Bile Beans was a widely advertised trade name for an herbal concoction popular in the early twentieth century touted as a cure for indigestion and "biliousness" – ailments that would have been likely to afflict the dour James Duffy.[24] Was the inclusion of the advertisement an "ironical moment" in Duffy's reflection on his own character or, as has been suggested, a correspondence with the "ordered Aristotelian view he tries to impose on the world"?[25] At some point following his breakup with Emily Sinico, Duffy adds to his bookshelves a copy of *Thus Spake Zarathustra*. One of Nietzsche's descriptive lines regarding the "superfluous" – "Diseased they ever are, they vomit bile and call it newspaper" – certainly provides an ironic connection between that advertisement early in the story and the newspaper account of Sinico's death later.[26] For the purposes of the present essay, the implications of the clipping are moot; the appearance of the advertisement is significant in the simple appearance of the clipping at an early stage in Joyce's writing and in its bracketing of the story between the introduction of Duffy and the climax in the newspaper account.

The three clippings enumerated and described in the "Ithaca" episode of *Ulysses* show the variety of uses to which they can be put. All three are contained in a table in the front room (otherwise unspecified) in two drawers whose contents are minutely enumerated. Two are located in the first drawer and the third is in the second. Joyce had a firm concept of the nature of these drawers' contents from early on in the composition of the episode. The draft in the "Ithaca" manuscript notebook, though in several places divergent from the sequence and content of the episode's final version, gives the text of the drawers' contents in a manner remarkably like the final result.[27] One notation is particularly revealing. At the top of the handwritten list of the first drawer's contents is written the word "sentimental". The term parallels the designation "documents" which begins the list of the second drawer's contents. "Documents" survived into the published work (*U* 17.1855), but "sentimental" was

24 As advertised in "A Story from Erin's Isle: Two Years of Indigestion and Liver Troubles – Then Bile Beans and Perfect Health", *Penny Illustrated Paper and Illustrated Times* 92, no. 2365 (22 September 1906): 192.

25 Mary Power, "The Bile Beans Advertisement", *James Joyce Quarterly* 13, no. 4 (Summer 1976): 462.

26 Friedrich Nietzsche, *Thus Spake Zarathustra: A Book for All and None*, trans. Alexander Tille (London: T. Fisher Unwin, 1899), 64. This is an edition that Joyce might well have had access to.

27 James Joyce, "II.ii.7. Partial draft: 'Ithaca'", The Joyce Papers 2002, MS 36,639/13, National Library of Ireland, Dublin.

dropped. These were the author's notes to himself, categorizing at the outset the distinct nature of each drawer's items. Though some additions (notably the clipping in the second drawer) were made to the lists after the composition of the notebooks, the structure of the contents remained remarkably the same through successive stages of manuscript and proof and first edition.

The sequence of the items is not as clear as that of other lists such as those in "Cyclops", where the items or persons enumerated tend to begin with straightforward elements and then deviate off into the farcical. The seemingly random sequence of the drawers' lists leaves the relations between items in the drawers uncertain. Yet a reader will make connections between adjacent elements in the lists – and there are relations or at least inferences to be made. For example, the magnifying glass immediately precedes Bloom's two pornographic photos. One might imagine Bloom peering intently through the magnifying glass at minute details of the photographs' actors. But is this why the magnifying glass is in the drawer? The first drawer, in particular, contains what seems to be the same kind of quotidian assortment that can be found in anyone's kitchen or desk drawer. Yet some of the objects in the drawer anchor indistinct references elsewhere in the book with "Ithaca's" typically minute detail (for example, the inventory of three letters sent by Martha Clifford to Henry Flower [*U* 17.1796–98]).

The first clipping, "from an English weekly periodical *Modern Society*, subject corporal chastisement in girls' schools" (*U* 17.1801–3), could be seen from several perspectives (see illustration 11.7). Extensive debates occurred throughout the early twentieth century British press regarding juvenile punishment – a

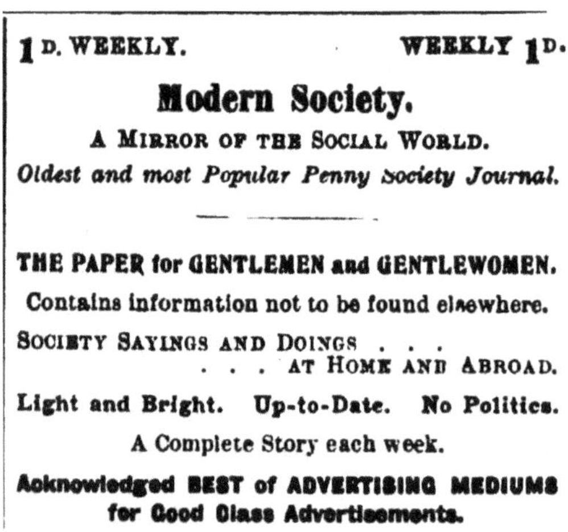

ILLUSTRATION 11.7
Advertisement for Modern Society. Newspaper Press Directory *(1905): 499.*
COURTESY OF HATHITRUST.

topic that Bloom in his role as reformer would have been attentive to.[28] As "a mirror of the social world", as the periodical advertised itself, it would have been likely to have published such an article. The clipping recalls the brutality of corporal punishment in the British navy as parodied in "Cyclops" (*U* 12.1333–59). Recalling the presence of Milly in the drawer's other objects (such as her "epistle" [*U* 17.1792]), it brings the issue home in a personal way to Bloom's fifteen year old daughter. But the clipping could take on a completely different cast in the context of the two erotic photocards in the drawer (*U* 17.1809). It could remind the reader of "The Honourable Mrs Mervyn Talboys" in "Circe" who asserted that Bloom sent her one of the erotic photographs featuring the señorita "practicing illicit intercourse" with the torero, and whom Bloom "implored" "to chastise him as he richly deserves" (*U* 15.1067–72).

The second clipping, "a press cutting of recipe for renovation of old tan boots" (*U* 17.1813–14), is an item of interest to a man who thinks earlier in the day "Mulch of dung. Best thing to clean ladies' kid gloves. Dirty cleans" (*U* 4.481), not to mention the dozens of other practical ideas that pop into his mind during the course of the day. This is the kind of everyday advice that filled many newspaper pages of the time. Bloom's idea of a recipe is formulaic: "Those homely recipes are often the best" he thinks as he negotiates the purchase of lotion from the chemist at Sweny's (*U* 5.496). Indeed, it fits in with numerous other instances of Bloom's wisdom as when "renovation" comes up earlier in "Ithaca":

> For what reason did he meditate on schemes so difficult of realisation?
> It was one of his axioms that similar meditations or the automatic relation to himself of a narrative concerning himself or tranquil recollection of the past when practised habitually before retiring for the night alleviated fatigue and produced as a result sound repose and renovated vitality.
> *U* 17.1754–58

Could this "renovated vitality" have a particular irony in the light of Blazes Boylan's signature "tan shoes", mentioned frequently enough in connection with him to anchor the association (*U* 8.1168; 10.307; 10.1241; 11.337; 11.761)?[29] Of

---

28 For example, in 1902 the "Society for the Reform of School Discipline" advertised as its first priority "the abolition of corporal punishment"; *The Reformers' Year Book* (1902), 143.

29 The relation of Bloom's cutting to Boylan's shoes is discussed by Mike Tierce, "'A press cutting of recipe for renovation of old tan boots': A Note on the Ending of Joyce's *Ulysses*", *James Joyce Quarterly* 21, no. 2 (Winter 1984): 176–77.

course, "Nausicaa's" Tommy Caffrey also wears tan shoes (*U* 13.77) which his sister is concerned might suffer if he urinates carelessly. In light of the damage done by Boylan to the Bloom household on 16 June, one might also recall the graphic image of Gretta's boots in "The Dead" – "One boot stood upright, its limp upper fallen down: the fellow of it lay upon its side" (*D* 15.1565–66) – echoing the position of Gretta on the bed and the standing Gabriel, "limp" after his wife's revelation of an earlier love.

The third clipping, a "local press cutting concerning change of name by deedpoll" (*U* 17.1866–67), is in some ways the most prosaic of the three, as "Ithaca" provides the text of the cutting, which is much like other similar notices of the period. A "deed poll" was a common way to accomplish a name change at the time and was often documented by a classified advertisement in a newspaper.[30] Virag's name change has already been reported in "Cyclops" by Martin Cunningham (*U* 12.1640). Quoting the text of the classified ad in "Ithaca" presents the statement as a performative act by Bloom's father and also preserves Virag's words in a way that recalls the gramophone recording of "poor old greatgrandfather" that Bloom imagines in "Hades" (*U* 6.964). This item encapsulates the dual roles of clippings, in this case firstly as news and a transformative event, and secondly as an archival document, its function having been changed into nostalgia. In Bloom's drawer, it coexists with various other items related to his father that launch Bloom into several pages of "reminiscences" (*U* 17.1887) and "remorse" (*U* 17.1893) and then into his consideration of departure from 7 Eccles Street (*U* 17.1958). This clipping further complicates the confusion of names in the two drawers. The sound of "deed poll" reverses "Poldy". Bloom's father begins his notice as "I, Rudolph Virag" (*U* 17.1769), using the anglicized form of his given name rather than "Rudolf", as he is scrupulously referred to elsewhere in the episode when his pre-name change status is intended (*U* 17.534, 17.622, 17.1637, 17.1875).[31]

Even more than with the newspaper headlines of "Aeolus", the questions of "Ithaca" break up the narrative. But of course there is a narrative underneath that carries Bloom and Stephen to Eccles Street, sees Stephen's departure, and takes Bloom upstairs and eventually into bed. So while the questions and inventories appear in the abstract, there is some congruence with a Bloomian consciousness and with Bloom's actions. That Bloom unlocks the first drawer

---

30 "A deed to which there is only one party; for example, one declaring a change of name", "Deed poll", in Jonathan Law, *A Dictionary of Law* (Oxford: Oxford University Press, 2015), online.

31 Hans Walter Gabler justifies this spelling as "anticipatory of Rudolf Virag's metamorphosis into Rudolph Bloom by the deedpoll quoted" (*U-G* 1752).

and looks into it becomes apparent when he adds to the accumulated letters from Martha the one received earlier in the narrative. The minute enumeration of items in the drawer is, however, the "Ithacan" compulsive voice taking over from what, on a narrative level, may be Bloom's mental review or visual scan of the objects in the drawer. It is as if he is scanning a page from a newspaper. Just as the objects in the two drawers have been extracted from Bloom's life, the three clippings in these two drawers have been extracted from newspapers.

News clippings are not as prominent in *Finnegans Wake* as in *Ulysses*, but they and remnants of press notices do appear in the text and serve in similar ways as floating documentary objects lost from their original context but used anew. Among the numerous items "persianly literatured" (FW 183.10) in Shem's house, the Haunted Inkbottle, are "tress clippings from right, lift and cintrum" (FW 183.29). This appears immediately following the "garters" of a list of a variety of women, emphasizing the female association. Joyce maintained that the long tresses of Livia Svevo (wife of his friend the author Italo Svevo) were an inspiration for the *Wake*'s Anna Livia Plurabelle (*JJ* II 561). Just as Joyce had gathered positive, middling, and negative reviews of *Ulysses* in the *Extracts*, Shem is equally open to all varieties of "clippings". Joyce must have saved for years a cutting of the *Times Literary Supplement*'s review of *Dubliners* which notes that "the reader's difficulty will be enhanced if he is ignorant of Dublin customs; if he does not know, for instance, that 'a curate' is a man who brings strong waters".[32] In the *Wake* this becomes part of a logical proposition: "Let a prostitute be whoso stands before a door and winks or parks herself in the fornix near a makeussin wall (sinsin! sinsin!) and the curate one who brings strong waters (gingin! gingin!)" (FW 116.16–19). Reference in the *Extracts from Press Notices of "Ulysses"* of the *Sporting Times*'s attack on *Ulysses* ("enough to make a Hottentot sick") appears in book 1, episode 7 of the *Wake* in Justius's condemnation of Mercius:

> Is it not the fact (gainsay me, cake-eater!) that, while whistlewhirling your crazy elegies around Templetombmount joyntstone, (let him pass, pleasegood-jesusalem, in a bundle of straw, he was balbettised after haymaking) you squandered among underlings the overload of your extravagance and made a hottentot of dulpeners crawsick with your crumbs?[33]
>
> *FW* 192.33–193.3

32 E.E. Mavrogordato, "*Dubliners*", *Times Literary Supplement* no. 648 (18 June 1914): 298.

33 *Extracts from Press Notices of "Ulysses"*, 4.

Recounted history and the process of archival accumulation come together in the *Wake*'s reference to "Clio's clippings" in II.1, the "children's games" chapter. Clio, of course, was one of the Muses, the goddess of memory. Fritz Senn points out that:

> in Antiquity what was known of the mythical past was attributed to the Muses, daughters of Memnosyne [sic] or Memory. Homer invokes them, and so does Hesiod. But Hesiod's omniscient historians give early warning: "We know how to speak many false things as though they were true: but we know, when we will, to utter true things".... So scepticism about truth goes far back to the sources.[34]

The scene is the winding down of the games after Shem had failed three times to guess the colour of Issy's underpants, and the "sudden and gigantesquesque appearance" of H.C.E. in his role as publican and father, "the largely longsuffering laird of Lucanhof" (*FW* 253.29–32). In the naturalistic sense, H.C.E. has emerged from the pub to the outdoor scene; in another sense he is embodying the reappearance of myth or history. And then the text asks how we are to think of him: "by mortisection or vivisuture, splitten up or recompounded", "how accountibus for him?" (*FW* 253.34–36). The text of the succeeding paragraph expands upon this question, offering two possibilities (*FW* 254.1–14). Perhaps, for one, he appeared suddenly, "pitssched", tossed out of the sea and on to the seawall by the ancient waves of Ireland or simply pissed against the wall ("dognosed"), in a way that might have occurred to anyone, from the "brutest" to the "princest"? Or perhaps, as another possibility, has he evolved through documented history, "yclept from Clio's clippings", accounted for by a chronicler, perhaps even "built with glue and clippings, scrawled or voided on a buttress"?[35] (*FW* 135.33–34). In the way that newspaper clippings extract themselves from their context and become elements of a chronicle, they are pieced together and "ayewitnessed" (*FW* 254.10). In this sentence are both A.L.P. ("ancients link with presents") and H.C.E. ("human chain extends"), expressing a historical sequence from generation to generation (*FW* 254.8–9). "Yclept" is

---

34 Fritz Senn, "Joycean Refractions: Around Several Corners", *Papers on Joyce* 10/11 (2004–2005), 209–39.

35 Though most published texts of *Finnegans Wake* give the word as "chroncher", editors Robbert-Jan Henkes and Erik Bindervoet correct this to "chronicler" in *Finnegans Wake* (Oxford: Oxford University Press, 2012), 637.

archaic for "called", yet it could also echo the 1920s slang term "clip" referring to something stolen.[36]

Press clippings inhabit Joyce's works and letters like other bits and pieces of media, part of the multitude of cultural references in the books. What Brandon Kershner points out regarding newspapers is even more the case with clippings:

> But Joyce's invocation of the newspapers of the time has a broader and more complicated significance for our reading of *Ulysses*, in that the newspapers themselves existed, quite literally, in a dialogical relationship with one another and with their readership, as well as with Joyce's novel itself, in which they represent a mixed chorus of contending voices.[37]

Like Bloom's thinking of the cleaning of corpses, "I believe they clip the nails and the hair. Keep a bit in an envelope" (*U* 6.19–20), hair and nails being transformed from living things into the stuff (literally) of history, clippings take on a historical significance from the moment they are extracted from their page of origin. Clippings are not news but the recirculated and repurposed extractions from the news which live on as history or evidence or commentary in a way that the news, aiming to be up to date, does not. The context in which the news stories originally appeared is lost and is largely irrelevant as the clippings take on their own independent meanings defined by the contexts of letters or of the fictional texts that they inhabit. What makes Joyce's involvement with news clippings distinctive is the life that he gives them. Far from being pasted into a scrapbook and put away in a closet, clippings are rhetorical signposts in his letters and vibrant images in his works. For Joyce they are scraps from real life, part of the flotsam of historical and topographical fact that underpins the fiction.

---

36 "Clip", *OED Online*, accessed 6 December 2016, http://oed.com.

37 Kershner, *The Culture of Joyce's "Ulysses"*, 96.

CHAPTER 12

The Ineluctable Modernity of the Visible: The Typographic Odyssey of *Ulysses* in Interwar Print Culture

Tekla Mecsnóber

Abstract

Joyce was not always directly involved in decisions regarding the material shape in which *Ulysses* reached potential readers, but his interest in visual aspects of the written word appears to have made its impact on the novel's text as well. Examining the specific significance of type choice – as part of the bibliographic code – in designing and promoting *Ulysses* as a printed text, this study traces some of the salient changes that accompanied the novel's development from its first serialisation in the little magazines of the 1910s to its appearance as book in various editions of the 1920s, 1930s and in 1940 (the last to be issued during Joyce's lifetime). It also draws upon contemporary and later assessments of the "character" of relevant typefaces and highlights the role of some influential European and American typographers, anchoring these early editions among the revivalist and modernist design trends of the interwar years. These analyses suggest that whereas the typography of most of the earlier editions, as well as their publicity materials, tended to rely on historicising typefaces to convey connotations of classic dignity, artistic quality and craftsmanship, editions in the 1930s began to borrow from modernist typographic trends to promote the book as a modern work.

Keywords

Ulysses – publicity – typography – typefaces – bibliographic codes – visual design – print culture – modernism – revival

On or about December 1932, the visual identity of Joyce's *Ulysses* changed. As was the case with the alteration of "human character" that Virginia Woolf

 | DOI 10.1163/9789004359062_014

famously dated to 1910,[1] this change was not sudden or definite. But a change there was: whereas the typography of most earlier *Ulysses* editions and publicity materials tended to evoke connotations of classic distinction or artistry and craftsmanship, the prospectus issued by the Odyssey Press between 12 October 1932 (when Joyce signed the contract)[2] and late December 1932 (when the first copies were ready) began to market the book as a "modern classic" not only in words but also in appearance (see illustration 12.1). Although making a gesture to ancient Greece through its meander border ornament, the leaflet was set entirely in the distinctive and extremely influential geometric modern typeface

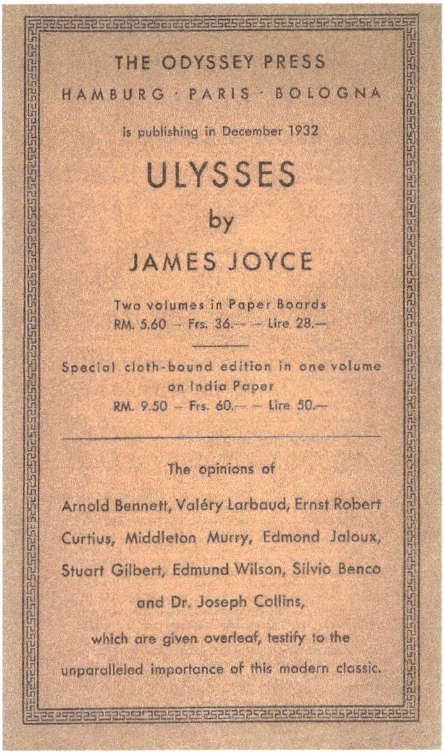

ILLUSTRATION 12.1
Prospectus issued by the Odyssey Press in 1932.[3]
FROM THE COLLECTION OF ALASTAIR JOLLANS.

1 Virginia Woolf, "Mr. Bennett and Mrs. Brown", *Nation and the Athenaeum* 34, no. 9 (1 December 1923): 342–43.

2 Luca Crispi, "*Ulysses* in the Marketplace: 1932", *Joyce Studies Annual* (2012): 51.

3 "Ulysses Publicity Leaflet Front", accessed 6 December 2016, https://paperbackrevolution.files.wordpress.com/2014/12/ulysses-publicity-leaflet-front.jpg.

Futura, issued in 1927 and marketed from the beginning as "the typeface of our time" ("die Schrift unserer Zeit").[4]

With this, *Ulysses* – described in the 1921 subscription prospectus of the first edition as "a contemporary of the future" and advertised in 1927 by the publisher of the German translation as the work of the "Homer of Our Time" ("der Homer unserer Zeit"),[5] entered the space of visual modernity. In Joyce's life, this look of modernity arguably culminated in the 1934 Random House edition, which was also negotiated in 1932,[6] advertised as "one of the monumental novels *of our time*",[7] and visually marketed through advertisements and a cover design that also relied on the same Futura type family to accentuate the message of the modernity of *Ulysses*.

This essay sets out to suggest that the typographic link between these first two large trade editions of the novel is not as accidental as it may seem. It will suggest that the inescapably visual nature of the written word became an increasingly visible motif in *Ulysses* as Joyce became involved in decisions regarding the material shape of his book. It will trace some of the salient changes in the typographic form that accompanied the odyssey of *Ulysses* in print from its first serialisation in the *Little Review* (March 1918 to September-December 1920) and the *Egoist* (January to December 1919) to the last version to appear in Joyce's lifetime, the 1940 Modern Library edition. It will highlight a number of visual clues that the typographic form of the novel and the printed publicity materials appear to have provided as to the nature and value – or, as Edward Bishop has argued using Pierre Bourdieu's concept, the cultural capital[8] – of the novel. In doing so, this essay focuses on a salient and purely visual aspect – typeface (font) choice – within what Jerome McGann called the bibliographic

4 Christopher Burke, *Paul Renner: The Art of Typography* (London: Hyphen Press, 1998), 86–87. Unless otherwise indicated, all type identifications are mine. For the standard names, designers and dates of typefaces, I have consulted *Encyclopaedia of Typefaces*, eds. W. Pincus Jaspert, W. Turner Berry and A.F. Johnson (55th anniversary edition, London: Cassell Illustrated, 2008). Exact font identifications are complicated by design differences between various sizes of the same typeface, the proliferation of authorised and unauthorised copies, the concomitant variety of alternative type shapes and names and, occasionally, the quality of the reproductions available.

5 *Der Homer Unserer Zeit: Deutschland in Erwartung des "Ulysses" von Joyce: Letzte Gelegenheit zur Subskription* (Basel: Rhein-Verlag, 1927). Subscription prospectus, Zurich James Joyce Foundation.

6 Crispi, "*Ulysses*", especially 35–38.

7 Random House display advertisement, *The New York Times Book Review* (28 January 1934): 21; my italics.

8 Edward L. Bishop, "Re: Covering *Ulysses*", *Joyce Studies Annual* 5 (1994): 22–55.

code, "the physical form of books and manuscripts (paper, ink, typefaces, layouts) or their prices, advertising mechanisms and distribution venues"[9] – as a foundational category in recent scholarship on the material aspects of literature. Drawing upon contemporary and later assessments of the "character" of relevant typefaces, the essay also anchors these early editions of Joyce's work among the design trends of the interwar years, during the increasingly mature and ultimately decisive emergence of a modern visual language in Europe and North America. Finally, it will attempt to briefly highlight the involvement of a number of influential European typographers and graphic designers in determining this form.

The Ineluctability of the Visible

Despite Stephen's memorable ruminations about the fundamental difference between the visible and the audible, between the spatial *nebeneinander* of visual arts and the temporal *nacheinander* of literature, visual characteristics of printed verbal matter appear to claim significant and ever increasing attention in the text of *Ulysses*. Stephen makes a connection between verbal content and visual appearance when the battered school book that describes the battle of Asculum is characterised as "gorescarred" (*U* 2.12). Later he seems to link the sensational content of a used book claiming to contain the "Eighth and ninth book of Moses. Secret of all secrets" to its visual design ("Seal of King David") and visual clues to its popular success ("Thumbed pages: read and read") (*U* 10.844–46). He interprets his sister Dilly's purchase of a "coverless" French primer as the token of a doomed aspiration to achieve common cultural capital with him and involve him in her "drowning" (*U* 10.867–76).

Like Howard Bridgewater, whose book on advertising Joyce is known to have perused with some attention,[10] Buck Mulligan is very much aware of the importance of suitable typography for business purposes. Amid the drunken revelry of the "Oxen of the Sun" episode, he establishes his credibility by producing "a set of pasteboard cards which he had had printed that day at

9 Jerome J. McGann, *The Textual Condition* (Princeton: Princeton University Press, 1991), 12. Although the terms "typeface" and "font" have slightly different definitions in typography, they will both be used in this essay to refer to the graphic shape of a set of characters.

10 Howard Bridgewater, *Advertising or the Art of Making Known* (London: Isaac Pitman & Sons, n.d., c. 1910) discusses the typography of letter headings and showcards (5–10) and newspaper advertisements (14, 19, 27–28, 30–31). For Joyce's interest in and use of advertising, see Sabrina Alonso's, Matthew Hayward's and David Spurr's essays in this volume.

Mr Quinnell's bearing a legend printed in fair italics: *Mr Malachi Mulligan. Fertiliser and Incubator. Lambay Island*" (U 14.658–60). The same episode also refers to a dubious plan to print and advertise an exclusive artisanal book edition that irreverently recalls those of the Dun Emer Press, run, following the example of William Morris and the advice of Emery Walker, by Yeats's sister Elizabeth and her friend Evelyn Gleeson in Dundrum: "To be printed and bound at the Druiddrum press by two designing females. Calf covers of pissedon green. Last word in art shades. Most beautiful book come out of Ireland my time" (U 14.1454–57).[11] The same passage also seems to evoke Mulligan's earlier comic critique of the pretensions of books with archaic colophons, claiming to have been printed "in the year of the big wind" – if not quite "by the weird sisters" (U 1.365–67) – as was the case with the first volume published at the Dun Emer Press, the 1903 edition of W.B. Yeats's collection *In the Seven Woods*.[12]

A similar appreciation of printed matter characterises Bloom, too. He spots the "crooked botched print" of the copy of Aristotle's *Masterpiece* as a sign of an inferior publication (U 10.585), and is reported to have spent "two bob" on a second-hand book with "fine plates in it worth double the money, the stars and the moon and comets with long tails" (U 10.526–28). Bloom's attention to bibliographic detail such as printing type, illustrations and cover and his passion for collecting fine printed matter is blown into hyperbolic proportions in the Ithacan list of the "visual impression" (U 17.1357) of the contents of Bloom's bookshelves. Understandably, these somewhat erratic descriptions focus first on the binding (Shakespeare's works bound in "dark crimson morocco, goldtooled" (U 17.1365); Spinoza bound in "maroon leather" (U 17.1372), but with a transition through the "black boards, Gothic characters" of Gustav Freytag's *Soll und Haben* (U 17.1383), they penetrate – rather less plausibly, for a mirror image – into the printed pages as well. The bibliographic precision culminates in an account of the various traditional type sizes used for printing *A Handbook of Astronomy* (with, indeed, "5 plates" [U 17.1391]) whose purchase M'Coy appears to have witnessed (U 10.528): "antique letterpress long primer [10 point], author's footnotes nonpareil [6 point], marginal clues brevier [8 point], captions small pica [11 point]" (U 17.1392–93). In the last and longest description, a book called *Short but yet Plain Elements of Geometry* is made to visually proclaim its age through the novel's use of archaic long "ſ"[s] characters in its rendition of the front matter ("printed for R. Knaplock at the Biſhop's Head, MDCCXI, with

11 See also Jerome J. McGann, *Black Riders: The Visible Language of Modernism* (Princeton: Princeton University Press, 1993), 5ff.

12 Cf. Don Gifford, *"Ulysses" Annotated: Notes for James Joyce's "Ulysses"*, 2nd ed. (Berkeley: University of California Press, 1988), 20.

dedicatory epiſtle to his worthy friend Charles Cox, eſquire", *U* 17.1398–1401) and handwritten note ("the property of Michael Gallagher ... carpenter, Dufery Gate, Enniſcorthy, county Wicklow, the fineſt place in the world", *U* 17.1403–7) to be found in it. As the habit of using this alternative shape for s was discontinued in standard English printing between 1785 and the 1810s,[13] the text of *Ulysses* reinforces the eighteenth-century origin of Bloom's book through this subtle visual clue.

Special typographic characters like the archaic long ſ in the description above or the various diacritics[14] that Joyce inserted into his text as purely visual clues have formed some of the more obvious (although not necessarily recognised)[15] typographic challenges of the book. There is, however, a passage in the novel where the role of typography is not so striking, but still crucial to the understanding of the "content" itself. In "Lestrygonians", Bloom reminisces about the stickers that he used to see on the walls of public toilets, advertising bogus medicine to cure gonorrhoea:

> All kinds of places are good for ads. That quack doctor for the clap used to be stuck up in all the greenhouses. Never see it now. Strictly confidential. Dr Hy Franks. ... Got fellows to stick them up or stick them up himself for that matter on the q. t. running in to loosen a button. Flybynight. Just the place too. POST NO BILLS. POST I I O PILLS.
>
> *U* 8.95–101

The capitalised part of this passage is a translation crux and a typographic crux as well. The suggestion seems to be that the loss of a few lines in the lettering forbidding advertisements on the wall can turn the official injunction into a potential promise to send medicine by mail (in the same way as Bloom received his "rubber preservatives" and his Wonderworker [*U* 17.1804, 1819–22]). This interpretation depends crucially on the recognition of the possibility of visually

13 Michael Twyman, *Printing 1770–1970: An Illustrated History of Its Development and Uses in England* (London: Eyre & Spottiswoode, 1970), 77–78.

14 See Tekla Mecsnóber, "Diacritic Aspirations and Servile Letters: Alphabets and National Identities in Joyce's Europe", in *Doubtful Points: Joyce and Punctuation*, eds. Elizabeth M. Bonapfel and Tim Conley, European Joyce Studies 23 (Amsterdam: Rodopi, 2014), 167–88.

15 John Ryder does not mention these aspects at all in "Editing *Ulysses* Typographically", *Scholarly Publishing* 18, no. 2 (1987): 108–24. Bernard Benstock provides a thorough interpretative account of many typographic peculiarities of *Ulysses*, but not these; "Bedeviling the Typographer's Ass: *Ulysses* and *Finnegans Wake*", *Journal of Modern Literature* 12, no. 1 (March 1985): 3–33.

transforming the word NO into something that can be read as the number 110. This possibility is, as the following excerpts from early *Ulysses* editions show, largely determined by the choice of the text type and, consequently, of the kind of capitals and numerals used.

Closely supervised by Joyce, the 1922 Shakespeare and Company edition created as good a solution as was possible with the text typeface used (see illustration 12.2 below). The small capitals chosen match the size of the old style (ranging, lower case) numerals, the zero is not too different from the O and (apparently by default)[16] the space between the two 1s is sufficient for a defective N. The fact that some of the serifs in 11 (top left, bottom right) could not have been there in a stipulated original N in the case of most serif typefaces suggests that Bloom may have visualised an inscription in sans serif letters, but this suggestion does not seem to have been taken up by printers. Although the O/o connection is made clear, the 1932 Odyssey Press edition[17] (and the 1936 Bodley Head edition[18]) use capitals of unequal height and thus weaken the connection between the capital N and the lower-case 11, threatening to block the interpretative association between the two sentences (see illustration 12.3).

This typographic puzzle may be seen as another example of the attention that the text of *Ulysses* appears to pay to the ineluctably visual nature of the written word. That this attention seems to culminate in the detailed bibliographic descriptions and typographic imitation of the penultimate episode and in the

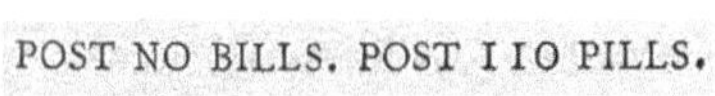
POST NO BILLS. POST I IO PILLS.

ILLUSTRATION 12.2
Type used for the "POST NO BILLS" passage in the first edition of Ulysses *printed in 1922 by Shakespeare and Company (page 146).*
COURTESY PRIVATE COLLECTION.

No Bills. Post 110 Pills.

ILLUSTRATION 12.3
Type used for the "POST NO BILLS" passage in the 1932 Odyssey Press edition (page 156).
COURTESY PRIVATE COLLECTION.

16 The page number on page 110 of the novel is practically identical to the characters displayed in POST IIO PILLS in this edition.

17 James Joyce, *Ulysses* (Hamburg: Odyssey Press, 1932), 156. The 2nd and subsequent impressions (1933–39) "corrected" the second sentence to read: "Post No Pills", and this reading was transmitted to the Random House edition as well, although set entirely in small caps: "POST NO PILLS" (151).

18 James Joyce, *Ulysses* (London: The Bodley Head, 1936), 142. Some modern editions use lower case numerals in combination with regular capitals but thus lose both the N/11 and the O/o association and effectively efface all visual clues.

wilful expulsion of purely visual (visible but inaudible) signs like apostrophes from the last episode is unlikely to be accidental. It was during the drafting of the "Ithaca" episode between February and October 1921 (*JJII* 442) that, arguably for the first time in his life, Joyce was given a chance to become actively involved in the visual design of his own work. After the serialisation of *Ulysses* was made impossible in the *Little Review* by a decision of the Court of Special Sessions (21 February 1921; *JJII* 503) and the refusal of New York publisher W.B. Huebsch to publish the text without alterations (5 April 1921, *JJII* 504), Joyce's agreement with Paris bookshop and lending library owner Sylvia Beach offered him a unique opportunity to shape not only the verbal but also the visual substance of the novel. The well-documented gusto with which Joyce proceeded to insist on a particular shade of blue for the paper cover to evoke the Greek flag (*JJII* 524)[19] and the less well-known care with which he suggested, with his printer's consent, typographic details like replacing the Grasset type of the headings of "Aeolus" in the Shakespeare and Company edition (February 1922) with "block capitals" in the Egoist Press edition (October 1922) – "especially as these are the type used by newspapers"[20] – suggest that by this time, Joyce was very much aware of the effect that the "visual impression" of the bibliographic code could have on the reception of his work.

The *Little Review* (1918–20)

As suggested above, Joyce did not always have so much influence on the visual connotations of his text, and this was very much the case when *Ulysses* was serialised. Focusing on the August 1917 issue, Edward Bishop has argued that this magazine was "frankly amateur" and was meant to look like it, too: "there are no pretensions to fine printing here, and the cover is not a cover", adhering to Ezra Pound's advice that "The plain exterior and the coloured label, are right".[21] If one focuses on the appearance – in both senses – of *Ulysses* in the *Little Review*, however, the picture becomes more complex. Readers who encountered the first instalment of *Ulysses* in the March 1918 issue found a visually more striking but arguably also more professional-looking review (see illustration 12.4). Sporting a masthead printed in bold and condensed capitals of the extremely

---

19 See also Sylvia Beach, *Shakespeare and Company* (London: Faber and Faber, 1960), 72.

20 James Joyce to Harriet Shaw Weaver, 17 October 1922, Harriet Shaw Weaver Papers, Add MS 57346, British Library, London.

21 Edward Bishop, "Re: Covering Modernism – Format and Function in the Little Magazines", in *Modernist Writers and the Marketplace*, eds. Ian R. Willison, Warwick Gould and Warren Chernaik (New York: St. Martin's Press, 1996), 307.

ILLUSTRATION 12.4
Front cover for the Little Review *of March 1918.*
COURTESY OF THE MODERNIST JOURNALS PROJECT.

successful commercial type family Cheltenham,[22] the new cover was literally much bolder than previous versions, with the colour of the paper (purple, pale green, bright orange, yellow, deep blue) providing an ever more powerful visual effect.

An even bolder and, this time, rugged and individual effect was achieved by the cover design introduced in May 1919, in the issue that also contained the second part of episode 9 of Joyce's novel. This new design was not unlike the lettering on the cover of *The Seven Arts* (1916–17), a (similarly) New York-based little magazine that the editors of the *Little Review* followed with some interest.[23] It used chunky woodcut-like letters for the name of the magazine and bold sans serif capitals and a heavy rule to – literally – underline its self-definition: "A MAGAZINE OF THE ARTS / MAKING NO COMPROMISE WITH THE

22 Stanley Morison, *A Tally of Types*, ed. Brooke Crutchley, new ed. (Cambridge: Cambridge University Press, 1973), 19.

23 See Ezra Pound, *Pound/The Little Review: The Letters of Ezra Pound to Margaret Anderson: "The Little Review" Correspondence*, eds. Thomas L. Scott and Melvin J. Friedman, with the assistance of Jackson R. Bryer (London: Faber and Faber, 1988), especially 143.

ILLUSTRATION 12.5
Front cover for the Little Review *of July 1919.*
COURTESY OF THE MODERNIST JOURNALS PROJECT.

PUBLIC TASTE" (see illustration 12.5). The freedom from conventional forms of visual harmony was made more striking in the first few months of the new cover design (May to July 1919) by the choice of patterned (flowery or striped) cover paper as the background to the blocky lettering. By this time, as the June 1919 issue announced, "Ezra Pound has abdicated and gone to Persia"[24] and the influence of Jane Heap, a visual artist by training and a future art gallery manager (1924–27[25]), had increased.

---

24 *Little Review* 6, no. 2 (June 1919): verso of the cover. Pound went to France and Italy with his wife and was, for a time, foreign correspondent for the *Dial*; see Pound, *Pound/The Little Review*, 259.

25 On Heap's involvement with modern visual arts, see Susan Noyes Platt, "Mysticism in the Machine Age: Jane Heap and *The Little Review*", *20/1: Twentieth-Century Art & Culture* 1, no. 1 (1990): 18–44. Platt attributes an earlier (summer-autumn 1916) change in the design of the magazine (from "drab brown cover to brilliantly coloured jackets and bolder typefaces") to the influence of Jane Heap, who became involved with Anderson and the *Little Review* at that time; see Susan Noyes Platt, "*The Little Review*: Early Years and Avant-Garde Ideas", in *The Old Guard and the Avant-Garde: Modernism in Chicago, 1910–1940*, ed. Sue Ann Prince (Chicago: University of Chicago Press, 1990), 152. In fact, the change in the magazine's design was a more gradual process: coloured labels appeared on the cover in August 1916, but bolder type only in October 1917.

There was a parallel change between the covers: the makeshift and somewhat cheap look of the March 1918 issue (with its mix of typefaces, the slightly condensed text face, closely printed lines, almost total lack of images) developed, by the end of 1919, into a more generously proportioned Caslon-like text face, wider line spacing and four-line capitals to mark the beginning of sections. Reproductions of art works were introduced in the November 1917 issue, were approved by Pound and readers alike[26] and, together with author portraits, contributed to the increasing visual distinction of the magazine. *Ulysses* was here, then, part of a visual bibliographic environment that was quite complex: visually appealing and at once emphatically non-defiant (on the cover) and respectable (inside), but neither obviously modern, nor obviously classic.

The *Egoist* (1919)

Readers who encountered *Ulysses* in the London-based magazine the *Egoist* between January and December 1919 faced perhaps less complex but none

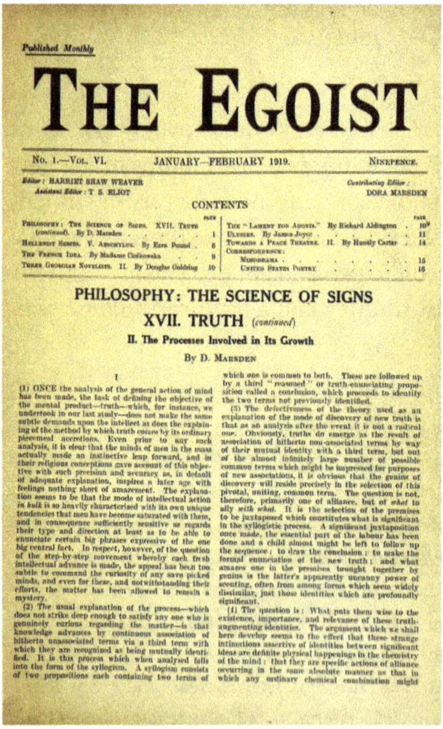

Published Monthly

THE EGOIST

No. 1.—Vol. VI. JANUARY—FEBRUARY 1919. Ninepence.

Editor: HARRIET SHAW WEAVER
Assistant Editor: T. S. ELIOT
Contributing Editor: DORA MARSDEN

CONTENTS

	PAGE		PAGE
Philosophy: The Science of Signs. XVII. Truth (*continued*). By D. Marsden	1	The "Lament for Adonis." By Richard Aldington	10
Hellenist Series. V. Aeschylus. By Ezra Pound	6	Ulysses. By James Joyce	11
The French Idea. By Madame Ciolkowska	9	Towards a Peace Theatre. II. By Huntly Carter	14
Three Georgian Novelists. II. By Douglas Goldring	10	Correspondence:	
		Monodrama	15
		United States Poetry	16

PHILOSOPHY: THE SCIENCE OF SIGNS

XVII. TRUTH (*continued*)

II. The Processes Involved in Its Growth

By D. Marsden

I

(1) ONCE the analysis of the general action of mind has been made, the task of defining the objective of the mental product—truth—which, for instance, we undertook in our last study—does not make the same subtle demands upon the intellect as does the explaining of the method by which truth comes by its ordinary piecemeal accretions. Even prior to any such analysis, it is clear that the minds of men in the mass actually made an instinctive leap forward, and in their religious conceptions gave account of this objective with such precision and accuracy as, in default of adequate explanation, inspires a later age with feelings nothing short of amazement. The explanation seems to be that the mode of intellectual action *in bulk* is so heavily characterized with its own unique tendencies that men have become saturated with them, and in consequence sufficiently sensitive as regards their type and direction at least as to be able to enunciate certain big phrases expressive of the one big central fact. In respect, however, of the question of the step-by-step movement whereby each fresh intellectual advance is made, the appeal has been too subtle to command the curiosity of any save picked minds, and even for these, and notwithstanding their efforts, the matter has been allowed to remain a mystery.

(2) The usual explanation of the process—which does not strike deep enough to satisfy any one who is genuinely curious regarding the matter—is that knowledge advances by continuous association of hitherto unassociated terms via a third term with which they are recognized as being mutually identified. It is this process which when analysed falls into the form of the syllogism. A syllogism consists of two propositions each containing two terms of which one is common to both. These are followed up by a third "reasoned" or truth-enunciating proposition called a conclusion, which proceeds to identify the two terms not previously identified.

(3) The defectiveness of the theory used as an explanation of the mode of discovery of new truth is that as an analysis after the event it is not a radical one. Obviously, truths do emerge as the result of association of hitherto non-associated terms by way of their mutual identity with a third term, but out of the almost infinitely large number of possible common terms which might be impressed for purposes of new associations, it is obvious that the genius of discovery will reside precisely in the selection of this pivotal, uniting, common term. The question is not, therefore, primarily one of alliance, but of *what* to ally *with what*. It is the selection of the premises to be juxtaposed which constitutes what is significant in the syllogistic process. A significant juxtaposition once made, the essential part of the labour has been done and a child almost might be left to follow up the sequence: to draw the conclusion: to make the formal enunciation of the new truth: and what amazes one in the premises brought together by genius is the latter's apparently uncanny power of scenting, often from among forms which seem widely dissimilar, just those identities which are profoundly significant.

(4) The question is: What puts them wise to the existence, importance, and relevance of these truth-augmenting identities. The argument which we shall here develop seems to the effect that these strange intimations assertive of identities between significant ideas are definite physical happenings in the chemistry of the mind: that they are specific actions of alliance occurring in the same absolute manner as that in which any ordinary chemical combination might

ILLUSTRATION 12.6
Front cover for the Egoist *of January–February 1919.*
COURTESY OF THE MODERNIST JOURNALS PROJECT.

26 See Pound, *Pound/The Little Review*, 164, 167.

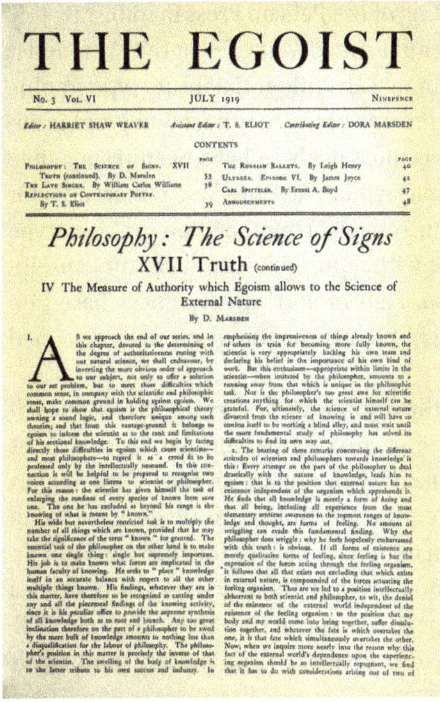

THE EGOIST

No. 3 Vol. VI JULY 1919 NINEPENCE

Editor: HARRIET SHAW WEAVER *Assistant Editor:* T. S. ELIOT *Contributing Editor:* DORA MARSDEN

CONTENTS

	PAGE		PAGE
PHILOSOPHY: THE SCIENCE OF SIGNS. XVII TRUTH (continued). By D. Marsden	33	THE RUSSIAN BALLETS. By Leigh Henry	40
THE LATE SINGER. By William Carlos Williams	38	ULYSSES. EPISODE VI. By James Joyce	42
REFLECTIONS ON CONTEMPORARY POETRY. By T. S. Eliot	39	CARL SPITTELER. By Ernest A. Boyd	47
		ANNOUNCEMENTS	48

Philosophy: The Science of Signs

XVII Truth (continued)

IV The Measure of Authority which Egoism allows to the Science of External Nature

By D. MARSDEN

ILLUSTRATION 12.7
Front cover for the Egoist *of July 1919.*
COURTESY OF THE MODERNIST JOURNALS PROJECT.

the less significant visual clues. As Edward Bishop has noted, this magazine underwent a change from the "punchy, bull-dog quality" associated with its treatment of controversial social subjects as well as the "heavy, barbed, Latin Antique typeface" of the masthead (see illustration 12.6), to a "more refined" character with more emphasis on literature and a more "slender and elegant" Caslon masthead (see illustration 12.7).[27]

A few points remain worth adding. For instance, the temporal gap and the dramatic visual differences between the March-April 1919 issue (which carried episode 3 of *Ulysses*) and the subsequent July 1919 issue of the – originally monthly – magazine may very well have been largely caused by Joyce's novel. In contrast to Ellmann's assertion that – after much difficulty – "one printer was prevailed upon to do a few episodes (II, III, VI, and X)" of *Ulysses* in the *Egoist* (*JJII* 443), the first two episodes published in the magazine (episodes 2 and 3) were actually published by a different printer (the Complete Press, West Norwood) than the issues containing the later episodes, printed at the Pelican Press in London. As the editors remained unchanged (Harriet Shaw Weaver, T.S. Eliot and Dora Marsden), the sudden typographic refinement of the magazine is likely due to the typographic excellence that manager Francis

27 Bishop, "Re: Covering Modernism", 300.

Meynell had aspired to since the founding of the Pelican Press in 1916.[28] By July 1919, Stanley Morison acted as "Designer of Printed Matter"[29] at the Press and it is thus Morison, soon to become the immensely influential future typographic advisor of the Monotype Corporation and one of the foremost typographic authorities of the United Kingdom, who is most likely to have been responsible for the sudden visual overhaul of the magazine. The Press was remarkable for combining the advantages of modern mechanical composition on Monotype machines with a selection of typefaces with a pre-nineteenth century, pre-industrial character (Monotype Venetian, Plantin and two typefaces based on Caslon: Old Face and Imprint), for which they also acquired specially designed extra letters and ligatures.[30]

The shift in both the masthead and the text body from graceless and quotidian nineteenth-century typefaces (like the spiky Latin Antique) to conscious revivals of earlier designs (like Caslon) was symptomatic of one of the important typographic trends of the age. An early eighteenth-century design, Caslon was revived (complete with the by then defunct long ſ) in the 1840s to print literary (and devotional) texts with a "period" flavour[31] and by the 1900s became a marker of literary quality: it was the type used to print G.B. Shaw's plays,[32] W.B. Yeats's poetry (at the Dun Emer and Cuala Presses[33]) and literary periodicals

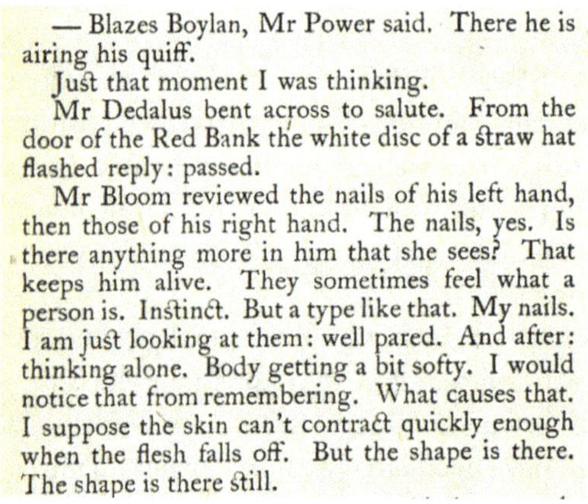

— Blazes Boylan, Mr Power said. There he is airing his quiff.

Just that moment I was thinking.

Mr Dedalus bent across to salute. From the door of the Red Bank the white disc of a straw hat flashed reply: passed.

Mr Bloom reviewed the nails of his left hand, then those of his right hand. The nails, yes. Is there anything more in him that she sees? That keeps him alive. They sometimes feel what a person is. Instinct. But a type like that. My nails. I am just looking at them: well pared. And after: thinking alone. Body getting a bit softy. I would notice that from remembering. What causes that. I suppose the skin can't contract quickly enough when the flesh falls off. But the shape is there. The shape is there still.

ILLUSTRATION 12.8
Extract from page 44 of the "Hades" episode printed in the Egoist *issue of July 1919, set in Caslon and using archaic ligatures.*
COURTESY OF THE MODERNIST JOURNALS PROJECT.

28 Nicolas Barker, *Stanley Morison* (London: MacMillan, 1972), 70–71.

29 Barker, *Morison,* 83–84.

30 Barker, *Morison,* 84.

31 Robin Kinross, *Modern Typography: An Essay in Critical History,* 2nd ed. (London: Hyphen Press, 2010), 39. See also Twyman, *Printing,* 78.

32 Sebastian Carter, "Typeface Design for the Monotype Corporation", in *History of the Monotype Corporation,* eds. Andrew Boag and Christopher Burke (London: Printing Historical Society; Woodstock: Vanbrugh Press, 2014), 204.

33 McGann, *Black Riders,* 16.

like the *Yellow Book, Samhain* or the *English Review*. By switching to Caslon, the *Egoist* also became associated with this sense of quality – but arguably also with a nostalgic longing for a pre-industrial world of dignified artistry and craftsmanship that had induced William Morris's printing revival at the Kelmscott Press as well. Thus, it may have come as even more of a surprise to readers of the previous two episodes of *Ulysses* that the text of the "Hades" episode, like most of the newly designed July 1919 issue, was not only set in Caslon, but also generously sprinkled with ligatures (tied letter combinations for *ct, st, is* and *in*), as shown in illustration 12.8.

It was thus given a distinctly archaic – and rather anachronistic – flavour, which appears to have had little to do with the early twentieth-century Dublin colloquial language that the text relies on here. Ligatures survived into the second half of "Hades", published in the September issue, but by the time "Wandering Rocks" (episode 10) began in the last issue of the magazine in December 1919, the anachronistic ligatures were withdrawn from most of the magazine, including Joyce's text (as well as, more debatably, from T.S. Eliot's "Tradition and the Individual Talent"). Having swung from visually indifferent to preciously archaic, the typographic form of *Ulysses* in the *Egoist* settled to give a suggestion of solid literary quality, just before the serialisation was abandoned.

Shakespeare and Co. and Egoist Press (1922–30)

As suggested above, the first book edition of *Ulysses* also provided Joyce with the chance to rescue the visual form of his work from the power of editors, printers and typographic designers: design decisions were made by Lyon master printer Maurice Darantiere in close consultation with Joyce and first-time publisher Sylvia Beach. The outcome of these negotiations was an impressively large and squarish volume whose typographic virtues have been the subject of some debate.[34] Despite the questionable utility of the book as reading matter, it does seem to make a more unified visual statement than either of the previous, rather protean serialisations. The types used to define the visual identity of the first edition of *Ulysses* appear to counter the degradation involved in the charge of obscenity by making the novel look indisputably dignified and classic. Thus, the minimalistic front cover carries, against a blue background,

34 See Peter de Voogd, "Joycean Typeface", in *Aspects of Modernism: Studies in Honour of Max Nänny*, eds. Andreas Fischer, Martin Heusser and Thomas Hermann (Tubingen: Gunter Narr Verlag, 1997), 203–18; Bishop, "Re: Covering *Ulysses*", 22–55; Glenn Storhaug, "'Seems to See with his Fingers': The Printing of Joyce's *Ulysses*", in *Type & Typography: Highlights from "Matrix", the Review for Printers and Bibliophiles* (West New York: Mark Batty Publisher, 2003), 323–31; John Ryder, "Editing", 108–24.

ILLUSTRATION 12.9
Front cover of the first edition of Ulysses *published by Shakespeare and Company in 1922.*
COURTESY OF THE MODERNIST VERSIONS PROJECT (MVP.UVIC.CA). MADE POSSIBLE BY THE GENEROUS SUPPORT OF THE SOCIAL SCIENCES AND HUMANITIES RESEARCH COUNCIL (SSHRC) OF CANADA.

the words "ULYSSES / BY / JAMES JOYCE" in white capital letters modelled on formal square capitals as used on antique Roman monuments (see illustration 12.9).

Designed in 1846 by Louis Perrin of Lyons as "charactères augustaux" and also known as Lyons titling, these august capitals constitute a perfect match with the type in which the text was set. The text type is a member of the "Elzévir" family of fonts,[35] which were developed from Perrin's designs and which copied his capitals rather faithfully.[36] The first Shakespeare and Company edition possessed, then, a typographic unity, and was evocative – through the classic letter shapes and all-capital setting of the cover page – of the dignity of Roman antiquity in a way appropriate for a book called *Ulysses*.[37] (There is, of course, quite some cognitive dissonance between the quasi-Arnoldian "high seriousness" of the visual appearance of the book and the comedy and contingency of much of the verbal substance.) The text type had similarly serious historic

35 John Ryder identified the type as Ancien Romain by Deberny ("Editing", 118), while Joyce and Darantiere used the (generic) name Elzévir. I rely on Ryder's work for the identification of the typefaces of the body text and "Aeolus" headings in the book editions (1922–1936).

36 G.W. Ovink, "Nineteenth-Century Reactions against the Didone Type Model – II", *Quaerendo* 1, no. 4 (October 1971): 282–301.

37 This was by no means Darantiere's default style: his covers for Ernest Hemingway's *Three Stories and Ten Poems* (1923) and Rudyard Kipling's *Sept poèmes des Barracks Room Ballads* (1925) are both strikingly different.

associations. In parallel with the revival of Caslon typefaces in England and the United States, the "Elzévirs" were designed in mid-nineteenth-century France with the intention of returning to pre-industrial (this time, seventeenth-century) models and breaking the monopoly of "modern" (Didot-inspired) types. (With their relatively thick vertical strokes, thin horizontal lines and serifs and geometric construction, "modern" types could suffer from low legibility and a monotonous appearance.) As was the case with Caslon, the Elzévirs were often used in the late nineteenth-century for high-quality literary texts and works with a "period" flavour. What Sylvia Beach has called Darantiere's "famous type"[38] was, then, like the Caslon used in the later issues of the *Little Review* and the *Egoist*, a conscious claim for visual distinction: in the words of one of the standard typographic works of the age, Elzévirs commanded "high respect" and were to be used on "special occasions".[39]

Another effect of the close collaboration of printer, publisher and author is the matching design of the subscription prospectus (see illustration 12.10). Printed in the same Elzévir typeface, this is in perfect harmony with the visual form of the first edition of *Ulysses*.

ILLUSTRATION 12.10
Subscription prospectus for the 1922 edition of Ulysses *issued by Shakespeare and Company.*
COURTESY OF SPECIAL COLLECTIONS, UNIVERSITY OF WISCONSIN-MILWAUKEE LIBRARIES.

38 Beach, *Shakespeare and Company*, 58.

39 Daniel Berkeley Updike, *Printing Types, Their History, Forms, and Use: A Study in Survivals* (Cambridge: Harvard University Press, 1922), 232. In contradistinction, Ovink suggests that "the elzévirs lost their special appeal at the turn of the century"; Ovink, "Nineteenth-Century Reactions – II", 301.

In the hands of Beach, *Ulysses* thus received a unified visual identity, making claims for links with classical antiquity and special literary value. This unity did not remain intact in subsequent editions. The October 1922 edition by the Egoist Press, for instance, relied on the design, printing plates and printer of the Shakespeare and Company edition, but the publicity flyer made a different visual statement. Printed in a type inspired by eighteenth-century engraved characters (issued as "Nicholas Cochin" in 1912), this flyer seems to downplay classical connotations in favour of connotations of a more generalised artistic quality.[40]

Two Worlds Monthly (1925–26)

The trend for nostalgic pre-industrial visual connotations, present in the *Egoist* serialisation and the Egoist Press publicity material, continued in Samuel Roth's enthusiastic but not quite authorised serialization of the first fourteen episodes in his *Two Worlds Monthly* between July 1926 and October 1927 (see illustration 12.11).[41] Printed on good paper using prestigious typefaces like Caslon, sold for a respectable 50 cents (just like the double issue of the *Little Review* that carried the last *Ulysses* instalment) and boasting a list of famous names (Arthur Symons, Arthur Schnitzler, T.S. Eliot, Ezra Pound), the magazine presented itself as a carrier of indisputable literary value. (This is somewhat incongruous with its being, as the subtitle claimed, "Devoted to the Increase of the Gaiety of Nations".) In harmony with the conscious attempt at "old style" typographic refinement in the publication, *Ulysses* was advertised at the top of the cover in the first three issues in a type (Pabst Oldstyle, 1902) that was supposed to attract "the eye of the man who knows" and "give an air of distinction to the best of work".[42]

With its distinctive shapes, strong tone and slightly irregular outline, the letters used by Roth clearly meant to evoke the solid craftsmanship and artistry associated with historicising printing, visually linking the magazine to his more exclusive quarterly, *Two Worlds*, and embodying his claims about the

40 The complete resetting of the text for a new Shakespeare and Company edition in 1926 also disturbed the unified look insofar as the text face was changed. In addition, Beach's *Ulysses* advertisements began to use more commercial types as well.

41 For a recent account of Roth's complex dealings with Joyce, see Jay A. Gertzman, *Samuel Roth: Infamous Modernist* (Gainesville: University Press of Florida, 2013), 63–100.

42 *American Specimen Book of Type Styles* (Jersey City: American Type Founders Company, 1912), 413. The type is also known as Pabst Roman.

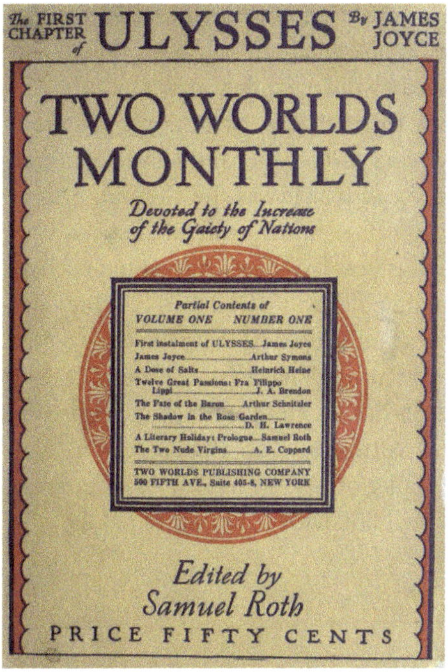

ILLUSTRATION 12.11
Front cover of the first (July 1926) issue of Samuel Roth's Two Worlds Monthly, *advertising "The FIRST CHAPTER of ULYSSES By JAMES JOYCE". The issue contained the first three episodes.*
COURTESY OF THE MODERNIST VERSIONS PROJECT (MVP.UVIC.CA). MADE POSSIBLE BY THE GENEROUS SUPPORT OF THE SOCIAL SCIENCES AND HUMANITIES RESEARCH COUNCIL (SSHRC) OF CANADA.

"excellence" and "permanent value" of his monthly magazine.[43] In contrast, when Roth issued a full book edition of *Ulysses* in 1929, he practically forged the 1927 Paris impression. Copying the understated classicism of the original, he abandoned the conscious and somewhat nostalgic flavour carried by his serialised version.

Odyssey Press (1932–39)

It was the Odyssey Press (a purpose-made imprint of the newly established paperback publisher, the Albatross Press)[44] that – at least among the English-language editions – first made an unmistakable gesture towards modernity in

43 Call for subscription, *Two Worlds Monthly* 1, no. 1 (July 1926): 4.

44 For detailed discussions of the establishment and significance of the Albatross Press, see Alistair McCleery's "Tauchnitz and Albatross: A 'Community of Interests' in English-Language Paperback Publishing, 1934–51", *Library* 7, no. 3 (2006): 297–316, and "The Paperback Evolution: Tauchnitz, Albatross and Penguin", in *Judging a Book by Its Cover: Fans, Publishers, Designers, and the Marketing of Fiction*, eds. Nicole Matthews and Nickianne Moody (Aldershot: Ashgate, 2007), 3–18.

the visual identity of *Ulysses*. As suggested above, not only did the prospectus call Joyce's work a "modern classic", it also made it look both classic and modern: the former quality was suggested by the meander border and the traditional symmetrical layout, the latter by the exclusive use of the iconic modernist Futura typeface, designed a few years earlier (1927) and as exemplified above in illustration 12.1. It is useful to recall that it was the German printer of the first impressions of the book, Jakob Hegner, who had encouraged Paul Renner to design an entirely modern sans serif typeface that would eschew the intensely and increasingly political dichotomy of "German" (Gothic) and "non-German" (serifed Roman) typefaces and who appears to have suggested the slogan "the typeface of our time" to Renner.[45] Futura soon became part of the international language of modern design and was sold or copied by all major type foundries in Europe and North America. The use of this type for the conspicuous reddish publicity leaflet of *Ulysses* has an air of international modernism, but also creates a visual link with the other initial flagship

ILLUSTRATION 12.12
Cover for Dubliners *published by Albatross Press in 1932.*[46]
FROM THE COLLECTION OF ALASTAIR JOLLANS.

45 Burke, *Paul Renner,* 81ff.

46 "Albatross Dubliners", accessed 6 December 2016, https://paperbackrevolution.files.wordpress.com/2014/12/albatross-1-dubliners.jpg.

modernist publication of Albatross Press, Joyce's *Dubliners* (1932). Published a few months before *Ulysses* as the inaugural volume of Albatross's "Modern Continental Library" and printed in Italy, *Dubliners* – like subsequent volumes of the press – physically embodied modernity not only in being machine-composed and mass-produced, but also in looking new (see illustration 12.12). Designed by renowned typographer and printer of fine books Giovanni (earlier Hans) Mardersteig, titles in the series sported striking colour-coded paper covers, displaying freshly designed sans serif typefaces like Futura, Gill Sans (1928) or, in the case of *Dubliners*, the Italian Semplicità (1931).

The 1932 Odyssey Press edition was also the first to realise Joyce's suggestion that the headings of "Aeolus" should follow the example of newspapers and should be printed neither in a serif type richer in tone than the text type (as was the case with the headings of the 1922 to 1925 editions, set in Grasset, as reproduced in chapter 10, illustration 10.2) nor in capitals of the text type (as happened in the 1926 reset Shakespeare and Company text), but in sans serif "block capitals" (see illustration 12.13). To create the visual association with newspaper headings, the 1932 edition used a carefully designed but not overly innovative sans serif (Reform Grotesk). By choosing this type, designed in 1904 (and reissued in 1932), the designer created a visual reference that could encompass the early 1900s but would still feel sufficiently contemporary.

The professional appearance of the book was completed by the neat typeface of the main text (Monotype Baskerville, cut in 1923 as part of the revival programme initiated by the same Stanley Morison who most probably designed the last three instalments of the novel in the *Egoist*), also used in the cloth-bound one-volume limitation on the modest sand-coloured binding. The lettering on two-volume versions, printed in bright red on a grey paper board,

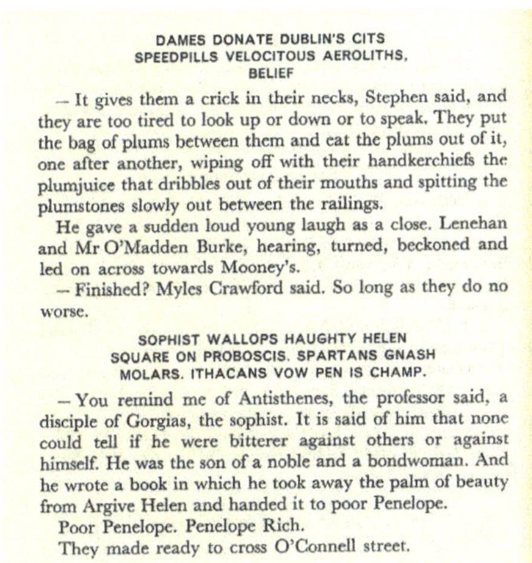

DAMES DONATE DUBLIN'S CITS
SPEEDPILLS VELOCITOUS AEROLITHS,
BELIEF

– It gives them a crick in their necks, Stephen said, and they are too tired to look up or down or to speak. They put the bag of plums between them and eat the plums out of it, one after another, wiping off with their handkerchiefs the plumjuice that dribbles out of their mouths and spitting the plumstones slowly out between the railings.

He gave a sudden loud young laugh as a close. Lenehan and Mr O'Madden Burke, hearing, turned, beckoned and led on across towards Mooney's.

– Finished? Myles Crawford said. So long as they do no worse.

SOPHIST WALLOPS HAUGHTY HELEN
SQUARE ON PROBOSCIS. SPARTANS GNASH
MOLARS. ITHACANS VOW PEN IS CHAMP.

– You remind me of Antisthenes, the professor said, a disciple of Gorgias, the sophist. It is said of him that none could tell if he were bitterer against others or against himself. He was the son of a noble and a bondwoman. And he wrote a book in which he took away the palm of beauty from Argive Helen and handed it to poor Penelope.

Poor Penelope. Penelope Rich.

They made ready to cross O'Connell street.

ILLUSTRATION 12.13
Sans serif block capitals used for the headings of "Aeolus" in the Odyssey Press edition of 1932.
COURTESY PRIVATE COLLECTION.

made a more pronounced gesture towards the pre-industrial past by using a refined historicising open type (Naudin Champlevé, 1910s–1920s).

Random House (1934)

The Random House edition, brought out a few weeks after Judge Woolsey's decision to lift the ban on the text on 6 December 1933, continued to balance modernist visual features with the traditional and classic. Designer Ernst Reichl created a complex layered design. The hand-drawn elongated monoline black letters which spell out the book title on the front and spine of the celebrated dust jacket could be seen to evoke archaic Greek inscriptions as well as modern sans serif letters (see illustration 12.14). The asymmetrically placed rectangular red field draws attention to the author's name and could gesture towards the geometric abstract art of painters like Piet Mondriaan, while stencil-like geometric Futura Black (1930) letters in lower case echo the innovative visual language of the Bauhaus and the New Typography.

While repeating the red-black-cream colour scheme of the wrapper, the binding shifts the referential balance towards tradition and antiquity through the use of the slightly irregular, calligraphic capitals (Weiss Roman Initials, Series I, 1926) which playfully evoke ancient inscriptions of a less formal kind

ILLUSTRATION 12.14
Dust jacket design by Ernst Reichl for the Random House edition of Ulysses *published in 1934.*
COURTESY PRIVATE COLLECTION.

ILLUSTRATION 12.15
Title spread of the Random House edition of Ulysses *published in 1934.*
COURTESY PRIVATE COLLECTION.

and introduce a visual element that runs through the book (see illustration 12.15). The same initials crop up on the right side of the innovative title spread, the left page being occupied by a huge initial U in the same style. Similar enlarged initials mark the opening of the three main sections of the book, spreading the classical and calligraphic visual clue through the book, but also harmonising with the fine text type (Linotype Baskerville).

If the design of the first Random House edition blends visual references to modernity, antiquity and craftsmanship, the publicity focused on modernity and, more emphatically, on accessibility. As was the case with the Odyssey Press edition, the first authorised American edition was advertised as a "modern classic", but also claimed, more enticingly, that it was about "an average man", had been "suppressed for 20 years" and was now available in an "unexpurgated edition" and "in a format worthy of its contents" for $3.50.[47] The advertisement from which these descriptions are taken appeared in the *New York Times Book Review* three days after the novel was published and had to compete against dozens of book ads, often of a much larger size (see illustration 12.16). That it still managed to attract attention is to a large extent due to its distinctive design. While most advertisements used custom-made bold typefaces of the recent boom in display types that they helped to generate[48] (serifs like Cooper Black, geometric sans serifs like Cable, rugged angular sans serifs like Neuland, formal scripts like Bernhard Cursive Bold), the *Ulysses* advertisement was dominated by hand-drawn letters. As was the case with

47 *New York Times Book Review* (28 January 1934): 21.

48 Advertisements in the news section of the same issue of the *New York Times* (28 January 1934) made copious use of other recent popular types inspired by Futura, Cable and Bodoni Ultra to promote, chiefly, luxury items like fur coats (4–6). Bold versions of the Cheltenham family were used in advertisements as well as news headlines.

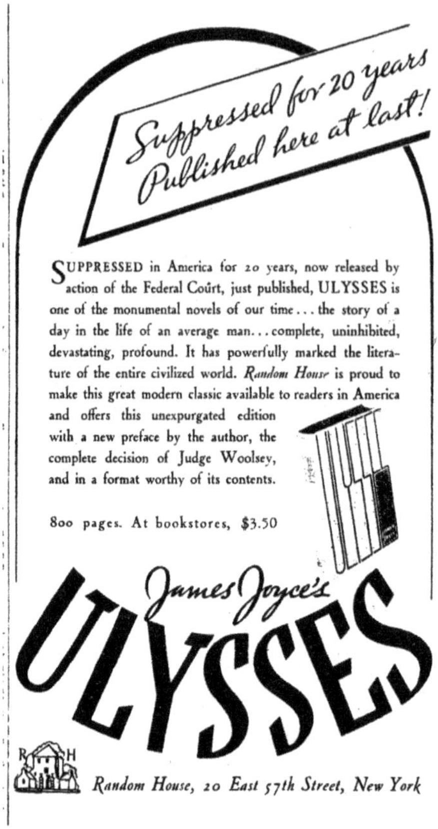

ILLUSTRATION 12.16
Random House advertisement for Ulysses *placed in the* New York Times Book Review *issue of 28 January 1934.*

some of the other book advertisements that also displayed book covers,[49] an attempt was made to create a recognisable visual identity through matching the typography of the advertisement with that of the cover design. The word ULYSSES, which occupies about a fifth of the entire advertisement space, is displayed, accordingly, in long, individual, pen-written capitals that managed to strike a visual balance between the delicate elongated lettering on the dust jacket depicted above it, and the informal script in which Joyce's name and the hyperbolic initial announcement ("*Suppressed for 20 years / Published here at last!*") was given.

49 E.g. the advertisements for Pearl Buck's *The Mother* and Sinclair Lewis's *Work of Art* in the same issue of the *New York Times Book Review* (28 January 1934): 11, 13. There were of course limitations to the extent of matching: a technical limitation would have been the availability of type, a practical one the visual salience of letter styles used on the cover. In the case of *Ulysses*, for instance, using the delicate thin lettering of the dust jacket in the ad would have produced a rather weak visual impact.

The same informal-looking script and the pen-drawn capitals were to serve as part of the promotional visual identity of the edition: they were used, occasionally in a slightly modified form or with different advertising texts, in several other newspaper ads.[50] The design can be seen as adding a low-key personal touch to the advertising materials, bringing the "modern classic" closer to the "average man". As Catherine Turner suggested with reference to the double-page ad in the 10 February 1934 issue of the *Saturday Review of Literature,* the script "looked inviting, almost like a letter".[51] Similar script and pen-drawn capitals were used on the cover of the reading aid that Random House issued as a separate folder (see illustration 12.17).[52] Created by Aaron Sussman,[53] the folder displayed, inside, a prominent hand-lettered title "How to enjoy JAMES JOYCE'S great novel ULYSSES", mixing the script used on the cover with long slab serif capitals which create a ready connection with the dust jacket, depicted prominently in the bottom right corner. As a third salient typographic style, modernism also appeared in the folder: the note referring readers to the list of other Random House books inside and all further information on the cover were couched in a recent Futura-inspired type (Metroblack, 1929–30).

The message of accessibility was apparently successful: an ad in the 18 March 1934 issue of the *New York Times Book Review* boasted of high sales ("Now 35th thousand") and cited a more accurate publication history ("After thirteen years, a best seller everywhere!"), while preserving the lure of a "complete, unexpurgated" edition (see illustration 12.18).[54] Listing six "Random House Successes", with *Ulysses* at the top, this advertisement made modernity its dominant characteristic. It uses the striking and very recent Futura Display face (1932) to focus attention on the publisher's name and the book titles,

50 E.g. *New York Times Book Review* (11 February 1934): 19 and (11 March 1934): 24. The advertisement published in the 18 February 1934 issue of the *New York Times Book Review* (18) has the same overall design – with a triple display of the pen-drawn ULYSSES logo – as the pre-publication announcement that appeared in the *Saturday Review of Literature* 30, no. 27 (20 January 1934); see the image reproduced in Catherine Turner, *Marketing Modernism between the Two World Wars* (Amherst: University of Massachusetts Press, 2003), 203. Turner reproduces two further advertisements from the same paper (*The Saturday Review of Literature*, 27 January and 10 February; see Turner, *Marketing,* 202, 206) using modified lettering.

51 Turner, *Marketing*, 207–8.

52 The inside of the folder was identical with the advertisement in the *Saturday Review of Literature* 10, no. 30 (10 February 1934): 474–75.

53 Turner, *Marketing*, 205.

54 *New York Times Book Review* (18 March 1934): 16.

ILLUSTRATION 12.17
Random House promotional folder for the 1934 Ulysses.[55]
COURTESY OF DARTMOUTH COLLEGE LIBRARY.

with a type of the recent slab serif revival (Stymie, 1931) providing the authors' names and advertising copy.

Limited Editions Club (1935)

The *Ulysses* of the Limited Editions Club, designed by publisher George Macy and containing a variety of typographic styles, has received some criticism, being described as a typographic farce[56] and as a coffee-table book.[57] The fact that the text was introduced by the most widely recognised Joyce scholar of the age, Stuart Gilbert, and contained special textual corrections[58] suggests, however, that the publisher was aiming at some intellectual distinction as well. The cover carries the names of the author and of the illustrator (Henri Matisse) and an image that is not obviously related to the text, echoing Matisse's "illustration"

55 *How to Enjoy James Joyce's Ulysses* (New York: Random House, 1934).

56 Ryder, "Editing", 113; see also 122.

57 Sam Slote, *"Ulysses" in the Plural: The Variable Editions of Joyce's Novel* (Dublin: National Library of Ireland, 2004), 22; Slote also quotes Ryder.

58 Slote, *"Ulysses"*, 22–23.

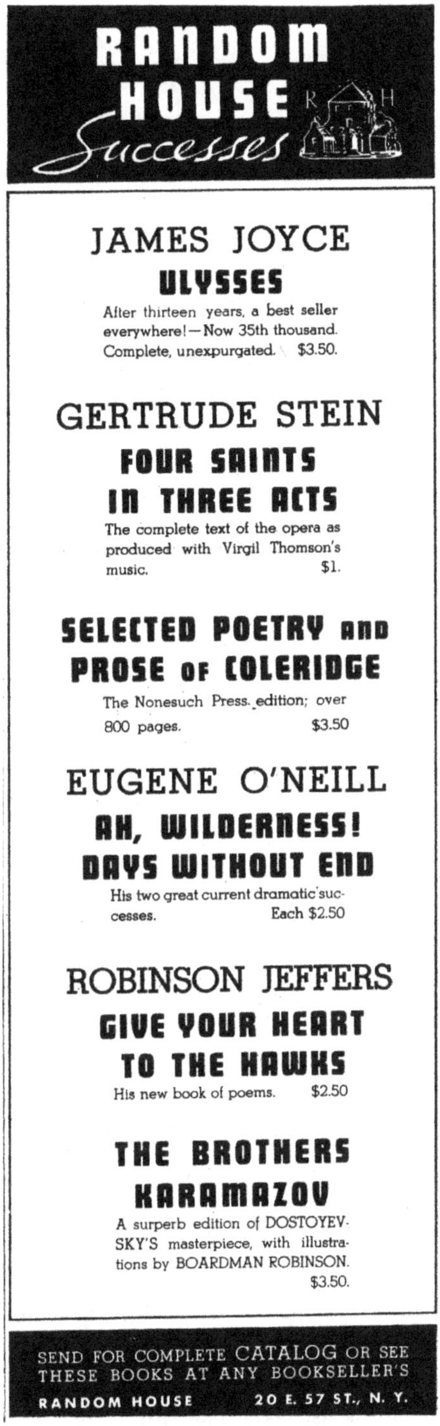

ILLUSTRATION 12.18
Random House advertisement for Ulysses *placed in the* New York Times Book Review *issue of 18 March 1934.*

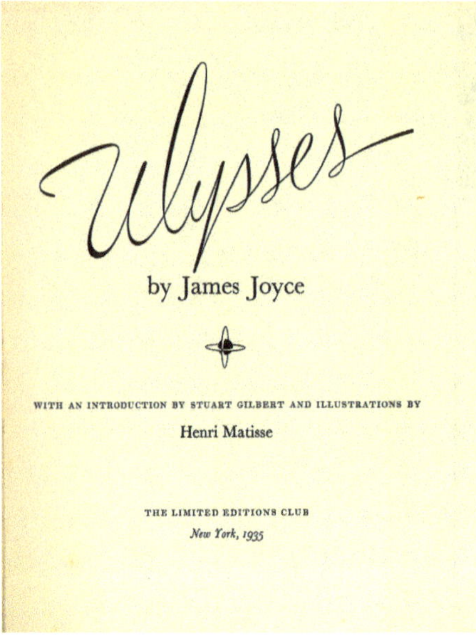
Ulysses

by James Joyce

WITH AN INTRODUCTION BY STUART GILBERT AND ILLUSTRATIONS BY

Henri Matisse

THE LIMITED EDITIONS CLUB

New York, 1935

ILLUSTRATION 12.19
Title page of the Limited Editions Club Ulysses *issued in 1935.*
COURTESY OF THE ZURICH JAMES JOYCE FOUNDATION.

of the meeting of a Homeric Nausicaa and Odysseus. With its gilt-stamped and embossed design, the cover emphasises antique associations and the sheer lavishness of the production. This latter feature returns on the pages of the book: the title page is dominated by a finely drawn script, creating a visual clue of intimacy and delicacy which is present on the spine, recurs on every page and also marks the commencement of sections (see illustration 12.19).

While the text face is a regular but not especially refined Scotch Roman, the "Aeolus" chapter revels in setting the headings in an unprecedented variety of typefaces, including blackletter, nineteenth-century French script designs (like Typo Upright, also known as Parisian Ronde), early twentieth-century American commercial high-flyers (like Cheltenham Bold Condensed) as well as German-made geometric modernist sans serifs (like Cable), a sample of which is shown in illustration 12.20.

Although this multiplicity has been severely criticised by typographers who prefer a more understated style, it does playfully but strikingly recall the extreme diversity – as well as some specific typefaces – of American newspaper typography in the mid-1930s, especially as regards advertising. It thus introduces an unexpectedly frivolous visual motif, which is also congruous with the kaleidoscopic nature and stylistic multiplicity of Joyce's text. Avowedly exclusive and respectable in its intention, the design of the book becomes playfully experimental here, and may be linked to such previous examples of uninhibited typographic eclecticism as Dadaist texts (like Hugo Ball's 1916

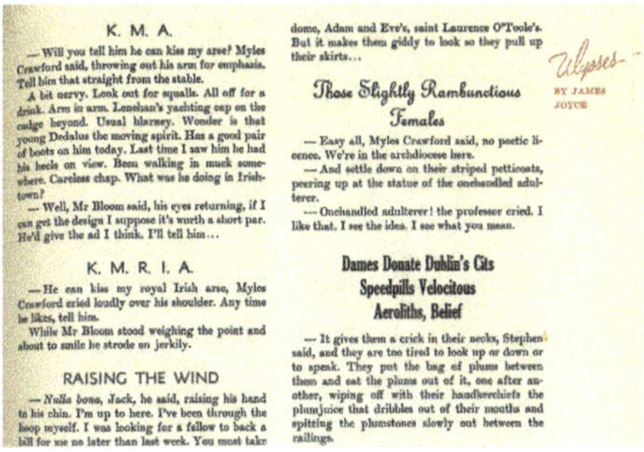

K. M. A.

—Will you tell him he can kiss my arse? Myles Crawford said, throwing out his arm for emphasis. Tell him that straight from the stable.

A bit nervy. Look out for squalls. All off for a drink. Arm in arm. Lenehan's yachting cap on the cadge beyond. Usual blarney. Wonder is that young Dedalus the moving spirit. Has a good pair of boots on him today. Last time I saw him he had his heels on view. Been walking in muck somewhere. Careless chap. What was he doing in Irishtown?

—Well, Mr Bloom said, his eyes returning, if I can get the design I suppose it's worth a short par. He'd give the ad I think. I'll tell him...

K. M. R. I. A.

—He can kiss my royal Irish arse, Myles Crawford cried loudly over his shoulder. Any time he likes, tell him.

While Mr Bloom stood weighing the point and about to smile he strode on jerkily.

RAISING THE WIND

—*Nulla bona*, Jack, he said, raising his hand to his chin. I'm up to here. I've been through the hoop myself. I was looking for a fellow to back a bill for me no later than last week. You must take

dome, Adam and Eve's, saint Laurence O'Toole's. But it makes them giddy to look so they pull up their skirts...

Those Slightly Rambunctious Females

—Easy all, Myles Crawford said, no poetic licence. We're in the archdiocese here.

—And settle down on their striped petticoats, peering up at the statue of the onehandled adulterer.

—Onehandled adulterer! the professor cried. I like that. I see the idea. I see what you mean.

Dames Donate Dublin's Cits Speedpills Velocitous Aerolites, Belief

—It gives them a crick in their necks, Stephen said, and they are too tired to look up or down or to speak. They put the bag of plums between them and eat the plums out of it, one after another, wiping off with their handkerchiefs the plumjuice that dribbles out of their mouths and spitting the plumstones slowly out between the railings.

Ulysses

BY JAMES JOYCE

ILLUSTRATION 12.20
Headlines of the "Aeolus" episode printed in the Limited Editions Club Ulysses.
COURTESY OF THE ZURICH JAMES JOYCE FOUNDATION.

poem "Karawane") or the yellow-black-magenta book jackets that Stanley Morison, an otherwise very refined arbiter of taste, designed in the 1930s for Victor Gollancz's popular Mundanus books.[59]

Bodley Head (1936)

If the typographic clues associated with the first authorised American edition were confident in their complexity, and the second authorised edition exuded exclusivity but revelled in variety, the first edition printed in England struck a more cautious, but also more unified, visual note. Designed by Eric Gill, the green linen front cover carried no words, only a gilt-stamped bow, subtly orienting the reader towards Homer's heroic epics.[60] The white dust wrapper repeated the antique bow reference on the spine and allowed the front to be dominated by the title and Joyce's name, printed in black. The typography is reminiscent of the 1922 edition in its proportions, placement and shape, although Joyce's name has been made relatively more prominent. The type, however, is actually a recent design: Eric Gill's Perpetua (released in 1932). Rooted in Gill's practice of stone lettering, these crisp titling capitals gesture towards formal Roman inscriptions, creating an effect that is at once fresh and evocative. Although Gill is usually credited only with designing the cover,[61] his influence appears to reach further: the half-title and the title page echo the dust cover in using Perpetua (and its italic version), as shown in illustration 12.21, while the

59 Alan Powers, *Front Cover: Great Book Jackets and Cover Design* (London: Beazley, 2001), 22–23; Barker, *Morison*, 238.

60 One hundred copies were bound in white calf vellum.

61 For instance, John J. Slocum and Herbert Cahoon, *A Bibliography of James Joyce, 1882–1941* (New Haven: Yale University Press, 1953), 34. The newspaper advertisement announcing the Bodley Head edition in the *Observer* made the same assertion: "Binding design by Eric Gill", (11 October 1936): 11.

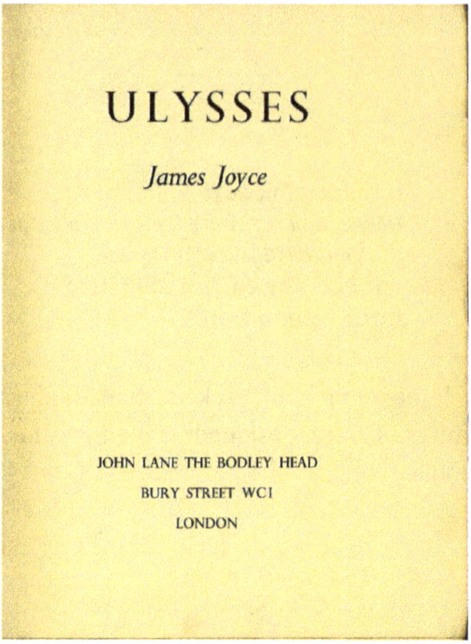

ILLUSTRATION 12.21
Title page of the Bodley Head edition of 1936.
COURTESY OF THE ZURICH JAMES JOYCE FOUNDATION.

headings of "Aeolus" are set in Gill's celebrated and characteristic humanist sans serif, Gill Sans. Arguably, this use of Gill Sans is somewhat anachronistic (as the type was released in 1928) and slightly incongruous (as it was used in newspapers mostly for advertising, rather than article headlines),[62] but it did add a touch of sleek newspaper modernity to a book otherwise dominated by the classic reminiscences of Perpetua and the time-tested English literary associations of the Caslon text face.

Described by Morison as "artistic", "literary" and "distinguished",[63] Perpetua seems to have been the most prominent type in the newspaper advertisements announcing the book as well, suggesting that it was meant as part of the visual identity of the book (see illustration 12.22). A comparison with the other book ads that surround them does indeed reveal how "classic" the look of the *Ulysses* announcements is. In, for instance, the 11 October 1936 issue of the *Observer*, all the other advertising on page 13 uses strikingly black titling faces like the "modernised" Monotype Bodoni Ultra Bold or the rugged modern sans serif

62 The Gill Sans type family was represented on almost all pages of the book advertising section of the 11 October 1936 issue of the *Observer*. By this time, Gill Sans was widely used in a range of other contexts, having also become part of the visual identity of railway companies as well as, since 1935, Bodley Head's Penguin paperbacks; see Barker, *Morison*, 350; Powers, *Front Cover*, 30–31.

63 Morison, *Tally*, 104.

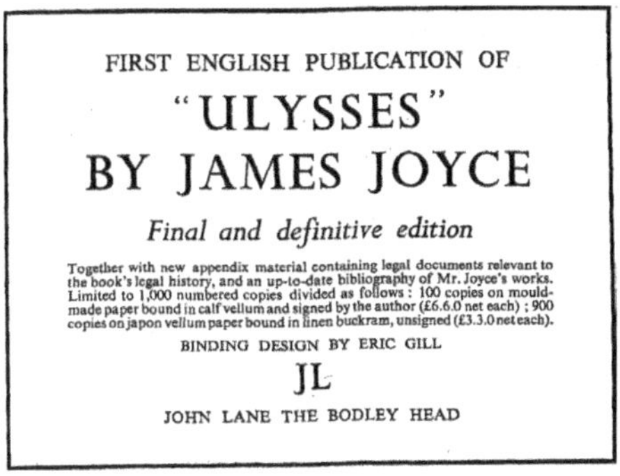

ILLUSTRATION 12.22
Bodley Head advertisement for Ulysses *placed in the* Observer *issue of 11 October 1936.*
IMAGE PUBLISHED WITH PERMISSION OF PROQUEST LLC. FURTHER REPRODUCTION IS PROHIBITED WITHOUT PERMISSION.

Othello or the somewhat more refined Gill Extra Bold, and even the relatively modestly designed other Bodley Head announcements resort to Bodoni Bold italics. In comparison, the *Ulysses* announcement, printed in crisp and classic Perpetua and the similarly recent, crisp and classic-looking Times New Roman (1931, 1933), makes a particularly dignified impression.

The visual clues that characterised the first British *Ulysses* are, then, rather homogeneous, stressing associations of classic perfection and literary distinction, with just a hint of modernity. It is tempting to conjecture that the fact that this edition may have intended to convey the same message with British types as the 1922 edition did with French types may have something to do with the uncertainty of the legal situation surrounding them, in which a serious work of recognisable artistic value may – as was the case after the 1933 Woolsey decision – be more immune to charges of obscenity.

Modern Library (1940)

The reissue of *Ulysses* by Random House as a Modern Library Giant in 1940 deserves attention not only because it completed the shift towards mass appeal but also introduced a new visual element that is still relevant. While most of the book design was identical to the 1934 version (although some misprints had been corrected),[64] the dust jacket was redesigned (see illustration 12.23). Presenting "Ulysses" in an informal script style, with ascenders and descenders reaching from the top to almost the bottom, the dust jacket seems to focus on accessibility. Joyce's name, however, is spelled out in more solemn hand-drawn capitals, among which the round E may have been intended to rhyme with ancient Greek epsilons or Irish half-uncials. Having served as a typographic

64 Slote, "*Ulysses*", 21.

ILLUSTRATION 12.23
Dust jacket (front and spine) for the reissue of Ulysses *in the Modern Library series of 1940.*
COURTESY PRIVATE COLLECTION.

sign of "Irishness" since the mid-nineteenth century, half-uncial and uncial lettering was to become a recurring element of the visual identity of many later Joyce editions (as was the case with editions of Viking in the 1960s or Dover in the 1990s). The spine of the Modern Library dust jacket, on the other hand, gives author and title in the signature modernist face Cable (1927), a geometric contemporary and rival of Futura. The cover thus reiterates elements of the visual presentation of the previous Random House edition, and appears to add a novel reference to Irishness, but the message of accessibility has by now fairly conquered the dust jacket.[65]

Conclusion

Ernst Reichl's 1934 *Ulysses* dust jacket has been hailed by design historians as "a striking cover that foreshadowed the rigorous formal and conceptual experimentation of American design in the coming decades".[66] Giovanni Mardersteig's refined classic modernist cover for Joyce's *Dubliners* in the Albatross series has also been seen as a trendsetter that served as inspiration for the design of the immensely successful and influential Penguin books.[67] While these designs appear to have exerted a wider influence, the typographic

65 This is seen as a sign of "middlebrow" by Edward Bishop ("Re: Covering *Ulysses*", 43) and a case of "suburban blandness" by Ned Drew and Paul Sternberger, *By Its Cover: Modern American Book Cover Design* (New York: Princeton Architectural Press, 2005), 15.

66 Drew and Sternberger, *By Its Cover*, 12.

67 Powers, *Front Cover*, 30.

form of most interwar editions of *Ulysses* were not so much pioneers as participants in the momentous graphic developments of the age, which have left an indelible stamp on the visual characteristics of all written communication today. Thus, *Ulysses* in print shows – and in some cases reflects on – the profusion of newly designed revivalist and modernist typefaces that catered for the need created by such technological innovations of the nineteenth-century as machine composition and high-speed dry-paper printing.[68] As the creator of advertising agent Bloom and one-time reader of advertising manuals, Joyce would have been interested to know that as *Ulysses* took ever newer material shapes, many of the types characteristic of the print culture of the interwar years were beginning to be experimentally tested with regard to their semantic associations and "appropriateness".[69] Such scholarly publications provided evidence for what printers, publishers and advertising professionals had thought for a long time: in the ineluctable visibility of the printed word, typography is a decisive factor.

Ulysses is remarkable for receiving attention from some of the century's most seminal typographers, thus illustrating the emergence of typographic design as a distinct profession,[70] called forth by the proliferation of relevant designs and information. Like so many other participants in the print culture of the age, these typographers often formed networks of collaboration and influence: Stanley Morison (probable designer of the last issues of the *Egoist*) worked together with Giovanni Mardersteig (designer of the Albatross *Dubliners*) in the 1920s and had a crucial role, as advisor to the Monotype Corporation, in the commissioning and introduction of Eric Gill's Perpetua and Gill Sans typefaces (prominently used in the Bodley Head *Ulysses*); Ernst Reichl (designer of the Random House *Ulysses*) received his early editorial training in Germany at the same publisher (Kurt Wolff) with whom Mardersteig had also worked and formed a lifelong friendship[71] – and whom Joyce had unsuccessfully approached in 1920 about a German translation of the *Portrait*.[72] These designers also illustrate the decisive influence of many European artists

68 See, for instance, Twyman, *Printing*, 79; Ovink, G.W., "Nineteenth-Century Reactions against the Didone Type Model – I", *Quaerendo* 1, no. 2 (April 1971): 18–19.

69 See, for instance A.T. Poffenberger and R.B. Franken, "A Study of the Appropriateness of Type Faces", *Journal of Applied Psychology*, 7, no. 4 (December 1923): 312–29.

70 Kinross, *Modern Typography*, 67–69.

71 Marshall Lee, "Ernst Reichl", *Fine Print: A Review for the Arts of the Book* 7, no. 3 (July 1981): 106; Giovanni Mardersteig, *Ein Leben den Büchern gewidmet* (Mainz: Gutenberg-Gesellschaft, 1968), 4.

72 Kurt Wolff, *Kurt Wolff: A Portrait in Essays & Letters*, ed. Michael Ermarth, tr. Deborah Lucas Schneider (Chicago: University of Chicago Press, 1991), 45–46.

in shaping the form in which early readers encountered Joyce's text, but also the profoundly international nature of modern graphic design, in which type designs, trends and typographers moved between different cultures with ease and success.

Most of the typefaces that were used to print, cover and advertise *Ulysses* in Joyce's life are, chiefly in digitalised versions, still part of our typographic landscape. This is so because the revivalist and modernist typographic trends of the 1920s and 30s, exemplified by the visual identities devised and rehearsed for the early *Ulysses* editions, have created lasting designs and protocols. The typographic odyssey of *Ulysses* is certainly not over, but the modernity of the visible has proved ineluctable.

Acknowledgements

This study would not have been possible without the generosity of the Zurich James Joyce Foundation, and especially Fritz Senn, who provided research time and access to the Foundation's invaluable collection of early Joyce editions and publicity materials.

Index

acronym: *see* alphabet
acrostic cipher: *see* alphabet
advertisements featuring in *Ulysses*
  Barclay & Cook shoes 126
  "Cigars of Joy" 15
  classified ad (deed poll) 188
  classified ad searching for Bloom ("£5 reward") 82
  classified ad ("Wanted, smart lady typist") 78–79, 83, 88
  College sports 60, 113
  E. Griffiths Hughes hair dye 15
  Elija throwaway 108–9
  "Eyebrowleine" 102n38, 103–4, 118
  Hely's 109, 125
  imaginary 127
  "Iron Jelloids" 99, 102
  "Kemp's Whoopaline" 15
  Keyes 59, 124, 158
  Kino's 59, 115
  mity cheese 123
  Mulligans visiting card 195–96
  nose shaper 119
  patent medicine 96
  "Plumtree's Potted Meat" 59, 122–23
  portable trouser stretcher 15
  Procter and Gamble 99
  safety pins 15
  Sandow 121
  "Science-applied suspenders" 15
  travelling showcart 110–12
  Trinity College bicycle race 113–14
  "Widow Welch's" female pills 102
  "Wonderworker" 121
  advertising used as code: *see* code
advertising for *Ulysses* 183–84, 193, 194n7, 195, 207–8, 210, 213–21, 223–24
  see also "Extracts from Press Notices"
advertising: historical development (1910–1920)
  design 127, 128n37
  guidebooks 99–100, 112
  keywords (or watchwords) 100–102, 104
  religion and 108, 110, 121, 123
  techniques and theories 110, 112–18, 124–27, 129
  theorists (Gale, Harlow; Scott, Walter Dill) 112
  classified ad 77–79, 82, 84, 86, 88
  language: *see* advertising; gender
  targeting women: *see* gender
  used as code: *see* code
  Joyce's notes on advertising: *see* Joyce
Alake of Abeokuta 101, 101n34
Albatross Press 209–11, 222–23
Alberti's cipher disc: *see* alphabet
Allen, Grant 15
alphabet
  alphabet for secret communication
    acronym 68
    acrostic 66
    anagram 61, 67
    Athbash 61
    boustrophedon: *see* boustrophedon
    cipher 62
    crab 63
    cryptogram 60–61, 163
    encryption 60
    Ogham 68–70
    secret writing 63
    semagram 63–64, 67n32
    steganography: *see* steganography
    Temurah 61
  alphabet open communication
    arrangement of letters 56, 61–62
    evolution 60
    see also language
anagram: *see* alphabet
Anderson, Margaret 182
Antheil, George 24, 184
Aristotle 145, 196
Aristotle's Masterpiece 42
Arnold, Matthew 13
Athbash: *see* alphabet
attention (attract in advertising) 108–9, 112–15, 117, 123, 126–27
  see also perception
Attridge, Derek 66, 29, 166

Ball, Hugo 218
Bauhaus 212
Baron, Scarlett 61n7
Barrès-Baker, M. C. 78
Bauer, Friedrich L. 61–65
Beach, Sylvia 24, 153n35, 173, 199, 205, 207–8
Beaufoy, Philip 31–37
  address 35–36
  "For Vera's Sake" 34
  "Matcham's Masterstroke" 20–21
  Prize Tit-Bit stories 21, 44–46
"beautiful" or "beauty" (as advertising keywords) 101–4
  see also advertising keywords (or watchwords)
Beck, Harald 118–19, 124, 162, 171n34
Bell, Vanessa 34n20
Bergson, Michael 32n13
Bibliographic codes (McGann) 194–96, 199, 202
Bishop, Edward L. 194, 199, 203
Bloom, Leopold 11, 13–18, 21, 22–27, 48, 55, 73, 78–81, 96–98, 130–41, 149–52, 157–58, 162–71, 186–89, 191, 196–98
Bloom, Molly 23, 72–73, 82, 94, 97, 102–4
Bobrikoff, Nikolai Ivanovitch 48
Bodkin, Matthias McDonnell 138–39
boustrophedon 61, 61n7, 163–64
Bowlby, Rachel 91n11
Brayden, William 55, 135
Breen, Josie 94
Bridgewater, Howard 112, 116–18, 124
Bridgwater (schooner Rosevean) 118n20
British Library 26
Brockman, William S. 128n38
Brody, Daniel 183
Budgen, Frank 24, 38, 40, 91
Burns, Robert 177
Byron, George Gordon 51, 184

Caffrey, Cissy 105
Chamber Music 183–84
cipher: *see* alphabet
circularity of text 149, 154, 158–60, 165–74
  see also linearity
classified advertising: *see* advertising
Clifford, Martha 72–73, 79–80
clippings: *see* press clippings
clothes 93–96, 99–100, 102
Clutton-Brock, Arthur 181
code
  advertisement used as code 56, 79, 81
  jargon 63–65
  spatial coding 52
  see also alphabet; secrecy
commodity 169–70
commodity culture 90–91
Complete Press 203
Conley, Tim 74n47
Conmee, John, S.J. 48
consumerism 90–93, 97, 99, 113
  female consumer 91–92, 98–100, 105
  male consumer 99–100
  see also gender; advertising and religion
Costello, Peter 21
covers of *Ulysses* editions 192–224
  see also materiality
crab: *see* alphabet
Crawford, Myles 52–53
crossheads: *see* headlines
crux (typographical) 198
cryptogram: *see* alphabet
Cuala Press 204
Cuddon, J. A. 69
Cummins, Maria 90
cuttings: *see* press clippings

Darantiere, Maurice 205–7
Dawson, Dan 51, 54
"The Dead": see *Dubliners*
Deasy, Garrett 51, 171
deception: *see* code; secrecy; steganography
Dedalus, Simon 51
Dedalus, Stephen 171–72, 188, 195
  Avoids "The Ship" 51
  Invited to write for the newspaper 52
Delany, Richard 134
désoeuvrement 85
Devlin, Kimberly 90
dialogism 154, 191
Dignam, Patrick 59, 81n4, 123, 150, 151n31, 157, 163n18, 164, 177n4
Dubliners 59, 182, 184, 189, 210–11, 222–23
  "The Boarding House" 80
  "The Dead" 43, 98, 188
  "A Painful Case" 184–85
Dun Emer Press 196, 204
Dunne, Miss 98–99

Easter Rising, 1916 132
Egoist Press 199, 208
Eliot, T. S. 203, 205, 208
Ellmann, Maud 169–70
Ellmann, Richard 33, 165, 203
encoding: *see* code; secrecy
encryption: *see* alphabet
errors 73–74, 152–53, 160, 163–64
Eveline 106
Exiles 179, 182–83
"Extracts from Press Notices" (1907–1922) 129n38, 183–84, 189
  see also press clippings

female language: *see* gender
female mode of consumption: *see* gender
fetishisation of advertising language 84–85, 88
fine printing 199, 205
Finnegans Wake 20, 56, 80, 83–85, 87–88, 174, 189–91
Fitzharris, James: *see* Skin-the-Goat
Fleischmann, Martha 74
Francini Bruni, Alessandro 36n25
Fraser, W. Hamish 28
Freud, Sigmund 84–85, 87, 91, 91n11
Friederichs, Hulda 31n12

Gale, Harlow 112
Gallaher, Ignatius 52
Garvey, Ellen Gruber 100
gender
  language (of women's ads) 91–92, 99–100, 102–6
  mode of consumption 93–96, 105
General Slocum disaster 47–49
Gibson, Andrew 90, 101, 105–6
Gifford, Don 13n5, 24, 73n45, 118n20, 160n11, 165, 170n31, 172n36, 196n12
Gilbert, Stuart 216
  schema for *Ulysses* 160
Gill, Eric 219–20, 222–23
  see also typefaces, Gill Sans
Gissing, George 30n8
Glasheen, Adaline 68n33
Gordon, John 60n5
graphics of print: *see* materiality; typography; visuality
Gray, John 140
Griffith, Arthur 27
Gula, Marianna 69n36
Gunn, Ian, and Alistair McCleery 83

Harmsworth, Alfred 19–20
Harmsworth, Desmond 28
Hart, Clive 68n33
Hayward, Matthew 110n4, 110n5, 112–13, 120n25, 123, 125–27
headlines (headers, crossheads) 144, 146–47, 153, 158, 160, 170–71, 199
Heap, Jane 182, 201
Hegner, Jakob 210
Heller-Roazen, Daniel 63n19
Hely: *see* advertising
Henke, Suzette 90–91
Herodotus 61, 62n12
Herring, Phillip F. 101n34
Historicism, typographic: *see* typography
Holmes, Sherlock (Arthur Conan Doyle) 16–17
Huebsch, Benjamin W. 182, 199

interruption: *see* narrative
intertextuality 90–91, 99, 105
Invincibles 53

Jackson, John Wyse, and Peter Costello 21, 30n10
Jackson, Kate 11–13, 29
Jones, Francis P. 135
Josephine, Aunt: *see* Murray
Joyce, James
  engagement with letter puzzles 57–58
  fascination with the press 59, 181
  memory of *Freeman's Journal* offices 136
  "Notes on Business and Commerce" 107, 112, 115–18
  scissors and paste man 24, 184
  spurious submission to *Tit-Bits* 20–21
  talent for journalism 24
  use of Dublin newspapers and magazines 24, 38, 40, 50, 101–2, 181–83, 191
Joyce, John Stanislaus 20, 30–31
Joyce, Nora 43, 74, 179
Joyce, Stanislaus 20–21, 24, 31n11, 98, 179, 181

Kahn, David 61–64, 69–70
Kavanagh, Michael 52

Kenner, Hugh 73, 89, 91, 174
Kernan, Thomas 49–50
Kershner, R. Brandon 101n32, 102n38, 105, 181n14, 191
Killeen, Terence 71n41, 146n11, 156n1, 159n9
Kipling, Rudyard 30n8

Lawrence, Karen 89–91
language 167, 172–74
  circulation of 162, 167, 170, 173
  Greek 163–64
  Hebrew 163–64
  Irish (Gaelic) 164, 172–73
  origin of 172–74
  of machines 150, 165–67
  see also advertising; alphabet; gender; letters; onomatopoeia; orthography; phonemes; rhetoric
Le Fanu, Joseph Sheridan 30
Lenehan, T. 54–55, 171–72
Leonard, Garry 90–95, 108n2, 113, 120
Leslie, Shane 184
letter puzzles: *see* puzzles
letters (alphabet) 162–66, 173
  Gaelic 164, 221–22
  Greek 163–64, 212, 221
  Hebrew 163–64
  Roman (antique) 219
  see also errors; orthography; typesetting; typography
letters (correspondence) 163, 181
Leys, John K. 21
Lily 98
Limited Editions Club 216, 218–19
Linati scheme for *Ulysses* 160, 168
linearity of text 147, 153
  see also circularity
Linotype 162n13, 164n20, 213
Longfellow, Henry Wadsworth 37
Lucas, W. 39

Macalister, R. A. Stewart 68, 70
MacDonald, J. Angus 100
MacDowell, Gerty 89–106, 118–20, 122
  naturalistic reading of 90–92, 105–6
  syntax 96–98
MacHugh, Roland 172
MacManus, L. 135
Macy, George 216
Marathon (battle) 51
March of Intellect 29
Mardersteig, Giovanni (Hans) 211, 222–23
Marsden, Dora 203
Marsh, Tess 41
"Matcham's Masterstroke" 33–37
materiality 59, 160–61, 164–65, 172, 174, 194, 196
  see also covers; paper; typography; visuality
Matisse, Henri 216–17
McCarthy, Patrick 73n47
McGann, Jerome 194
McLuhan, Marshall 157
Menton, John Henry 162
metamorphosis (transformation) 108, 114, 120–22, 128–29
Meynell, Francis 203–4
Milton, John 55
Mirus bazaar 101
modernism 146, 210, 212, 215, 224
modernity 148, 152, 193–95, 202, 209–10, 213, 215, 220–21, 224
Monotype 162n13, 204, 211, 220, 223
Monroe, Harriet 184
montage 120, 123n30
Moran, James 136n7
Morison, Stanley 204, 211, 218–20, 223
Morris, William 196, 205
motion (wandering) 108–9, 111, 114–15, 122, 123n30, 129
Mulligan, Malachi "Buck" 195–96
Mullin, Katherine 90
Murphy, William Martin 27–28
Murray, John Valentine "Red" 135
Murray, Mrs. William (Aunt Josephine) 175
Mutoscope 17–18

Nadel, Ira 60
Naether, Carl A. 100–103
Nannetti, Joseph Patrick 136
Narrative
  closure 143–55
  interruption 143, 147–49, 151–54
naturalism: *see* MacDowell
Nelson's Pillar 133
New Journalism 13

Newnes, Frank 18
Newnes, George 11–20, 28–29, 37
  on journalism 16
newspapers and periodicals 144, 146n14, 153, 156–60, 173–74, 176, 199
  accuracy 52–53
  advertising in 42–43
  Ally Sloper's Half-Holiday 26
  Answers to Correspondents 20, 26, 28
  as archive 176, 188, 190–91
  Bits of Fun 39–40
  clipping services: *see* press clippings
  Comic Cuts 20
  Daily Express 19, 24
  Daily Mail 26
  Daily Mirror 20
  Daily Nation 27
  Dublin Penny Journal 139
  Dublin Review 184
  Egoist 194, 202–5, 207, 211, 223
  English Review 205
  Era nuova 179, 180
  Evening Telegraph 49–50, 78, 86, 133, 138–39, 156–58
  Feuille du Bureau d'adresses 78
  Freeman's Journal 26, 27, 48–50, 52, 58, 73–74, 78–80, 110, 130–31, 133–35, 137–38, 140, 156, 158, 164n20, 165, 170, 172, 184
  Gentlewoman 104
  Good Housekeeping 102
  Illustrated London News 26
  Irish Cyclist 26
  Irish Daily Independent 28
  Irish Independent 27
  Irish Times 49–50, 78–81
  Lloyd's Weekly 23–24
  Ladies' Home Journal 102
  Lady's Pictorial 100–102, 104
  Little Review 148n20, 158–60, 182, 194, 199–202, 207
  London Times 19
  Mainly about People 18
  Modern Society 81, 186
  Morning Herald 19
  New York Times, New York Times Book Review 182, 194n7, 213–15, 217
  New York World 52
  Observer 20, 219n61, 220–21
  Pearson's Magazine 19
  Pearson's Weekly 19, 28
  penny weeklies 25, 28
  Photo Bits 2, 39
  Piccolo della sera 24, 179n10, 181
  Poetry 184
  Princess Novelette 101–3, 118
  Review of Reviews 16
  Samhain 205
  Seven Arts 200
  Shamrock 23
  Sinn Féin 184
  Sporting Times 189
  Star 18
  Strand Magazine 16
  Sun 18, 26
  Sunday Chronicle 184
  Thom's Official Directory 26, 141
  Times 20
  Times Literary Supplement 20, 181, 189
  Tit-Bits 11–17, 20, 24–25, 28–39
    prizes 14–16, 31–32, 38
    "Inquiry" column 37–38
    Tit-Bitites 30–31, 38
    train-accident insurance policy 14
  T. P.'s Weekly 18
  Two Worlds Monthly 208–9
  United Irishman 27
  Vogue 102
  Weekly Sun 18
  Westminster Gazette 17
  World 178
  Yellow Book 205
New Typography 212
Nietzsche, Friedrich 185

obscenity cases against *Ulysses* 182, 199, 205, 212, 221
O'Connor, T. P. 18
O'Connor (widower in *Ulysses*) 119
Ogham: *see* alphabet
O'Molloy, J. J. 48, 51n2
onomatopoeia 66, 71, 146, 148, 152–53, 161–62, 165–66
orthography 152, 161–64, 167, 170
Orwell, George 30n8
Osteen, Mark 60, 110–14, 169–70, 121n26

"A Painful Case": *see Dubliners*
paper 27, 152, 195, 200–201, 208
 see also newspapers and periodicals; materiality
paralysis 149–50
Parnell, Charles Stewart 27
parody (and satire) 86–88, 91
Pearson, Arthur 19–20
Pelican Press 203–4
penny weeklies: *see* newspapers and periodicals
perception 108, 115–17
periodicals: *see* newspapers and periodicals
perspective of narrative (Bloom's; Gerty's) 92–94, 106
Peterson, Joseph H. 62n13
Phoenix Park murders 52–53
phonemes 162, 167
Photo Bits: *see* newspapers and periodicals
photographs 186–87
Pierce, David 136n8
Pigott, Richard 23
Plock, Vike Martina 122
A Portrait of the Artist as a Young Man 65, 88, 179, 181–83, 223
POST NO BILLS (*Ulysses*) 164, 197
Pound, Ezra 181, 199, 201, 208
press clippings 175–91
 press clipping services 176–77, 182–83
 Joyce's use of press clippings 175–91
 see also "Extracts from Press Notices"
Price, Leah 26n2
Prince's Stores 134–35
printing presses 147–53, 160–61, 165, 204
Purefoy, Mina 72
puzzles (letter puzzles contests) 57–58, 161–62, 167, 171–72

Quinn, John 182

Reichl, Ernst 212, 222–23
Renner, Paul 210
 see also typefaces, Futura
"respectable" and "respectability" 78–80, 83, 86–88
 see also advertising keywords; advertising
reviews 177, 181–84, 189
rhetoric 144, 160–61, 165, 170–72
Richards, Grant 59, 184
riddles: *see* puzzles
Richards, Thomas 90–92, 96–99
Romeike, George 177
Romeike, Henry 177–78
Rose, Danis 52n3
Roth, Samuel 208
Rowntree, B. Seebohm 86

Salisbury, Lord 14
Schnitzler, Arthur 208
Schwarz, Oscar 179
Scott, Walter Dill 112
secrecy 52, 72–73, 80–83
secret writing: *see* alphabet; steganography
self-advertising (Joyce's): *see* advertisements; press clippings; "Extracts from Press Notices"
self-reflexivity 152–53, 156–74
semagram: *see* alphabet
Senn, Fritz 27n4, 67, 98, 107–9, 120, 129, 146n10, 146n14, 146n15, 147n15, 150n27, 190
 superimposition 52–56
Shaw, George Bernard 204
Sheehy, Eugene 30
Sheehy Skeffington, Francis 59
showcart: *see* advertisements featuring in *Ulysses*
Simmel, Georg 154
Simpson, John 22, 32n13
Skeat, Walter W. 64
Skin-the-Goat 53
"smart" or "smartness" (as advertising catchword) 78–79, 100–101, 104, 110, 110n5
 see also advertising keywords (or watchwords)
Smith, Barbara Herrnstein 144
Smith, W. H. 13–14
Solomon, Howard M. 78
spelling: *see* orthography
Spurr, David 110n5, 128n37, 149n25, 149n26, 150n28
Stead, William T. 16
steganography 58, 61–75
Strachan, John 124n32
superimposition 52–56
Symons, Arthur 208

Tacitus, Aeneas 63n17
Taxes on Knowledge 26

Taylor, John F. 54, 160, 170, 172
technology 13, 26–27, 148–52, 223
see also printing presses
teleology 150, 153–54
Temurah: *see* alphabet
toilet paper 21
Trithemius 62, 62n13, 75
Turner, Catherine 215
Twigg, Lizzie 79
typefaces
Baskerville 211, 213
Cable (Kabel) 213, 218, 222
Caslon 203–4, 207–8, 220
Cheltenham 200, 213n48, 218
Cochin 208
Elzévir 206–7
Futura 193–94, 210–12, 215, 222
Gill Sans 211, 219–20, 223
Grasset 199, 211
Latin Antique 203–4
Lyons Titling 206
Metroblack 215
Pabst Oldstyle 208
Perpetua 219–21
Reform Grotesk 211
sans serifs 198, 200, 210–13, 218
Scotch Roman 218
Script faces 218
Semplicitá 211
Stymie 216
Times New Roman 211
Weiss Roman 212–13
typesetting 152, 161–65
see also errors; linotype; monotype; typography
typography 146, 152, 163–65, 192–224
classic 193, 202, 205–6, 210–13, 220–22
craftsmanship 193, 205, 208, 213
distinction through 193, 202, 208, 221
handwritten letters 213–15, 218, 221–22
historicism, typographic 196–98, 204–6, 212, 224
readability 221–22
visual identity 192, 205, 208, 210, 214, 223–24
see also typefaces; visuality

Ulysses
Episode 1 ("Telemachus") 196
Episode 2 ("Nestor") 53, 195
Episode 3 ("Proteus") 153
Episode 4 ("Calypso") 21, 33, 41, 56
Episode 5 ("Lotus Eaters") 80, 169, 27
Episode 6 ("Hades") 49, 70, 162, 165, 167, 188, 205
Episode 7 ("Aeolus") 14–19, 24, 48, 50–55, 70, 130–41, 143–55, 156–74, 211
Episode 8 ("Lestrygonians") 48, 108–10, 114–15, 122–23, 167–68, 196
Episode 9 ("Scylla and Charybdis") 48
Episode 10 ("Wandering Rocks") 48–49, 168, 195, 196, 205
Episode 11 ("Sirens") 30, 34, 80, 166, 169, 182
Episode 12 ("Cyclops") 65, 69, 154, 186, 188
Episode 13 ("Nausicaa") 18, 39, 56, 89–106, 110n5, 119, 120n25, 167, 178, 188
Episode 14 ("Oxen of the Sun") 56, 196
Episode 15 ("Circe") 35–37, 39, 42–44, 79–81, 94–95, 105, 167
Episode 16 ("Eumaeus") 17, 22–23, 34, 35, 49, 78, 167
Episode 17 ("Ithaca") 13, 17, 23, 31, 81, 110, 121–22, 127, 143, 154, 163, 169, 185–89, 196–97
Episode 18 ("Penelope") 23, 40, 81, 97–98, 102, 104, 153, 168, 170
Ulysses, early editions 192–224
Bodley Head 198, 219–21, 223
Egoist Press 199, 208
Modern Library 221–22
Odyssey Press 193, 198, 209–12
Random House 212–17, 223
Shakespeare and Company 198–99, 205–8
see also Albatross Press; newspapers and periodicals (*The Egoist, Little Review, Two Worlds Monthly*)

Victoria (Queen) 26
Virag, Rudolf 188
visuality 60, 63, 145–46, 192–94

Walker, Emery 196
Wawrzycka, Jolanta 69n35
Weaver, Harriet Shaw 179, 181–82, 184, 203

weeklies: *see* newspapers and periodicals
Wells, H. G. 30n8
Wolfe, Charles 37
Wolff, Kurt 223
women's magazines: *see* newspapers and periodicals
Woolf, Virginia 34, 192–93
"Work in Progress": *see Finnegans Wake*
Wylie, Reggy 94, 118

Yared, Aida 74n49
Yeats, W. B. 172, 196, 204